The Misery Merchants

First published by Jacana Media (Pty) Ltd in 2020
Second impression 2023

10 Orange Street
Sunnyside
Auckland Park 2092
South Africa
+2711 628 3200
www.jacana.co.za

© Ruth Hopkins, 2020

All rights reserved.

ISBN 978-1-4314-2936-3

Also available as an ebook.

Cover design by publicide
Editing by Megan Mance
Layout by Aimèe Armstrong
Proofreading by Lara Jacob
Index by Megan Mance
Set in Ehrhardt MT Std 11.5/15.5pt
Printed by Inside Data, Cape Town
Job no. 004025

See a complete list of Jacana titles at www.jacana.co.za

The Misery Merchants
Life and death in a private South African prison

Ruth Hopkins

To my parents, Brian and Janet

Contents

Author's note		ix
1	How I ended up in prison in South Africa	1
2	Lwazi's list of the dead	11
3	The Madiba clansman – Dan	17
4	Chasing Setlai	29
5	Chemical silencing – zombies and robots	43
6	Death in the dark room	67
7	Dust to dust – Tebogo Bereng	83
8	Don't call me farm boy	95
9	The strike	109
10	Keeping it tight: The Department of Correctional Services	129
11	Zach 'No blood on the ground' Modise	143
12	Power in numbers	157
13	The shareholders, the contract and the government	171
14	G4S in South Africa	181
15	Plus ça change…	193
16	Fight or flight?	213
17	Interconnectedness-towards-wholeness	225
A word of thanks		243
Appendix		247
Notes		249
Postscript		253
Index		275

Author's note

FROM 2012 TO 2020, I INVESTIGATED allegations of abuse at Mangaung Correctional Centre in Bloemfontein, South Africa. Over the years, I interviewed approximately 100 inmates and 30 guards at the prison, as well as multiple government and G4S sources. Some sources leaked information: video footage, reports, photos, emails, affidavits and other records. Others provided eyewitness accounts of alleged assaults and other forms of abuse. I received confidential material from sources who have chosen to remain anonymous, because they fear reprisals. I have corroborated the allegations put forward by named and anonymous sources, as much as possible. I have opted to refer to most sources by their last name. I refer to some sources in this book by their first name only. This is because I have come to know these people well during my investigation and I never addressed them with their last names when I met them.

I provided the Department of Correctional Services (DCS), G4S and shareholders of the prison contract, Bloemfontein Correctional Services (BCC), an opportunity to respond to the allegations contained in this book. I sent them twenty pages of questions, including various allegations, ranging from well-documented cases of abuse to hearsay I picked up in the prison. G4S's spokesperson Heinrich Hoffman wrote in an email to me on 2 July 2019: 'we are unable to comment on your questions because the shareholders in Bloemfontein Correctional Contracts (BCC), including G4S and its employees, are contractually prohibited from providing comment without the express approval of the Department of Correctional Services.' Spokesperson for the department Logan Maistry wrote in an email to me on 9 July 2019 that the matter was before court, so he also declined comment. Lastly, Pappie Mokoena, the chair of BCC, also declined to comment, other than to point out: 'The allegations made in the Right to Reply document are of a contentious and serious nature. As we have advised you in the past, we would not condone nor tolerate abuse at the Mangaung Correctional Centre and would deal with any such conduct should we become aware of it. Based on our previous engagements with you we do not believe that you intend to give BCC a fair opportunity to respond or that you intend to report in a balanced manner on matters that relate to the Mangaung Correctional Centre. You have in the past also undertaken to provide detailed information or proof of your allegations but have failed to do so, despite the gravity of the alleged acts.'

I will make most source documents available at www.ruth-hopkins.com subsequent to the publication of this book. I will also share the full text of DCS's, G4S's and BCC's responses to questions I sent to them, because I believe transparency is crucial to both democracy and journalism.

Journalists exercise their democratic role in society by holding those in power to account. People have the right to know why and how their government spends tax money on the for-profit incarceration of citizens. Both the Department of Correctional Services and G4S have not been transparent about this. For five and a half years the department and the company were in court opposing an application to access the DCS investigation report on the human rights violations that took place in the prison and that are detailed in this book. G4S's first motion, after it applied to be added to the case, was to request that the underlying evidence in the report – medical records, affidavits and other documentation – would be subject to a 'judicial peek'. This means the judge would have a secret review of the evidence to determine whether the justification for the denial of access was valid or not. In other words, the evidence of maltreatment would not be discussed in an open court. However, on 7 February 2020, the High Court in Pretoria rejected the application for a 'judicial peek' and instructed the department to publish an unredacted report.[1] Judge Pierre Rabie

Author's note

ordered the department to release the report within 15 days. Time will tell if and how the department will publish this report. At the time of writing, the department had not responded to the ruling.[2]

G4S however, did respond. On 10 February 2020, they released a strange statement, which I have added as an appendix to this book. 'In 1998, G4S South Africa became a minority shareholder in Bloemfontein Correctional Contracts (BCC) – the concessionaire company responsible for the management of MCC. It is anticipated that G4S South Africa's investment will end in 2026, when BCC's contract expires. In line with the G4S Group strategy, G4S South Africa has no plans to invest further in correctional services in South Africa,' the statement reads.

The company stated in relation to my investigation and the contentious DCS report: 'In 2013, G4S South Africa received reports of alleged mistreatment of prisoners at MCC and, in response, proposed that a retired judge carry out an independent investigation into the allegations. In the event, BCC reviewed the allegations and concluded that there was no evidence to support the allegations.'

This evident lack of transparency is worrying, because it pervades the entire prison privatisation project in South Africa. The privatisation of correctional facilities was pushed through parliament in record time, with barely any discussion around the morality or desirability of the proposed project. Time has shown that this was an ill-informed, costly decision, not only in terms of public finance. The human cost of electroshocking, forcibly medicating and indefinitely segregating incarcerated people is huge. Not just for the people held in this prison, but for society at large. Because the men harmed in prison will re-enter society and most probably cause more harm. An uninterrupted cycle of violence inevitably leads to more violence. This book aims to expose and eventually interrupt the cycle of violence.

And this is why speaking truth to power is so important, especially when political governance and commercial incentives have become indistinguishable bed fellows. As Maria Ressa, a fearless journalist from the Philippines and editor of online news site Rappler[3] stated in her keynote speech at the 11th Global Conference on Investigative

Journalism held in September 2019 in Hamburg:[4] "Without facts, we don't have truth. Without truth, there is no trust. Without all three, you can't have democracy. This is why democracy is broken around the world."

So who is speaking truth to powerful multinationals like G4S? In an age where political leaders seem obsessed with austerity measures and public sector cost cutting – and not much else – it should come as no surprise that they will not do this. What is it then that we, the people, can do? How do we want to organise the punishment of people who have transgressed certain norms in society? Should governments award profitable contracts to multinational enterprises that are mostly focused on their share price and have very little concern for the humanity of the people they interact with? I hope this book will lead to a discussion of these ethical and moral issues and that it will energise people to think and to speak out.

This book is an invitation to reclaim the democratic debate around the privatisation of prisons specifically and the entire private security industry generally. We, the people, should not be ignored and misinformed. We should have our say.

1

How I ended up in prison in South Africa

THE WOODEN BENCH IS designed to feel uncomfortable. I'm sitting bolt upright, shifting uncomfortably, facing the reception area of the prison. A young woman with tightly braided hair and wearing a bright red and blue G4S uniform answers a telephone behind a counter. A man in his mid-twenties stands behind her, chatting to another woman, who is a bit plumper than the first.

Adjacent to the reception desk is a security area. A bored G4S guard feeds all incoming items through an X-ray machine. A row of lockers to the side provides a secure space for visitor belongings as they venture into this maximum-security prison, which houses just under 3 000 prisoners, in Bloemfontein, Free State. It is August 2012, and I am visiting this modern and privatised prison for the second time.

G4S is a multinational security company with a presence in 90 countries, employing about 550 000 people. It boasts on its website that Mangaung prison is the second biggest maximum-security prison in the world.[5] G4S also provides security and cash-in-transit services and runs prisons in the UK, Australia and South Africa. It claims to be South Africa's and Africa's biggest private employer.[6]

A woman walks towards me. This must be Anneke, I think. When

I arrived at the prison the guards asked me to wait, because Anneke la Grange, the security manager, wanted to speak to me.

She has very coiffed, medium-length hair in different shades: a shock of blondish hair frames the right side of her face, the rest is of a copper/purplish shade. She takes a seat on the bench and faces me. Her make-up is as manicured as her hairdo: shades above her eyes fade into each other like a sunset, her shiny lipstick has been applied with precision.

After some friendly chitchat, she asks me why I'm here.

'I work for the Wits Justice Project,' I say, hoping that might suffice. 'We investigate legal matters. Prisoners write to us about their legal problems, and we help them find lawyers.'

Working closely with lawyers, the Wits Justice Project (WJP) focuses on the criminal justice system. During my time with the WJP, it was an all-woman team, and we often talked about the South African criminal justice system being broken – and mainly failing the poor.

I tell her that the letters prisoners send us speak of wide-ranging concerns: expired medication, lost transcripts, appealing old cases, torture, court delays, wrongful convictions, prosecutorial misconduct and many others. Many letters we receive at the WJP come from people held at Mangaung.

I expect her to throw me out, but she nods, and when I'm done explaining, she says it's fine, she understands. My heart is beating so loudly in my ears, I can barely hear her. Trembling slightly, I put all my possessions save for my notebook and pen in the locker. The bored guard runs my notebook and pen through the X-ray machine. I step into one of two cubicles behind the machine. A female warder follows me in, draws the blue curtain and pats me down. I get the all-clear and can leave the cubicle.

A direct supervision officer (DSO), as G4S calls their prison guards, leads me through heavy double doors into a square space without windows. The posters on the wall are the only distractions, showing objects you're not allowed to bring in, warnings about TB and HIV, and listing the clothing rules (no short skirts) and visiting hours.

A second door springs open. It's clearly operated remotely, as the DSO didn't touch anything. The courtyard on the other side is bathed in harsh sunlight. As I walk across, I see the gardens. Men in blue uniforms push wheelbarrows into a polytunnel. A chain-link fence separates the garden from the fields. Men carrying spades and rakes pass through a narrow gate in the fence.

The units in Mangaung prison are named after prisons G4S ran, and mostly still runs, in the UK and Australia. The two units named after G4S-run Australian prisons are Mount Gambier[7] – which accommodates prisoners who are studying, either remotely or through on-site programmes – and Port Phillip. The units with 'UK' names are Altcourse, Buckley Hall, Rye Hill and Wolds. Altcourse was named after a prison G4S opened in Lancashire in 1997.[8] Buckley Hall was named after a prison that Group 4 – G4S's predecessor – ran in Rochdale until 2000,[9] when the state took over the management of the prison. The Wolds unit is named after a Yorkshire prison G4S ran until 2012 when it lost the contract after the Inspectorate for Prisons found that: 'performance had deteriorated and we expressed concerns about a number of issues, including the availability of drugs, a lack of staff confidence in confronting poor behaviour, weaknesses in the promotion of diversity and limited work and training provision'.[10] The Wolds unit is where troublemakers are sent. In Wolds, you either stay in a cell with three other cellmates on a 'street', which is a corridor with cells on both sides, or alone in one of the isolation cells, known as 'intermediate'.

And then, finally, there is a unit not named after existing prisons elsewhere but after one of the most famous streets in the world – Broadway. It is made up entirely of isolation cells. This is where you'll find those prisoners needing protection as well as those from whom others need to be protected. An isolation unit, where people sit alone in their cells all day, named after a place, famed for its entertainment and art. I wonder what the corporate officials tasked with providing names for prison units were thinking...

The prison faces the main thoroughfare, Dewetsdorp Road, in the distance. I walk past a set of toilets into the visitation building and hand the receptionist a list of prisoners I'd faxed through the day before. She runs the details through the resident administration system.

Lwazi's* mugshot pops up on her computer screen. He is clean-shaven, but his piercing eyes are deep set and his stare menacing: 'What the fuck are you looking at?' His eyebrows are scrunched together into a frown, his personal information framing his face. Race: black. Nationality: Xhosa. Age: 38.

With its high ceilings, whitewashed walls and white furniture, the sparse visiting hall feels clinical. There are two vending machines at the back: one with chips and sweets and the other with cooldrinks. The space is empty. I walk past two guards slouched in their chairs to the interview 'rooms', which are not really rooms, as they look like phone booths dating back to before cell phones. The interview booths all have windows through which you can see the visiting room. Inside each booth, a table and worn office chairs are squeezed together.

I take a seat behind the table.

I read through my notes while I wait for Lwazi and think back to the first time I came here, in early 2012. I had just been hired by the WJP and was eager to get stuck into an interesting case, a challenging investigation. When Bernard, a Mangaung prisoner originally from Tanzania, wrote to us that he had been wrongfully convicted of a murder in Fish Hoek, Cape Town, I wanted that to be it. I would dissect and pull apart the miscarriage of justice – and write about it, beautifully. I would leave no stone unturned, and the rays of justice would shine through the cracks of the broken criminal justice system to expose the glaring wrongdoing.

I met with Bernard in one of these not-so-well-aerated booths. Wide-eyed and wildly, Bernard emptied the contents of a plastic bag on the table. His papers lay between us like a sacrificial offering, and he picked up letter after document after letter, passionately pleading his case. His despair caught on, because I started believing him, not because the evidence was weak or strong, but because he *seemed* so innocent, so honest.

---

*   Not his real name

After that visit, he wrote to me: 'You're an angel, sent by God.' I flew to Cape Town only to find out that Bernard had known the murder victim before his death and that his palm print had been found in the house of the murder victim. I interviewed his best friend who told me he had noticed that Bernard was acting weirdly a few months before the murder, only to disappear after the crime was committed. The investigating officer told me he had attempted several times to locate the alibi Bernard provided, to no avail.

So, Bernard had thoroughly hoodwinked me. I learned an important lesson from this rookie mistake: never judge anyone by their appearance. The facts and evidence are all that count.

I'm still thinking about not judging anyone by their appearance when Lwazi enters the interview room. He's tall, with a two-day stubble and some patches of grey hair on his chin. It is August 2012, and a pinch of winter still lurks, creeping into joints. In winter, the Mangaung prisoners each get a blue polyester fleece jacket, which they wear over of their cotton pants and shirts, which are a shade fainter than the jacket. The pastel assemblage seems too cute and sweet for prison.

Nothing about Lwazi is cute or sweet. He doesn't look at me, he glares.

'Hi, I'm Lwazi.' His voice is surprisingly soft and gentle.

He scans the room before he sits down. His glare is measured and calculating. Then he starts interrogating me: who am I, what is the WJP, and why am I here? What are my aims? Lwazi had written to the Wits Justice Project, as had many other Mangaung inmates who I had put on the visiting list that I had faxed. But Lwazi is clearly not a trusting person.

I try to answer his questions. Then there is silence, and we look at each other uncomfortably. Small talk will break the ice, I reckon. Pointing at his tattoos, I ask him how he feels about his gang affiliation. He is a general in the 26s.

The 26, 27 and 28 prison gangs rely on a set of rules and codes of conduct that were established and developed about a century ago. Mostly unwritten myth has it that around 1900, Nongoloza, who roamed the hills of what is now Gauteng, formed a gang, which later split into three separate gangs: the 26s, 27s and 28s. They lived according to an elaborate set of rules governing honour, sexual relationships, money, rank and information. Nowadays the rules of the gangs have evolved differently in each prison.[11]

'Twenty-six is the camp of "Grey". The 26 deal with money and dagga and are not too much into blood. Unless there is a need.' Grey, I later quickly google, was a man Nongoloza met in prison. Grey headed a group of eight men who became gangsters – the 26s – to protect themselves against the violence and sexual threats of Nongoloza's men.

Lwazi has warmed up. He ventures deeper and deeper into the nooks and crannies of the endless folklore of Nongoloza's men, their allies and enemies.

'When Grey and his eight men were in prison, Nongoloza asked him, "Who are you?"

'"I am Grey," he answered, "with the crown", which was a reference to money. This is why the 26 gang is also called "Grey" and why we're known for our love of money,' Lwazi continues. His eyes sparkle above his gap-toothed smile. Suddenly he looks a lot less menacing.

Lwazi has a tattoo of a scorpion on his lower left arm. He got it because he was chased by the Directorate of Special Operations, commonly called the Scorpions, before his arrest for murder, he says. The Scorpions investigated organised crime and corruption during the first decade of the new millennium before they were disbanded in 2009.

He catches me looking at the roughly drawn image. 'I have another one,' he says and rolls up his right sleeve. A dark blob on his upper right arm looks like a Rorschach test. 'This is the beast,' he says, laughing at me as I try to make out a figure.

'It refers to an ox that was stolen from a white farmer, a retired cop who used to patrol the mines where Paul Mambazo, also known as Po, used to work and where the 26s, 27s and 28s started. And see this ...' He points to some faded letters next to 'the beast'. I can barely make them out: 'Fuck yu.'

In the late 1980s, while Lwazi was still at high school, in Mthatha in the Eastern Cape, he joined Umkhonto we Sizwe (MK), the armed wing of the African National Congress (ANC). He served under Ronnie Matshaya, who would later become Nelson Mandela's bodyguard.

'In the afternoons after school, I was carrying guns for the ANC, and this led to mischief for survival,' he continues. 'I was driving stolen cars, and there were lots of girls chasing me. I used to park those cars in the school's staff parking lot. That didn't go down well with the teachers. In those days, they still used corporal punishment, and one teacher tried it on me. It was unconstitutional, what he did. I manhandled that teacher.' Lwazi was expelled. He was 15.

Lwazi's family home in Mthatha was situated right next to a military base. This is the base where 18 people died in November 1990 during a failed military bid to overthrow former homeland military ruler Bantu Holomisa.[12] Lwazi says the gunshots that rang out that day 'riveted' him. 'After that coup, there were a lot of machine guns dropped by soldiers running away,' he remembers.

Around the time Nelson Mandela became state president in 1994, Lwazi got a job in the army and completed his military training at Port St Johns. But by 1996, disillusionment set in, and he lost faith in the ANC. 'If you fail to take care of soldiers,' he says, 'you invite trouble.'

Lwazi got involved in an armed robbery and he shot and killed someone. It led to a life sentence.

'You changed from being a soldier to a perpetrator in a matter of months,' I remark.

'I became a gang inside,' Lwazi responds.

A warder knocks on the window. I have become lost in the twists and turns of Lwazi's tales.

The guard says other prisoners are waiting for me. I think of the names on the list I had faxed through, names that belong to people who are now in the adjacent room, where the shackled and unshackled – depending on their disciplinary record – men sit and wait for their visitors. Men who probably haven't had a visit in months.

'Can we continue this discussion about your background later?' I ask, just as Lwazi is explaining that he is a Grey 26 with a 'white stamp'. This means he deals with money.

It is all about blood, fights, honour and money. But I am not here to learn more about the numbers gangs. I want to know what is happening in Mangaung prison.

I ask Lwazi what kind of information he has for me.

'Deaths in prison,' he says, deadpan.

He tells me that he has drawn up lists with detailed information on the abuse that is taking place. That he has a 'soldier' in every unit in the prison, a 26-gang member feeding him information.

'They are murdering us,' he adds as he scrunches up his eyebrows, making his eyes look even more fox-like.

'In that prison hospital,' he says, pointing in its direction, 'people are being poisoned, injected, beaten up. I've lost count of the body bags.'

I instinctively lower my voice. 'What proof do you have?' I whisper.

'I have smuggled information out of the prison. You can pick it up at a lawyer's office in Johannesburg. Ask for Rachel. She works there as a receptionist.'

Lwazi gets up. I stand up as well and shake his hand. He slips out the door, and I am left behind in the stuffy room, with yellowish foam spilling out of holes in the upholstery leaving foam crumbs on the armrests and my shirt.

2

Lwazi's list of the dead

I PICK UP LWAZI'S envelope from the small lawyer's office in Sandton. It is an upmarket practice. Among the many shiny luxury cars in the reserved parking bays in a leafy garden surrounding the office, my dusty, clapped-out, 1985 Mercedes looks like a time traveller. I sit and wait until a smartly dressed Rachel appears, hands me the envelope, and then disappears.

Most of the prisoners I spoke to before meeting Lwazi told me about assaults, electroshocking and forced medication. They also told me about suicides and prisoners dying following torture or abuse. Lwazi said he had compiled lists of names of people who had experienced some or all of these things.

Back at my office, I open the envelope. It contains one letter, about 20 handwritten pages, written in clear and regular capital letters, giving every word a measure of urgency.

Lwazi starts the letter by explaining what, in his view, lies at the root of the problems at Mangaung prison: 'This institution provides a platform for certain individuals to flout rules as they please for their financial gain.'

He writes about a prisoner who died in September 2012. He had stabbed a female DSO, and that had landed him in 'intermediate'. In the early morning hours, the night patrol discovered his body, allegedly hanging from a window.

'This inmate's height is 1.8m, and the height of cell windows is 2m, so it is highly unlikely for an inmate of that height to be able to hang himself,' Lwazi points out in the letter.

The man's cellmate at the time claimed that he was in the cell while his co-inhabitant was committing suicide but that he neither heard nor saw anything.

'This cellmate said that the suicide happened at 9 pm, whereas the night patrol men maintained that they discovered it at 6 am, soon after he warned them, on the same day. It is clear this prisoner is hiding something,' Lwazi's letter continues.

I add the cellmate's name to the list of prisoners I wish to see at Mangaung the following day and fax it through.

The cellmate is a young man in his early thirties. He wears glasses and has a scar above his left eyebrow. Despite his gang affiliation, he is afraid of speaking about the cause of death of his cellmate. 'Because of my safety, I must be careful of what I say,' he explains.

He does agree to talk about his cellmate's last few weeks. He tells me how he had become increasingly desperate before he died. It had something to do, the cellmate says, with several blood tests – for a range of illnesses, including HIV – a dirty needle and test results not coming back on time. 'He asked me: "These people, will they help me or kill me?"'

Lwazi's notes are on various issues, ranging from exorbitant phone call costs to the quality of the food and prisoners dying like flies. It must have cost him days to compile them.

Isaac Nelani is the next prisoner on Lwazi's list of the dead. 'The safety of prisoners when they are in solitary confinement is not guaranteed,' he writes. 'An inmate by the name of Isaac Nelani, who was removed from his unit to the Broadway unit, was assaulted and electroshocked and died there in 2005.'

Karel Laaken* is next. Lwazi alleges that he died after being injected with an unknown substance. Another inmate allegedly ended up in a wheelchair. Lwazi claims another inmate died when he was left inside a cell with a rival gang member, and the warder apparently watched while he was being slaughtered.

Lwazi smuggles more information out of the prison. Every time we meet, he presents a new case. He says Pappie Botha** underwent an operation on his stomach, yet he is still suffering from extreme abdominal pains, following complications. Despite Zoli Zali's 'reclassification' as a medium-security prisoner, the transfer to this kind of facility is yet to happen. Another inmate was allegedly raped by his cellmate. I write down all the details to follow up later.

Lwazi's advocacy on behalf of his fellow incarcerated men seems at odds with his carefully crafted image as a ruthless thug.

But then I remember his remark, at our very first meeting, that his decision to join the 26s did not originate from his love of the gangster life. It was motivated by a desire to help and protect others. He told me how he saw a young boy being raped by a 28-gang member and the helplessness he felt because he couldn't do anything to stop it. He asked other offenders what he could do to fight prison rape. They said, 'Nothing, unless you join a gang.'

Lwazi took to the 26s' lifestyle. He was promoted several times. 'I worked myself through the ranks, from stone yard [a prisoner with no rank] to soldier, mountain, sergeant, major, captain, inspector and eventually made the top rank of general,' he says. His gang career has, however, ended in remorse. Lwazi, who at the time of writing is

---

*   Not his real name
**   Not his real name

waiting to be released on parole, has rejected his gang affiliation and expressed remorse for the hurt he caused.

Karel Laaken's family wants nothing to do with an inquest into his death, they tell me when a colleague phones them. He had raped and killed his own sister. The family never wanted to hear his name again. I also fail to corroborate the other names on Lwazi's list.

These dead ends in my death investigations are overshadowed by Isaac Nelani, whose death was so dark, unforgiving and unresolved, I become obsessed with it.

G4S: The biggest company you have never heard of

The company that runs Mangaung prison, G4S, is the largest company you have never heard of. It claims to be one of South Africa's biggest employers, with approximately 15 000 people on its payroll.[13] In addition to running the Bloemfontein prison, G4S offers guarding, cash-in-transit services and security technology. It has contracts with embassies, government departments and private companies in South Africa. G4S also provided security for the infamous Indian Gupta family who stand accused of looting South African state coffers.

Once you've seen them, it is hard to unsee them. In Johannesburg, the ubiquitous cash-in-transit vans suddenly appear from nowhere. The black-and-red G4S logo is unmistakeable – and it seems to be everywhere.

Yet while the company is everywhere, it is also invisible. Like furniture blending into the background, G4S is omnipresent but barely noticeable. During my investigation, I never see the managers or directors of Mangaung prison. G4S's South African head office routinely refers all media inquiries – including my own – to the Department of Correctional Services (DCS).

3

The Madiba clansman – Dan

'When an animal stops being tame, should it be put down?'

WITH ITS BROWN, BEIGE, cream and white interior, the Urban Hotel is Bloemfontein's most earnest attempt at being cool. The rooms are lush and simple at the same time. There are framed oval rugs on the walls. A glass wall divides the shower and bedroom. While most other accommodation in Bloemfontein is characterised by a twee homeliness, the Urban Hotel is decidedly trendy, nearly aloof.

In the tiny suave bar on the first floor, a barman serves beer, cold drinks and wine. He places the glasses on paper coasters. There's a tinny rumble coming from the television, with some sport on.

I arrange to meet Dan Mbelwane, a warder at Mangaung, at the bar, as the dry air inside the hotel makes me thirsty. It's late in 2012.

Dan sits opposite me in a hip transparent plastic chair. He spreads his legs and cocks his head. It feels like he's assessing me like Tony Soprano, trying to decide whether I will live or die.

In his early thirties, Dan has piercing eyes and a permanent scowl. His head is shaven. A thin goatee lines his jaw, and he has a moustache.

Dan tells me he doesn't trust white people. 'What are your terms of reference?' he asks me, more than once. 'What is it that you want?'

I explain, again, that I am a journalist. That Lwazi recommended I speak to him. That Lwazi had told me that a warder by the name of Dan is organising resistance among prisoners and warders in the prison, that he is forging a pact between them. This sparked my interest because I had never come across prisoners and warders working together.

I tell Dan I have stories about unimaginable abuse, suffering and torture happening in Mangaung prison, that I want to write them down and that I'm hoping he can help me find further evidence.

He just looks at me while I explain. I'm not sure he's even listening.

'Medical files,' I say, taking to a direct approach. 'Can you access them?'

'Of what?' he asks.

'Of the injuries, of course.'

'I can get those,' he says, confidently.

Dan and I meet several times over the next few months. He usually shows up an hour, two hours late. Sometimes he doesn't turn up at all and turns off his phone. I have to practise patience, not one of my fortes.

We meet again at the Urban in February 2013. He's late, and I am on the verge of giving up on him when he arrives, with his wife in tow. She takes a seat next to him. She doesn't say a word but keeps a close eye on me.

I have nothing to trade with, nothing to convince Dan that he should trust me, other than that I keep showing up. I have been visiting Mangaung once or twice a month for the past year and have spoken to about 40 prisoners by now. Since I last saw Dan, I have more stories of prisoners who claim to have been electroshocked, beaten up, and who have shown me their scarred, swollen, bruised and, apparently, broken limbs. There are some who say they have been in isolation for as long as four years. I have watched prisoners stumble, appearing to be out of their minds, and I was told this was after they had been forcibly injected with something, a substance that made them 'robotic, zombie-like and very tired'. I tell Dan all of this.

He listens, and talks, but he doesn't really give me anything I can use.

Before he leaves, he waves a blue paper at me.

'You see, here's a medical file,' he says. 'Warders broke this prisoner's hand, but look, there is nothing, no mention of an injury. Nothing. That is how they cover up.'

And then: 'I have a lot of information. A lot. Everything you want.'

I really want that paper. I try to take it, but he quickly flicks it back in his pocket. I never see it again.

As he leaves, he remarks, casually: 'I once beat up an inmate and broke his hand.' He refuses to divulge anything further, and I'm not sure if it is a warning or if he'd just let it slip.

When I see him about a month later, he brings one of his sidekicks, a skinny guy with a wispy moustache who doesn't say much but nods a lot. They are both members of POPCRU, the Police and Prisons Civil Rights Union.

I tell Dan that Lwazi said he knows more about the case of Isaac Nelani, who allegedly died in solitary confinement after being assaulted. Some of the other prisoners I had interviewed had whispered Nelani's name, appearing to confirm what Lwazi had written in his notes. They say that on a cold winter's day in 2005, following Nelani's request for more blankets, guards beat him up so badly that he died.

The imprisoned men also allege prison management repositioned his body to make it look like a suicide.

'He didn't hang himself, that much I know,' Dan says. The skinny guy nods solemnly. 'But management made it look like suicide. They hung a jacket around his neck and attached it to the door.

'They keep prisoners like tamed animals in cages. When an animal stops being tame, should it be put down?' Dan asks me.

The skinny guy smirks, daring me to answer.

In April 2013, I return to Bloemfontein. By this time, the Urban's sense of cool has waned, and I opt for one of the many guesthouses run by an Afrikaans family: each individual homely interior feels more uniform at every visit. There is always an overweight sausage dog sniffing for food scraps, framed saccharine little mottos dot the walls, and Christian iconography adorn every corner of the house. But all this *truttigheid*, as their Dutch ancestors would have said, is actually, at the end of a long stressful day, quite comforting. More importantly, fresh air circulates through those houses, something that does require disconnecting the electric air freshener that spreads a sickly-sweet scent if left connected.

Since the hotel bar is no longer an option for meetings, I decide to hide in plain sight. I meet a string of sources at fast-food chain Wimpy in Mimosa Mall, one of Bloemfontein's busy, bustling shopping centres. All they have to offer a vegetarian is a soggy, toasted cheese sandwich – add salad and bread to that and you have the entire available vegetarian menu in Bloemfontein.

I'd been waiting for an hour at the Wimpy when Dan shows up with one of his 'soldiers', as he calls the small cabal of young men who work with him to 'bring down G4S'. He often says this in their presence. They sit at his side, silently. When Dan speaks, sparking hopes of a revolution, voicing disdain for the 'dogs of capitalism', they nod vigorously. They are disciplined and only speak when Dan asks them to.

The two men shuffle into the red pleather seats opposite me. I see it's the skinny guy again.

It is at this meeting that I notice for the first time that Dan now seems to be talking in the first-person plural, as if the two of us, we're a team: 'Don't worry. We'll get them.'

Perhaps it's because we're meeting in a public place for the first time, but I also become aware of how careful Dan is. He carries no phone and barely looks at me when he talks, scanning the steady stream of people coming through the revolving doors at the entrance of the mall. As we leave, I see he didn't come with a car.

Dan hates how G4S workers are treated at the prison. He speaks about racism, corruption and negligence. For years, they've been asking management to replace the ceramic toilets in the prison, for instance, because the shards often ended up in warders' arms, legs or hands.

A female warder has been raped. A male guard died, three months after the last of three stabbings that happened in the prison. Not one of the warders who were assaulted, stabbed, taken hostage or raped was apparently offered any significant counselling.

POPCRU compiled a list of 30 detailed complaints received from 2005 to 2012 about the unacceptable levels of violence in the prison:

DSO Kgopane was assaulted on the head and sustained serious head injuries, later passed away, after resigning.

DSO Tshepang Khaphe was stabbed in the head at Buckley Hall in January 2012 and was given one day leave and dismissed on [sic] 2012.

DSO Tutu Motshelamadi was assaulted with a pool ball in Port Phillip and sustained a serious head wound.[14]

The list of complaints goes on and on. I'm told it was sent to the prison management, but the problems were never really addressed. In addition, warder and guard salaries have not been raised in a decade.

Dan wants me to meet some of the G4S warders who feel that the company maltreated them. He introduces me to Pule Moholo and Dehlazwa Mdi, two former G4S DSOs who were on duty in the Broadway unit on 2 November 2009, when a hostage situation erupted. I had heard about it from some of the prisoners I interviewed before. These men told me that, following the incident, they were stripped naked, electroshocked and injected with 'zombie drugs'.

I meet Pule and Mdi – he goes by his last name – at the latter's house. We all sit down around a square coffee table, and Mdi starts talking. He has a raspy voice and is chatty. Pule, on the other hand, is shy and withdrawn. He seems to be deep in thought. When he finally speaks, he mumbles. Listening to his frightful story, I understand his reticence.

Around noon on the day of the hostage situation, Pule and Mdi did what they do every day at that time – they let the prisoners out into exercise cubicles to stretch their legs for an hour. A group of 11 prisoners overpowered Pule and forced him to unlock all the cells in Broadway. His arm was cut with a piece of broken glass in the scuffle, and he was cuffed.

Mdi was also assaulted and cuffed. 'Some of the prisoners said: "We just want a transfer out of this prison. Don't worry, we won't hurt you,"' Mdi remembers. 'But others disagreed and suggested that they should stab our eyes out or rape us.' The prisoners then locked him, Pule and another guard in an exercise cubicle.

The prisoners demanded that their transfer demands be heard before releasing the three hostages. They were pretty desperate. A hunger strike was happening around the same time, to draw attention to reclassification issues. After serving a set number of years of their sentence without incident, prisoners in South Africa should be reclassified from maximum-security to medium-security prisoners. Reclassification works much like parole; a file is kept on the prisoner containing information on the severity of the crimes committed, possible history of alcohol and/or drug abuse, disciplinary record in prison, evidence of participation in peer groups and programme involvement. Medium security means a wider choice of prisons and more lenient conditions. Reclassification often offers a chance to be closer to loved ones. It's a highly desired milestone in most prisoners' sentences. Yet in Mangaung, prisoners complained their reclassification never happened, despite clean records and completion of other programme elements. A DCS whistleblower had flagged irregular reclassification at Mangaung prison in 2009, but nothing had been done. The beds at Mangaung remained full, reclassification notwithstanding.

When negotiations between senior management at Mangaung and the hostage takers went nowhere, a special unit of the South African Police Service (SAPS) was called in. By the time the snipers were in place and the fully armed police officers entered the prison, the three hostages had been locked up for 16 hours.

Mdi first caught a rubber police bullet in his side and Pule took a blow from the butt of a police gun before G4S managers pointed out that they were warders. Prisoners had taken their uniforms. The three hostages were then finally taken to safety, and the prisoners subsequently became the prey in an orgy of violence meted out by the prison's internal emergency security team (EST).

Pule and Mdi were treated for 'minor injuries' in the prison hospital. 'We were told not to talk to anyone,' Pule remembers. 'They injected me in the buttocks.' The drugs put him to sleep immediately. When he woke up, he says he felt strange. He couldn't walk, talk or move properly. His thoughts were foggy, his balance was off. 'I was wheeled out of the prison in a wheelchair,' he says. When he got home, he slept for two days straight. His memory of those days is vague, he tells me.[15]

Mdi says he had similar symptoms. 'I felt very drowsy, and I slept for 24 hours when I got home,' he remembers. He puts it down to shock.

Not long after Pule arrived back home, he says G4S management visited him. They told him and his wife not to talk to the media about what had happened. They insisted he detail the events of that day in an affidavit, which he says made him realise something was off. Early in 2010, he was dismissed due to 'gross negligence' following a disciplinary hearing.

I'm startled to find out that G4S guards also claim to have been injected with the 'zombie' drug some of the prisoners have told me about. Both the incarcerated men and their guards seem expendable. A needle prick will even make them forget there was a problem.

'You were at the prison today,' Dan tells me as we sit down at the Wimpy again. It is May 2013, and he has brought one of his soldiers with him again. He rattles off a list names of prisoners I interviewed. 'My soldiers,' is all he says when I ask him how he knew I was there.

Dan's belief that the prisoners and their guards have to work together is unusual. I have seen prisoners and guards occasionally striking up individual friendships, but on the whole, they tend to dislike each other. But at Mangaung, the jailer and the jailbirds have now formed a team.

This unorthodox cooperation started when Dan met Lwazi. Like Lwazi, Dan is also from the Eastern Cape. 'They used to call out my clan name when they saw me: "Hey Madiba!"' Dan recalls. 'Lwazi approached me and asked me if he could trust me. I said that he should never trust me, because he is an inmate and I am an officer. Before we can talk, I told him, you need to contact all the high-ranking generals and tell them to stop stabbing guards. He's clever, and I believe I influenced him positively, and we started to have a workable understanding of the role of prisoners and the role of warders.' His soldier nods.

Dan speaks about the demographics in the prison a lot. Warders and the people placed in their care are black, whereas the prison management is predominantly white.

Through that racial lens Dan observed how white staff members either held administrative positions with minimal interaction with the prison population, or they were part of the heavily armed – and therefore relatively safe – EST, also known as the Ninjas or the Zulus. The warders or DSOs, who work in close quarters with violent prisoners, are unarmed and mostly black.

This obvious race-based inequality is one of the things that led Dan to start thinking differently about those in prison, to start seeing them not as animals, but as fellow human beings. He began initiating relationships with Lwazi and others.

Both parties – the prison generals and the prison warders – agreed early in 2013 that there was unchecked violence inflicted on prisoners. They also concluded that the warders were equally subjected to unnecessary levels of violence.

'G4S views both the workers and the prisoners as a commodity. The company doesn't care if we are safe or if our lives are protected. All black bodies are "cash cows" to them,' Dan explains.

'Lwazi was my messenger. He convinced the other generals that the stabbings had to stop. We had to stop killing each other, as this is exactly what we did during apartheid: black people were killing each other. But then they united and brought down the system. We wanted to work together to get rid of G4S, so the DCS could take over. That was our shared aim. We agreed there and then that no one shall be abused by either party anymore.'

Dan smiles.

'You know, if life had turned out differently for me, and I had ended up in prison, then I think I would have been a general. Being a leader is in my blood. It is written into my clan name.'

Dan and I meet again at the end of May 2013. This time he arrives alone. One-on-one, Dan doesn't shout from the pulpit as much. He is more personable and relaxed. He opens up and starts talking about his background and family – his roots.

Dan was part of the G4S warder class of 2008. A young gun at 23 years old, he loved the authority of prison work, the uniforms and adrenaline rush that came with it.

He passed the three-month induction training for prospective G4S guards with flying colours. But his classmates didn't fare that well. 'I remember HR Director Stephen Page entering the room and starting to shout at us. He said we were stupid and not worthy of being G4S employees. I immediately responded and told him that he cannot paint us all with the same brush, we worked hard and this is demoralising.'

Stephen Page noticed Dan and told him he should lead his classmates and make sure their results improved. After several weeks Dan says he had inspired everyone to improve their efforts and 90 per cent of trainees passed.

This interaction became a pattern in Dan's career. He would impress and stand out, because he spoke out fearlessly. His peers looked up to him. That, in turn, led to attempts to contain him when he would not back down or fall in line. 'If you are smart, critical or outspoken, the company either promotes or fires you,' Dan says.

During his training Dan was also offered membership of POPCRU, which was unusual, as membership is normally awarded to workers, not trainees. Stephen congratulated him and told him POPCRU shop stewards could become HR managers if they were good at their jobs.

Thabang Molise, POPCRU's institutional secretary at the time, also noticed Dan. He told him he was 'the future' of POPCRU. G4S later appointed Molise as a human resources manager.

What initially drew the prison management and the union to Dan is the same thing that ultimately repelled them. He is an assertive, well-read and conscious black man.

Dan grew up in Bloemfontein with a Xhosa father and a Sotho mother. 'I hail from the same tribe as Mandela. I'm a Dlomo, Madiba, Yem Yem, Uvelebambentsele, I'm from the Thembu clan. We are kings and chiefs.'

Dan looked up to his cousin, Lerato. 'Just after I had finished high school, my cousin gave me *I Write What I Like* by Steve Biko. It shook my world. I finally understood that no one has to feel inferior because of race. But first I was a bit afraid when I read that Biko believed Jesus didn't exist. I thought this man will take me straight to hell!

'Lerato said to me: "I think you should pursue politics. One day you will see yourself in parliament."' His cousin also recommended he read the *Mail & Guardian*, so that he could stay abreast of political developments in the country.

'I can tell you this, when I first arrived in the prison, during the first two weeks, and I brought my *M&G*, it raised eyebrows. Everyone was watching me,' he says.

After a while his colleagues started asking him what he was reading.

'I recommended *I Like What I Write* to everyone and told them: "Read it, understand the message. It will inspire you as a black person to believe in yourself." My cousin gave me the book for a purpose, and it made me what I am today. I followed that book.'

G4S the global giant

The British company describes itself as the world's leading security provider and one of the biggest private employers in the world,[16] earning £7.3 billion in annual revenue in 2018 and employing close to 550 000 people in 90 countries. The multinational claims to be Africa's biggest private employer.

G4S is a 'global giant' listed on the FTSE 250 Index. It has attracted transnational capital investment from major global fund managers such as Invesco and BlackRock. And while the top-level management of the company earns top-level salaries, their lower-level workers are not well paid. Corporate Watch calculated in 2018 that Ashley Almanza, G4S's CEO, earns 403 times the average G4S pay.[17]

'Securing your world' is G4S's corporate slogan. In 2012, the company commissioned US singer-songwriter Jon Christopher Davis, who calls himself an 'Americana artist with a lone star attitude', to write its theme tune: 'G4S Securing Your World'.[18] Sadly, Davis refused permission to reproduce the lyrics of the song, because, as he wrote in a Facebook message, he has 'no association with G4S and it's a jingle not a real song'.

4

Chasing Setlai

WHISTLEBLOWERS FORM AN invaluable part of my work and professional success. Without them, I would never have broken stories, exposed wrongdoings or even made a name for myself. In every investigation I have carried out, I worked alongside men and women who helped me uncover injustice.

What makes some people decide to blow a whistle and others keep their mouths shut? Every time I meet a source who is prepared to risk livelihood and security for elusive ideals such as 'the right thing' or 'justice denied', I am amazed. I have never been in a situation where I would have to make that choice.

But not all whistleblowers are filled with a sense of justice. I have met some along the way who were filled with feelings of revenge; they wanted to 'out' a particular person. Others had a distinct and acute moral objection and felt the need to bring to light more systemic forms of abuse. Others still wanted to feel important and sought the limelight, vicariously. This last group, without exception, consisted of people working on a book of their own.

Most whistleblowers I've met were bad sleepers. They had good, dysfunctional or no relationships; they were married, single, widowed or cheating on their partner. They were mostly cranky middle-aged men with beer bellies, bald spots and sometimes an alcohol problem. Their spouses often did not want to hear about their 'work problems' and told them to stop talking about 'those things'. This made them isolated and distrustful. What kept them awake at night was often the very reason they were talking to me.

Tatolo Setlai's motives were never clear to me; I didn't fully understand why he agreed to speak to me in the first place. Every time I managed to secure an appointment with him, he became more of a mystery. He was a reluctant whistleblower to start with and cancelled meeting after meeting, or just didn't show. Maybe jaded was a better word to describe him. That possibly stemmed from the fact that he had been blowing his whistle for too long.

Trying to meet with Setlai felt like the gender-reversed equivalent of a desperate young man trying to secure a date with a reluctant, arrogant yet beautiful girl. I chased him, he rejected me and instead of discouraging me, it invigorated me. I kept designing new strategies to persuade him to meet with me.

Dan and Lwazi, my main sources at the prison, had repeatedly mentioned Tatolo Setlai, who was a Department of Correctional Services (DCS) controller at Mangaung for 10 months from 2008 to 2009. 'He wrote a scathing report about the prison and was punished for it,' Lwazi had told me at the end of one of my visits. He'd leaned in towards me with more urgency than usual. 'He knows everything.'

As he passed me Setlai's phone number, I wondered how Lwazi knew so much.

After months of chasing him, we finally have a date. It's April 2013, and he's still working for the DCS in the Free State and the Northern Cape, so our conversations are off the record. Years later, after he retires, he will go on the record.

I arrive at the Wimpy in Mimosa Mall at the agreed time, order a coffee and wait. As the minutes and then the hours tick by, I realise he's not going to come. My phone calls and text messages go unanswered. When I feel sufficiently frustrated, I SMS him angrily that I've driven all the way from Johannesburg *just* for this meeting, which is a lie. It is nevertheless effective. Come by my office the next day, he responds.

When I enter his office in the DCS office on Zastron Street the next day, he's seated behind a large desk. A middle-aged, overweight man with a shiny bald head, a double chin and small eyes, he's in his brown DCS uniform, with several pips on his epaulettes. When he sees me, he raises his bushy eyebrows, straightens his back and quickly tries to close his unbuttoned jacket with one hand.

He motions at me to sit down. I instantly forget the introduction I'd composed in my head. I bumble, making incoherent small talk. He doesn't smile or further acknowledge me.

He seems uncomfortable. Over the phone he'd already expressed hesitation, repeatedly mentioning his upcoming retirement. In his office, he specifies: 'I know what they're capable of. I cannot risk losing my pension because of this.'

He has reason to fear the wrath of the DCS. In 2001, when he was the head of Grootvlei prison, situated right next door to Mangaung prison, he allowed prisoners to take a camera into the prison with which they recorded warders taking bribes, bringing in guns and physically abusing inmates. Taken as symptomatic of prevailing and widespread corruption in all South Africa's prisons, the video was leaked to the public broadcaster, the SABC. Setlai was transferred, and the Special Investigating Unit later arrested him on charges of corruption. The charges were dropped when it transpired that the prisoners who had testified against him had done so under duress.

No wonder the man has a constipated look about him.

'I heard you wrote a report about Mangaung prison?' I ask.

'Yes, I wrote one,' is all he concedes.

'So, what did you observe while you were working in the prison as a controller?'

'They paid prisoners to write false testimonies, if riots and assaults implicated G4S,' he starts. Then he stops and stares at me, and I feel like he is again reconsidering his decision to speak to me. 'The prisoners who didn't comply would be sent to Kokstad.'

In South Africa, there are medium- and maximum-security prisons, and then there is one so-called super-maximum correctional facility, the Kokstad Ebongweni Centre of Excellence, in KwaZulu-Natal. This prison, with only single cells, is where 'problematic' prisoners are transferred.

'At Mangaung, prisoners were placed in Broadway without the correct authorisation from the department or the Judicial Inspectorate for Correctional Services [JICS]. And I documented this and alerted the department in 2009. But they ignored me.'

Setlai speaks in a low voice, with guttural Gs and rolling Rs.

'What goes on in that prison is wrong and corrupt. For example, 90 per cent of the reclassification dates are incorrect,' he says, confirming what I have been hearing from the prisoners and Dan.

Setlai continues speaking, haltingly, but doesn't give me the report.

By bungling reclassification, Mangaung ensures its beds stay filled, I think as I drive back to Johannesburg on the seemingly endless N1 highway. On both sides of the road, flat yellow fields stretch out all the way to the horizon. Rusty windmills dot the landscape. The surroundings barely change as I drive and I feel hypnotised, as if I'm not moving.

I think about the bloody wars that had been fought in the landscape surrounding me. Wars that had drenched the land in blood long before apartheid had reached the country.

The uninteresting fields don't seem a likely setting for the battles that had taken place here. The Basotho people settled in what is now known as the Free State. The Basotho king, Moshoeshoe, of the Crocodile clan, fought and won battles with the British over the Warden Line, a border between British and Basotho territory. Moshoeshoe did not agree with the Line's trajectory and he armed his soldiers and gave them horses. Moshoeshoe's soldiers beat the British army twice, who ultimately decided to retreat and hand over the territory to the Boers.

The Boers reached the Free State when they crossed the Orange River during their Great Trek across the country. More armed battles followed, known as the three Basotho wars (1858–1868). Moshoeshoe lost the land to the Afrikaners in the three consecutive wars.

In the microcosm of the prison, this history feels absent yet alive. On the face of it, it might seem like it is the guards who are pitted against the inmates or the management against the workers. But ultimately what was taking place in Mangaung prison is in many ways racial. Most whites in the prison protect the interests of a British company, whereas most incarcerated and guarding Africans suffer at the hands of the same company.

The sun is dipping lower, spreading an orange glow over the fields, mixing pastel pink splashes into a crisp blue sky.

I feel my eyelids drooping, so I exit the highway and stop at a roadside restaurant in a small farming town to grab a cup of coffee. There are embroidered doilies on tables, shelves filled with chutneys, jams, pickles and other home-made products. An Afrikaans radio station burbles in the background. Three dogs run in and out of the place, as an old *tannie* enters the otherwise empty place to help me.

'Hoe gaan dit?' she asks, not even trying in English.

'Het gaan goed,' I try with my Dutch pronunciation, which must sound weird.

'Een koffie?' I try. Her facial expression tells me she knows what I mean.

She serves me the most disgusting instant coffee I ever had in my life, so I leave her little restaurant a bit disappointed.

Outside there is a fruit and vegetable stall, with massive butternuts and watermelons and bags of potatoes. Plastic bottles with ginger beer are stored in a fridge on the stoep. I see the raisins bobbing under the caps.

In 2015, the Free State Agriculture, a farmer representative organisation in the Free State, published a report which indicated that: '93% of the province was used for farming and 86.39% of the agricultural land in the Free State was white owned.'[19]

In the Free State, the *dorpies* I frequent while driving to Bloemfontein or where I end up for interviews with released inmates seem to be stuck in the past in other ways. A hotel I visited still had racially designated entrances and I once entered a bar with a framed old South African flag on the wall.

After our first meeting at the DCS, Setlai continues to be elusive. I keep contacting him, but my calls, voicemails and text messages are ignored, go unanswered. Then, in April 2013, he finally agrees to meet me again. This time he tells me to come to a guesthouse in Kroonstad, a medium-sized town about a two-hour drive from Johannesburg, about halfway between Johannesburg and Bloemfontein.

The guesthouse looks deserted. Setlai has a room on the first floor. The door is open, and I walk in. Setlai is sitting on an unmade bed in his DCS uniform. I sit in a chair opposite the bed and take out my notebook, a gesture aimed to expel the intimate sight and smell of an unmade bed in a guesthouse room, with this man sitting opposite me. Setlai doesn't say much. I wonder if he slept well. Then, he finally hands me a stack of papers, including the report he wrote during his 10-month stint as a controller at Mangaung in 2008 and 2009,[20] and several faxes. My patience has paid off.

Back in Johannesburg, I read through all the documents.

Controllers at private prisons are supposed to provide legal oversight. They have to report to the department on a wide array of issues related to prisoners' rights: healthcare, use of force, requests for transfers and such. As a DCS controller at Mangaung prison, Setlai did what he had done at Grootvlei prison before: he blew the whistle on abuse.

In September 2009, he notifies the deputy prison director Johan Theron of irregularities. 'Inmates are segregated [the legal term for isolation or solitary confinement] before the authorization document is signed, and the notification form that informs prisoners about their rights to appeal, should be attached to the segregation form,' one of the faxes reveals.[21]

According to the Department of Correctional Services Act and the Constitution – the legal framework that governs prison management – isolation is only allowed for an initial period of seven days and can only be extended – to a maximum of 30 days – after a hearing. The inspecting judge needs to be informed as well as the DCS, and a doctor has to examine the isolated prisoner every day. Setlai found these rights had been violated at Mangaung.

Moreover, he writes, isolation is used as punishment, a practice that became illegal after the dark days of apartheid, when political prisoners were held in isolation for years as punishment.

In a message addressed to Tertius du Toit, the G4S compliance manager, Setlai points out that the terms segregation, separation, solitary confinement, security classification and intermediate programme are being used interchangeably at Mangaung, yet they all reference the same thing: solitary confinement.[22] Setlai claims the G4S prison authorities semantically re-categorise the segregation of prisoners, in order to escape the legal prescriptions.

His attempts to address the unlawful isolation of prisoners were not well received. Setlai says G4S investigated him six times in six months for 'inciting prisoners to riot' and also reported him to the police for the same crime. 'All the allegations made against me by [G4S] are false,' he counters in an affidavit that also indicates his intention to further 'blow the whistle about what is happening in Mangaung Correctional Facility'.[23]

He does exactly that in the report he compiles for his employer, the DCS, late in 2010. He titles it 'Malfunctioning of private prison: Mangaung Correctional Centre'.

Here, he compares Mangaung with Guantanamo Bay, the infamous US military prison that is on Amnesty International's watchlist for human rights abuses, particularly long detention without trial and torture. He repeats his claim that prisoners are held in isolation unlawfully. 'Inmates are placed in single cells without the authorization of the Head [of prison] for more than 3 years without informing the DCS or the Inspecting Judge. Inmates are placed on "high risk" category without any explanation,' he writes.

The report names 62 prisoners who had been held in isolation for extended periods, ranging from two weeks to more than three years. Setlai claims that prisoners were locked up in isolation cells in Wolds 'for 23 hours a day without any programmes or activities as stipulated in [the DCS] agreement: this is regarded as gross human rights violation and should be reported to head office and Inspecting Judge.' Some of these men are apparently also denied life-saving medication for HIV and tuberculosis while they are in isolation.

Mangaung prison is in breach of its agreement with the DCS, Setlai continues. '[Mangaung prison management] don't do the job according to the contract,' he writes. 'Instead they are profit oriented, they use the cheapest methods in all spheres.' Elsewhere he writes how the state is 'milked' because of contractual obligations not being fulfilled. Essentially, work not done.

Zach Modise, the then DCS regional commissioner for the Free State, responds by reporting Setlai to the minister of correctional services and transferring him to another position within the department. The minister launches an investigation into his conduct, but the conclusion of the investigation is that Setlai did not do anything wrong. G4S also drops the criminal charges against him.

Whistleblowing has taken its toll, he tells me later. He's so anxious that he can't sleep at night. It has changed him, he says, he has become much more cynical and distrusting.

The report and faxes are a breakthrough in my investigation. Up until then I had driven to Bloemfontein once or twice a month to interview a long list of incarcerated men. Although the access and lack of scrutiny was amazing, it still hadn't led to any concrete evidence, other than the harrowing stories of the men and several guards. Now I have an official government report that not only backs the prisoners' allegations, it also proves that the department was aware of the chaos, violence and lawlessness in the prison. And, crucially, it has done nothing about it, rather choosing to cover it up.

After consulting with my team, I decide to write my first story on the prison. I choose to cover only the lengthy isolation and not the other forms of abuse. The reason is that there is detailed information in

Setlai's report on men who were held in isolation for up to four years. This strategy might also encourage or embolden other whistleblowers and sources to come forward.

The UN Special Rapporteur on Torture recognises prolonged isolation as a form of torture.[24] Solitary confinement, isolation, high care, segregation – these terms are all used to describe a situation where a prisoner is placed alone in a single cell and is not allowed any significant contact with the outside world. 'Privileges' are withdrawn, which can mean no contact visits, no access to radio, TV or newspapers. Once a day, the 'segregated' prisoners should be let out for exercise and a shower.

The absence of basic social interaction can lead to severe mental health symptoms. People who have experienced it complain of anxiety, depression and thoughts of – and attempts at – suicide. It reduces meaningful human contact to an absolute minimum. Even very brief isolation can lead to health problems. In an experiment conducted in 2008, volunteers who had been isolated for 48 hours 'suffered anxiety, extreme emotions, paranoia and significant deterioration in their mental functioning. They also hallucinated.'[25] Another study reveals more symptoms prolonged isolation can cause: 'hypersensitivity to external stimuli; perceptual disturbances, hallucinations, and derealisation experiences; affective disturbances, such as anxiety and panic attacks; difficulties with thinking, memory and concentration; the emergence of fantasies such as of revenge and torture of the guards; paranoia; problems with impulse control, and a rapid decrease in symptoms immediately following release from isolation.'[26]

I track down some of the prisoners on Setlai's list. Oupa Mabalane is one of them.

I visit him in the super-maximum prison in Kokstad. He was transferred there following his involvement in the 2009 hostage situation at Mangaung's Broadway unit.

'I was kept in Broadway for more than four years,' Mabalane tells me. 'They would come and beat me up whenever they wanted, because there were no cameras in the cells.' On the other side of the glass partition, his tattoo-covered hands nervously twitch on the table. But it was the isolation more than the violence that drove him 'insane', he says. He tells me he tried to kill himself because he couldn't stand being alone all day.

Thabang Nthabi is not on Setlai's list, but he did spend three unauthorised weeks in a Broadway cell. He's a lanky 30-something man with a few missing front teeth, and he greets me loudly when I arrive at his house, which is packed with visitors. House music thumps from a speaker.

In the silence and intimacy of my car, Thabang pours out his heart. For about three hours, he doesn't stop talking. He shouts and cries. Broadway is not only a place of isolation, it is also a stage set for violence, he says. Because there are no cameras in the cell and no cellmates or other potential eyewitnesses, it's the perfect setting for a thrashing with no record or consequences for the aggressor.

His nightmares only started after his release from Mangaung in 2012. 'I was so angry and frustrated, and I couldn't sleep. Terrible nightmares would wake me up, screaming and crying,' he says.

By the time he gets out of my car, he has calmed down. He's laughing again as he walks back to the house, a beer bottle swinging from side to side in his hand.

Shortly after receiving the list of 62 names from Setlai in 2013, I send it on to the JICS, which in turn forwards it to Mangaung, demanding the prison management confirms, denies or explains why these men were held in isolation for extended periods.

In response, G4S writes that it 'places a question mark' around whether the JICS really is 'in need of the information', since the requests 'are mostly signed by [JICS] administrative personnel'.[27]

In May 2013, the national manager for legal services at JICS Umesh Raga responds, noting the indignation evident in the G4S correspondence. 'It is apparent that the [Mangaung prison] Director takes umbrage at the Inspectorate's queries,' he writes. 'He then questions the authority and delegations within the Inspectorate and casts suspicions on the integrity of our staff and our mandate. We are indeed flummoxed by such aspersions.'[28]

Other than pointing out that the three men who were still being held in isolation at that time were there legally, the company completely ignores the Inspectorate's request. G4S argues that they are not segregated but 'high cared' due to a 'security risk', that emanated from their disciplinary record.

Shortly thereafter, my first article on Mangaung runs in the *City Press* locally and also in the *Guardian* in the UK.[29] It focuses on the 62 isolated prisoners and contains statements from three of them. The *Guardian* illustrates my story with a photograph of the late Pan African Congress leader Robert Sobukwe, who was in isolation for six years on Robben Island.

G4S responds to allegations in the article, by stating that 'the DCS controller approves the detention of all prisoners in single cells.'[30]

As expected, the prison doors also slam shut in my face. My number is blacklisted, so prisoners can't phone me anymore. A warder tells me that my picture is posted at reception, with a warning not to let anyone inside who looks like me.

But, as the cliché goes, when some doors shut, others will open. Suddenly, I'm on the map as a journalist investigating the prison.

Some time after the article appears, I receive a leaked confidential internal G4S email.

The email's subject line is 'High Care', and it's addressed to top-level directors and managers in the prison. In the mail, G4S compliance manager Tertius du Toit – who was Setlai's first port of call when he investigated abuse at Mangaung – reminds his colleagues of what South African law stipulates: 'The MD has decided that Highcare will not be utilized at [Mangaung prison] anymore for the foreseeable future. All instances where a need arises for an inmate to be placed in the Special Treatment Unit due to risk/aggression/violence, will be motivated in terms of Section 30 of the DCS Act.'[31] Section 30 of the Act, which governs the segregation of inmates, is attached to the email.

Setlai initially seems pleased with the publication of the article, but then he disappears again. He stops returning my phone calls or answering my messages.

Several months after the article is published, on 4 October 2013, a G4S press statement reveals that Setlai has been appointed as a consultant for the company. 'G4S has engaged the services of Tatolo Setlai to support the Centre as an Operational Advisor. Mr Setlai retired in June as the Provincial Head of Security, Free State Province. He was previously employed at MCC as a controller for the DCS. His experience and knowledge of MCC will bolster G4S's operational management cadre at this time.'[32]

Why would a whistleblower, who put his job on the line to expose a company, go and work for that same company? Did G4S make him an offer he could not refuse? Is he a double agent?

A rumour circulates that he is having an affair with one of the Mangaung prison managers. Maybe he just took the job to be close to her.

Dan, who put me in touch with Setlai in the first place, is also not impressed.

'We can't trust him,' he says the next time I see him.

The history of G4S

The company's roots stretch back to an era before the internet, video and television. In 1901 a group of 20 so-called nightwatchmen in Copenhagen decided to form the Kjøbenhavn Frederiksberg Nattevagt (the Copenhagen and Frederiksberg Night Watch). This security company earned money through individual contracts with households and businesses for the protection of their premises. A drapery wholesaler, Marius Hogrefe, and Jörgen Philip-Sörensen, a businessman, ran the company as it expanded throughout Denmark.

Hogrefe and Philip-Sörensen were not just the founders of a nightwatch, they were the architects of the modern-day private security industry. They were the founding fathers of three Scandinavian security multinationals: G4S, Securitas and ISS. It is ironic that the private security industry has roots in Scandinavia, which is currently one of the safest and most peaceful regions in the world.

In 1906 the nightwatchmen merged with the Danish Falck Group. As a 19-year-old, the founder Sophus Falck witnessed chaos ensuing after a fire broke out at the Christiansborg Castle in Copenhagen. He decided there and then that fire rescue services should be improved and several years later he founded the Falck group.

Falck started out as an ambulance and rescue service. In 1908, it offered the first ambulance services using automobiles in Denmark. By the end of that decade, Sophus Falck had expanded his business to cover all of Denmark.

A business strategy focused on expansion and buying up competitors was part of G4S's predecessors' corporate philosophy from day one. The Phillip-Sörensen family bought up many other nightwatch organisations. In 1934, Jörgen's son, Erik Philip-Sörensen, brought the company to Sweden. He founded Securitas, currently G4S's major competitor.

In the 1950s, the company started looking into expanding their business into the UK, after they had saturated the Danish and Swedish market. In 1968, the pater familias, who was in charge of the UK operation, merged their four British companies into one, naming the new company Group

4. In 1981 it was renamed Group 4 Securitas by Jörgen junior, who had taken over the British part of the business.

Jörgen had inherited his father's expansive hunger. He branched out into India in the 1980s. Group 4 gobbled up a huge chunk of the local security market. The company entered the American market when it bought American Magnetics Corporation in 1990. It also expanded deeper into Western and Eastern Europe. In 1991, Group 4 managed the first ever privatised prison in the UK, Wolds prison in Humberside. It later lost that contract due to poor contract compliance.

In 2000, Group 4 and Falck merged, forming Group 4 Falck. This move was sparked by the threat of global giant Securitas, which was dominating the global security market. Together, they continued a policy of 'aggressive acquisition', acquiring thousands of local smaller security companies. They steadily expanded across the globe. In no time, they were the second largest security company in the world, trailing behind Securitas. But they desperately wanted to become Numero Uno.

In 2001, Group 4 Falck bought businesses in South Africa, thereby entering the African market for the first time. In 2002, the company acquired Wackenhut, at the time the second largest security company in the United States.

In 2004, G4S was born when the British security provider Securicor merged with Group 4 Falck. It started trading on the London and Copenhagen stock exchanges. G4S was now the biggest security provider in the world.

5

Chemical silencing – zombies and robots

'I don't know what kind of illness they think I have.'

SILENCE IS A POWERFUL tool. It forms an insulating cloak around violence. If the victim of violence remains silent, the perpetrator of violence will get away with his or her crime. Victims of domestic violence and rape can take years to speak up about what happened to them. Similarly, the men I interview are ashamed and humiliated. It is hard for them – these mostly hardened, macho men – to admit to a woman that they have been abused and assaulted. Self-silencing is the first of three rings of silence.

The silencing around violence ripples, like Dante's hell, in concentric circles, writes feminist author Rebecca Solnit. In her at times hilarious and other times depressing book *Men Explain Things to Me*,[33] she opines: 'surrounding this circle (of self-silencing) are the forces who attempt to silence someone who speaks up anyway, whether by humiliating or bullying or outright violence, including violence unto death.' At Mangaung, prisoners who dare to file complaints are often bullied, ignored and sometimes beaten up.

The last ring of silence is society. 'Finally, in the outermost ring, when the story has been told and the speaker has not been directly silenced, tale and teller are discredited.' In South Africa, this is particularly true. Crime rates are high, and there is very little sympathy for the fate of those in prison. 'They always lie,' a police officer responsible for investigating crimes committed in Mangaung once told me, directing his sweeping statement at the prisoners without providing any evidence. Prisoners are guilty until proven otherwise. A similar thing happens when women attempt to report domestic violence. They are sent back home and told to 'fix things' with their partners.

In Mangaung prison, these three rings of silence seem to work perfectly to cover up the endemic violence marring the prison operation. And the for-profit prison deploys a cost-effective silencing weapon: prisoners who won't shut up are chemically silenced. They are forcibly medicated with antipsychotic drugs.

In November 2012, the WJP receives an anonymous letter from a Mangaung prisoner with an unimaginable allegation. I have to read and reread the sentence several times: 'G4S have a system they use by injecting prisoners with tranquilizers that are being used for animals. Just to think, it drops an elephant down, what about a human?'

This letter is among those that first inspire my investigation of Mangaung prison for a long list of allegations ranging from corruption to neglected transfer requests.

Most of the allegations sound sadly germane to South African prison life. But the reference to the use of animal tranquillisers stays with me. I had never come across anything like it.

The first prisoner to tell me about his experience with being injected in Mangaung is Thabo Godfrey Botsane.[34] Previous complaints about injections that allegedly made prisoners walk, talk and act like 'zombies or robots' had all come second-hand.

I meet Thabo in March 2013. He had just been released from Mangaung prison.

In a gravelly voice, tarred by years of heavy smoking, Thabo tells me what happened to him in 2009, when several inmates at the Broadway unit had decided to take Pule and Mdi and a third warder hostage, to protest the prison conditions. Thabo claims he had nothing to do with the hostage taking, but that he rather got swept up in it.

Once the hostages were freed, the Ninjas arrived. 'The EST guys came to my cell,' Thabo tells me. 'They stripped me naked, they poured water on me and then they started electroshocking me. I was lying naked, on the floor, face down, and they beat me, kicked me and beat me again. After that, a man who works for the intelligence unit in the prison, I think his name was Jacu, entered the cell and injected me in my buttocks. I tried to resist, but the Ninjas held me down. I fell asleep immediately and woke up feeling like a zombie. I felt lethargic, I couldn't move properly, I couldn't remember what had happened exactly. While I was in Broadway, I saw several inmates hang themselves. I started to think this might be the solution for me as well.'

Simphiwe Ambraal sends me a letter in early April 2013. He is serving a 12-year sentence for armed robbery. Stapled to the letter is a little plastic bag; it reads Mangaung prison pharmacy and gives the address of the prison. Inside, there are six Clomidep tablets and another bag with three tablets that look like paracetamol with the name Leponex printed across it.

'I quit taking these pills in May 2012, as they were making me feel [like] a zombie where I will always feel tired and delusional,' Ambraal writes in the letter. 'I sometimes will hallucinate and see things that are not there. My body will go numb and I will find it difficult to even raise my hands or wash myself. Then on 22 March 2013, I was forced to take them again but I refused and I was forcefully fed them [...] I'm a person who is not aggressive so I don't know why I am forced to take these pills as I am not on any medication for any illnesses, diseases or physical problems.'

Ambraal's letter and its contents provide the first clue as to what substances the prison is using to allegedly forcibly medicate the prisoners.

Leponex is used for schizophrenic patients who are treatment-resistant. Clomidep is marketed as a drug that treats obsessive-compulsive disorder. However, Ambraal claims he has no mental health issues. He was also considered mentally fit to stand trial back in 2007.

I see him the next time I visit Mangaung, later in April 2013. He is a big doe-eyed man who claims he requested a transfer after witnessing injections happening. 'I was afraid they were going to do to the same thing to me,' he explains.

His fear became a reality in May 2009, when the Ninjas fetched him from his cell, and he was held down as a nurse plunged a needle into his buttocks. He says the injection made him sleepy, gave him a dry mouth and made his jaws feel 'like they were crossing over each other'. From then on, he was injected every month, and when he protested, the Ninjas would tell him to shut up, because he was 'mad'.

'I saw the nurse shake a bottle. The fluid in the bottle would turn yellow. Then she would inject me with it,' is all that Ambraal remembers of the substance.

Then in 2010, the injections suddenly stopped. Not long after that, he was told to start taking the pills, the same as the ones he had sent me. But he refused, so they were force fed to him. He says he felt similar side effects after taking the pills to those he experienced following the injections.

'I don't feel like the same person anymore,' he says.

Lwazi, who says he has never been injected himself, had mentioned the 'zombies' and the 'robots'. He promises to smuggle out further information on prisoners being injected.

I pick up the second batch of letters at the lawyer's office in

Sandton in May 2013. Titled 'Victims of Injection', one of the letters lists seven Buckley Hall prisoners who are being injected. 'Buckley Hall has a housing capacity of 488 inmates. The question is, if one unit can have this number of inmates on injections, [then] how many inmates are there in other units who are also subjected to this illegal treatment? Mangaung has a total number of 2928 inmates.' Lwazi's maths suggests that, at any moment in time, there could be at least fifty inmates at Mangaung who are being injected with an unknown substance against their will.

The other forced injection stories to come across my path all follow a similar pattern. The Ninjas would be called to incidents – ranging from a dispute about food to a full-on prison riot – and escort the perceived culprit (of causing, inciting or aiding the incident) to the prison hospital. The culprit would be held down, so that the nurse or doctor could administer the injection in the buttocks. The doctors and nurses would not tell the man what kind of medication they were administering. The prisoners told me that the medical staff, employed by Faranani Healthcare Solutions, acted under the orders of prison management, who would approve injections for 'troublemakers'.

The list of prisoners claiming to have been injected with an unknown substance grows. Like Ambraal, some say they saw the nurse shake a bottle of transparent fluid, which made it turn yellow. Others say they were also force-fed tablets.

I list every single prisoner – approximately 20 – who claims to have been forcibly injected or given pills, and I see them in back-to-back meetings at the prison.

None of them can tell me what they were injected with. Yet all of them tell me the side effects are horrible.

'It feels like you're about to have a stroke,' Aubrey Buthelezi tells me when I ask him how he felt like after having an injection. 'My neck was permanently hanging to one side. I could barely speak. I couldn't feel my hands. All my muscles were stiff.' He describes the other side effects: dry mouth, poor concentration, loss of memory, jitteriness, fuzziness, excessive blinking and excessive sleeping.

A handsome, muscular man with delicate features that are offset by some missing front teeth, Buthelezi is one of the 20 men on my list. Like Ambraal, he was also considered mentally fit to stand trial and was convicted of an armed robbery in 2009. But in Mangaung, following a spat with a fellow prisoner, the Ninjas told him he was 'mad'.

After a mattress-burning incident in 2010, the Ninjas allegedly assaulted him before holding him down to get an injection in the buttocks. He then got a regular injection every week.

Buthelezi claims the injections stopped in 2012 and there was no replacement medication for his perceived 'illness'.

'They upped the dosage before they stopped injecting me, and I think they saw the side effects and decided to stop,' he speculates.

Prisoners and warders alike say James Mothulwe is worst off following the injections, with the side effects never really going away. 'His neck is paralysed,' one guard says. 'They overdosed him,' another claims.

On the day of our appointment in April 2013 Mothulwe limps towards me, his head lolling and bobbing back and forth and from side to side involuntarily despite the brace he wears around his neck in an attempt to keep it upright and stabilise it. His hands are shaking, and spit is dripping from the corner of his mouth. He shakes my hand and takes a seat opposite me.

Placed on the table, his left hand is twitching and moving erratically from side to side. I ask him what happened.

Mothulwe was also considered mentally fit to stand trial and was sentenced to 35 years in prison for rape. Following a suicide attempt in 2002, he was injected for the first time.

'The EST guys held me down, and the nurse came and injected me in the bum,' he stutters, spit dripping down his chin. 'After that, they injected me once a week.' Like with the other prisoners who spoke and wrote about injections, Mothulwe also didn't know what he was being given. He says he protested loudly and sometimes physically. His cries bounced off the hospital walls, no doubt instilling fear and dread in the others. The prison kept on forcing medication on him for five years, despite his dissent and the obvious side effects of the medication.

The substance started wreaking havoc on his body and mind. 'The side effects start about seven days after the injection,' he says. 'My body felt stiff. I became more depressed. I started shaking and getting nervous tics. In 2004, the side effects had become really bad. I started getting fits and couldn't move my body anymore. My left hand stopped working. Then the entire left side of my body became weak.'

I look at this hand, with the fingers hanging off the table. It's still twitching.

In 2007, the side effects became unmanageable, and the injections stopped. 'Someone in the hospital told me: "If they keep this up, you will die in here,"' Mothulwe says, pausing briefly, his hand still jerking involuntarily on the table. He was not given any medication to replace the injections.

His symptoms have all the hallmarks of tardive dyskinesia – a permanent disorder of the nervous system that can occur as a side effect when antipsychotic drugs are overdosed for long periods of time. There is no known cure.

It's six years since they stopped the injections, yet Mothulwe is still visibly struggling with spasms and loss of muscle control in his neck, face and hands.

One of the names that comes up is that of Dr Hellen Mngomezulu, the psychiatrist who apparently prescribed Mothulwe's medication and also gave him some tablets to mitigate the side effects. I phone her in April to try and get a response. 'No comment,' she says, quickly, before she hangs up on me.

Only much later, in 2017, do I get another chance to speak to a doctor who worked in the prison hospital. I catch Dr Emmanuel Mukahiwa as he leaves his surgery at the National District Hospital in Bloemfontein. At least I manage to exchange more words with him than with Dr Mngomezulu. Doctor Mukahiwa, according to inmates, had ordered and carried out many of the forced injections with antipsychotic drugs.

'We are bound by medical ethics,' he says when I ask him if he had ever injected a prisoner against their will. 'If I suspected any form of abuse ... I would never do that.'

'But they are mental people, and they have no judgement,' he continues. 'Go to any psychiatric institution, the state takes over, because the patients have no judgement. Sometimes, you see a person who has a clear judgement, and now they are saying: "Ah, I was injected by so and so," but in the moment, they can be a danger to themselves or a danger to others, and you have to consider those circumstances. We sedate people. Why? Because they are a danger to themselves or somebody else. We give them one or two injections, and they return to their normal self.'

I'm surprised by his statement that it's not unusual for medication primarily intended to treat mental illness to be administered outside of this diagnosis. 'There are indications for antipsychotic drugs outside of a psychosis,' he says. 'You need to assess the person and then decide.'

I ask him who authorises the administration of injections, and he says the doctors act independently in Mangaung, without the involvement of G4S. He also tells me that neither the diagnosis of a mental illness, nor the prescribed medication have to be reflected in prisoners' medical files.

When I ask what drugs they commonly use in these injections, he refuses to give me names. 'You can find it on the internet,' he says, before walking away into a throng of hospital patients.

I wonder about the idea of forced medication or drugging, also called involuntary treatment. In Mangaung, it appears to be commonplace; some EST members told me they were called in to help with injection administration 'about once a week'. In some instances, like in Thabo's case, drugs are given for a condition that has not even been diagnosed. But how about if there really does seem to be a mental illness? I think of Sello Mogale, a man who can barely remember his name. And Jan Botha, who spoke about spiders 'crawling into my brain'. Is it legal for them to be medicated without their consent?

South African law allows for forced medication, under very strict conditions. The Mental Health Care Act requires that the intended involuntary treatment is first approved by the head of the healthcare institution. At the time of the application, the mental health patient has to be incapable of making an informed decision and has to pose a danger to their own safety or that of others. A spouse, guardian, partner or parent may apply for medication to be administered. It is only when the spouse, guardian, etc. is unavailable or unwilling to make such an application that the healthcare facility may do so. Everything needs to be carefully documented: the reason for administering the treatment, as well as the period and nature of it. Two independent medical physicians then have to authorise the involuntary treatment.

I phone Marius Delport, a psychologist who worked for the DCS for a number of years, to ask for comment on the allegations from prisoners about forced injections. 'Medical health professionals are not allowed to give medication without having observed and assessed the patients,' he says. 'Who is prescribing this medication? These are not the type of drugs that should be freely available. Half a Valium pill would probably be more appropriate to the cases you described. Forced medication is rare and can only happen if the inmate is a danger to himself or others, when that person is no longer in touch with reality and therefore has no insight or he cannot argue. If this is not the case, and the conditions of the Mental Health Care Act are not met, then forced medication is a serious violation of human rights.'

Albert Janse van Rensburg, an associate professor in psychiatry at Wits, agrees. 'Two clinicians need to carry out an examination of the patient,' he explains to me. 'When all the requirements are met, the patient should be placed under observation for 72 hours while the medication is forcibly administered. Giving antipsychotic drugs to people to subdue them is hugely problematic.'

I phone JR, a nurse at the Mangaung prison hospital, to ask about medication and list several of the men who claimed to have been injected. When we meet, in May 2013, he grabs my notebook and starts scribbling. He hands it back. 'Clopixol Depot 50/25mg and a muscle relaxant,' it reads. 'Modecate, 0.5ml. Etomine: calms down, Risperdal ...' His list continues. He had checked the medical files of several men I'd spoken to, and this was the medication they were being given.

'They give them antipsychotic drugs and heavy tranquillisers,' he confirms when he has finished writing. I ask him who orders the injections.

'All injections are authorised by the prison management and the DCS controller.'

He tells me I should speak to his friend Sizwe*, who worked in the administrative office of the prison hospital from 2001 to 2012.

I meet Sizwe at the Urban bar. He's overweight and breathes heavily. A moustache of sweat drops lines his upper lip.

Prison managers and warders often handled the prisoners' medical files stored alphabetically in a filing cabinet in the office where he worked, he tells me. He saw them flipping out folders and inserting or taking out papers.

'After they assaulted an inmate, they bring him to the hospital,' he tells me. 'A few hours later, they return to see what the doctor has recorded in the medical files and then "correct" it to suit them.'

Sizwe shifts uncomfortably in his chair.

One of the prisoners told me that 'an overweight admin assistant' working in the hospital had injected him. He said the man wasn't a

---

*   Not his real name

nurse, yet he had administered the injection.

'Have you ever injected an inmate?' I ask Sizwe.

Sizwe looks at me and blinks a few times.

'No, never. I'm not qualified,' he says.

Sizwe was the only admin assistant working in the prison hospital, so either he was lying, or my source lied to me.

I asked him about James Mothulwe. He says he watched Mothulwe being injected, with increasing frequency, from 2005 to 2007.

'They overdosed him,' he says. 'That's why they stopped the injections in 2007. The drugs' side effects took over. He can't control the muscles in his neck. He was a quiet guy when he came into prison. The *tronk* made him go crazy. He was so stubborn. He was strong too! After the injections stopped, James was still a zombie, unable to hold his head up, unable to speak clearly.'

His leather jacket bulges on his meaty shoulders. His hand is wrapped around a Coke. Ice cubes tinkle as they collide against the sides of his glass.

Warders recommended I talk to a guy called Sampson*, who worked as a nurse in the prison hospital until 2012.

Sampson and I meet at a coffee shop at Loch Logan. The fancy shopping complex has what looks like marble floors, escalators and fairy lights, but its artificial lake (the mall is known in Bloemfontein as the Waterfront) looks dismal and forlorn.

In his forties, Sampson has a disarming smile. Not the type to administer forced medication, I think.

'Etomine will make a man go to sleep,' he says, after confirming he was regularly required to inject prisoners against their will. 'He will wake up and feel nice and dull and will not feel like doing anything,' he continues. 'There are two groups of inmates who receive the injections. Those with mental health issues and those who are being "difficult".'

---

*   Not his real name

'What do you mean by difficult?' I ask.

'There was an inmate called Bheki, a guy from KwaZulu-Natal,' Sampson answers. 'He used to make a lot of noise. They gave him antipsychotic drugs, and he became like a zombie.'

'Who orders these injections?'

'Faranani never take any decision on their own. They always take orders from the prison management.'

I look up the medication JR had written down in my notebook. They're described as antipsychotic drugs, mostly prescribed to treat schizophrenia. The different kinds of medication all have similar side effects: drowsiness, sleepiness, involuntary movements, weight gain, dry mouth, headache, anxiety and – in some cases – stroke and death.

Mangaung is not unique in its administration of this kind of medication. In Soviet Russia, during Joseph Stalin's reign, from the 1920s to the 1950s, political dissidents were sent to the work camps known as the Gulags in remote Siberia. Known as 'philosophical intoxication', political dissent was commonly classified as a psychiatric disorder. Dissidents were said to be injected with haloperidol, a first-generation antipsychotic drug. The Russian poet and essayist Joseph Brodsky, who's known for his political dissent, is said to have been injected with haloperidol for punitive purposes before being urged to leave the Soviet Union in the early 1970s.

More recently, in 2012, the US State Department was widely criticised following the surfacing of a Pentagon report[35] detailing forced administration of 'truth serum' to terrorist suspects at the notorious Guantanamo Bay prison, with the hope of extracting a confession during interrogation. Some prisoners said they were told they were being given a flu shot. Following the injection, prisoners felt 'groggy' and 'delusional'.

'Chemical isolation', as the use of antipsychotic drugs on prisoners is sometimes called, is actually a tested tool of prison authorities the world over.

Alleged forced administration of the schizophrenia medication Largactil[36] was also part of the intolerable conditions in the Strangeways Prison in Manchester that led to the infamous 25-day riots in 1990. The longest riot in British penal history, the Strangeways protest sparked numerous others around the country, culminating in a public inquiry chaired by Lord Harry Woolf. Following the inquiry, the Woolf Report[37] subsequently called the conditions in Strangeways unacceptable and recommended major reforms to the country's penal system.

Back in the US, former prisoner John Lash writes in a 2012 report that antipsychotic drugs were widely used as a form of crowd control in correctional facilities in which he did time for close to 25 years.[38] He specifically mentions the 'Thorazine shuffle' which alludes to the jerky uncoordinated movements of inmates on the antipsychotic drug Thorazine. He concludes that, by forcing antipsychotic medication on people who had not been diagnosed, mental illness had in effect become criminalised. Prison doctors were getting money from pharmaceutical companies for using their drugs, he claims. He also says many of his fellow prisoners were overdosed.

The issue of forced medication of inmates with psychotropic drugs made it all the way to the US Supreme Court of Appeal, in 1990. In *Washington vs Harper*[39] the court ruled that medication may only be administered to a prisoner, against their will if necessary, after a hearing with a lawyer, a psychiatrist and a psychologist as well as the prisoner and witnesses.

In 2014, claims surface that a large number of women in Canadian prisons are being prescribed 'mood-altering medication with life-threatening side effects [...] for years for unapproved purposes'.[40] The report claims that drugs such as quetiapine are frequently used 'off-label', meaning not for their intended purposes.

The next time I visit Lwazi, he slides some pills across the table. It's Leponex. Again. This still doesn't prove a lot, I think as I slip them into my pocket.

I realise I need hard proof of forced medication, so I arrange to see Egon Oswald. One of a handful of South African lawyers defending the human rights of prisoners, Oswald is well known for his attempts to get justice for 231 prisoners who were allegedly tortured in the St Albans correctional facility in Port Elizabeth. After pursuing the case through the domestic courts for 10 years, he finally dragged the South African government before the United Nations (UN) Human Rights Committee in Geneva in 2008. On 2 November 2010, Geneva concluded there were serious human rights violations requiring urgent redress.[41] The domestic courts, however, ignored the UN body, and a civil court ruled in favour of the state in May 2016.

'In all my years as a human rights lawyer, I have never come across forced medication with antipsychotic drugs on a prison inmate population,' Oswald tells me at our meeting in the boardroom of the journalism department at Wits in Johannesburg in February 2013 to go through my files and interview notes.

Oswald is well versed in prison torture. He knows physical evidence will make or break a case: the bruises, lesions, broken bones and teeth need to be documented before they heal, disappear or are replaced.

I already know the chances of accessing medical files confirming details of forced administration of antipsychotic drugs are extremely slim. Medical files are not readily available – I know prisoners failed to obtain their own documents – and tampering is known to happen after assaults.

But Oswald has a plan. Early in 2013, we head out to Bloemfontein to speak to the 'zombies'.

He'd asked to see the men as a group, to save time and allow for cross-referencing. We sit in one of the stuffy booths, waiting for them to arrive. In the adjacent waiting area, I see a huge man curled up on the bench, sleeping like a burly baby.

The men arrive. In comes Buthelezi, one of the first to describe the side effects of the medication to me in detail. And four others who're also on the list of 20 medicated men I originally drew up: David Kambule, Willem Boetie Vis, Joseph Maruping and Sello Mogale. All five of them look like they're floating. Their faces are vacant, they're docile and withdrawn. Their eyes are hazy. They stumble and file into the cramped booth.

Mogale is seated across from us, and half the table disappears under his huge forearms. Oswald asks him to describe the side effects, and they all start talking at the same time.

'My body is stiff.'

'I feel like a robot.'

'It makes you gain weight.'

'Makes me dizzy.'

'I don't know what kind of illness they think I have,' Buthelezi says.

Oswald leans in and tells them he wants to apply for an Anton Piller order.[42] 'If the judge grants it, I will be able to access your medical files and take a blood and hair sample, without the consent of the company,' he says. The men stare at him. Buthelezi nods. Mogale looks like he's falling asleep right there. 'We will take your blood and hair samples to find out what it is they're injecting you with,' Oswald continues.

My sources allege prison officials are destroying and tampering with medical files, and the incarcerated men tell me they tried and failed to access their own files. The company and Faranani Healthcare both deny access to medical files. All of this forms the rationale to apply for the order.

Within a few weeks, Oswald has drafted an application – which includes affidavits by Kambule, Vis, Maruping and Mogale, as they are being injected at the time and thus the medication would show up in their blood and hair. An affidavit from Mothulwe is added because of the enduring side effects he's been experiencing.

'The last occasion when involuntary treatment was attempted was during February 2013,' Kambule states in his affidavit. 'When I was summoned for my injection, I told the nursing staff that I had seen my attorney of record and that he was intending to go to Court to stop them. This had an immediate effect and they let me go without administering the injection.'

Maruping's affidavit reads: 'The medication consists of a clear liquid contained in a vial. When this vial is shaken, it becomes yellow and foamy. I am not sure of the name of the substance injected into me, but I believe that it might be the antipsychotic drug known as haloperidol.' Oswald includes this because the description matches the properties of haloperidol when shaken.

The court application heightens my expectations. I hope it leads to indisputable evidence of what the men are alleging.

On 2 April 2013, a High Court judge in Bloemfontein denies the application, likening it to a 'fishing expedition'.[43] Piller is consistently misspelled as 'Pillar' in his ruling, which concludes: 'The applicants alleged that upon ascertaining the exact nature of the treatment rendered to them, they propose to instruct their attorney to launch applications [...] It is clear that they wanted to go on a fishing expedition in order to see whether there is any incriminating evidence.'

The rejection of the application comes as no surprise, but it dampens my mood. I have stories, some pills in a bag and confirmation from EST members and nurses that men are being injected against their will.

What I need is absolute proof that this private facility is indeed injecting prisoners with antipsychotic drugs, against their will and not for medical treatment.

Some months later, that incriminating evidence lands in my lap through an entirely different channel. I'm finally handed the long-awaiting smoking gun. One day in July 2013, Dan and I are in POPCRU's Bloemfontein office when he disappears with my external hard drive. He reappears a few minutes later and hands it back.

'This is what you've been looking for,' he says.

It's a batch of videos showing EST members going about their daily business in Mangaung. They're legally obliged to film their actions every time management approves the use of force, and this is the evidence.

With an intern at the WJP, I watch the blood and gore spilling onto my screen. The Ninjas are regularly called to violent and bloody fights. With ceramic shards from broken toilets, the prisoners stab each other and the warders. There is footage of nurses stitching up raw wounds and the Ninjas interrogating the prisoners in an attempt to establish who was the aggressor and why the attack took place.

When Bheki Dlamini appears on my screen, I run to find my colleagues. I remember Sampson the nurse mentioning his name, claiming he was forcibly medicated because he was difficult and 'made a lot of noise'.

My colleagues and I crowd into my office and watch the video together. It starts with a close-up of a warder; other guards call him André. The camera is so close, his face is distorted.

'We are in Altcourse unit to pick up inmate Dlamini, who has disturbed the peace,' he announces matter of factly. For a moment, André then films his face from below. It looks like a scene from a horror movie.

He announces that planned use of force has been approved. In prison speak, this means an application had been made to the prison management as well as the DCS controller stationed at the prison to use minimum force on an inmate. He flips the camera to the 'core' of the prison unit, the communal space where inmates sit and eat or just hang out.

The men in black are everywhere. The men in blue all quickly disappear into their cells as the Ninjas move around, their electrified riot shields hanging from their sides. The shields release an electric shock when a button is pressed. The camera swerves around the unit and stops at Dlamini packing away his lunch plate. He's speaking with one of the Ninjas. Dlamini ambles over to his cell, yelling something at someone in the distance and waving his hand. In his cell, he starts packing his stuff into a bag.

A warder tells the camera: 'We are going to remove B. Dlamini. He is disturbing the peace and the good order of the prison. That is why we are removing him to healthcare, for him to get his medication.'

The camera zooms in on André's face again, who adds: 'The inmate is aggressive and mentally unstable. So, let's negotiate.'

Thus far, the video has no evidence of Dlamini being aggressive or mentally unstable.

The camera swerves to Dlamini's cell, but six armed Ninjas block the view. They're crowding around the entrance, craning their necks to see what's going on. Dlamini is seen having a discussion with Power Maluleke, the supervisor of the unit. Maluleke turns away from Dlamini, who's packing his bag, and says to the camera: 'Guys, we're taking him to Mount Gambier. Apparently, he has made an application to be moved to Mount Gambier, and we are moving the inmate there.'

Dlamini continues packing. He takes his pictures off the wall, unplugs his radio and wraps up some food that is on his desk.

Dlamini thinks he's getting ready to be moved to Mount Gambier, which houses those prisoners enrolled in educational programmes, as per his request. But he's mistaken.

André and Maluleke discuss their next move.

André: 'What are we going to do with him afterwards?'

Maluleke: 'From here, we are going to the core, from the core we are going to healthcare, but we will tell him that we are taking him to Mount Gambier.'

'But after healthcare, what then, do we bring him back?'

'They have to bring him back. But, even when you talk to him, he will never understand. It's useless.'

While they're talking, Dlamini is on his knees, looking under the bed. Final checks that he has everything.

'Are we going to keep him in healthcare for the night?'

Chemical silencing – zombies and robots

The discussion between André and Maluleke continues.
'Yes.'
'Because this kind of drugs takes a while for it to kick in – maybe a week.'
'He is someone who is sick. He is not a danger to us.'
'Hey, supervisor!' Dlamini has his stuff in his hands, and he's facing the camera.
'I have a size 40 trousers.'
'Size 40. Don't worry,' Maluleke reassures him.

Dlamini slings a bag across his back, grabs a black bin bag and some loose items and starts walking out of the cell, escorted by eight Ninjas. As he's collecting his stuff, André can be heard reminding his colleagues: 'We have to play his game. The wheel is spinning, but there is no driver.' There is laughter.

The gaggle of men then leave, and Dlamini can be heard speaking loudly and the Ninjas laughing at him behind his back.

Outside the unit, Maluleke once more faces the camera and repeats that he told Dlamini that he was going to Mount Gambier, but that the real mission is to get him to healthcare, where he would be injected.

The next shot is in the prison hospital. Maluleke again faces the camera.

'Confirmation to inject the inmate. Apparently, it is confirmed. I just want to inform the inmate about it.'

At his side, Dlamini is protesting loudly. He has apparently just realised he is not being taken to Mount Gambier.

Maluleke informs Dlamini he's going to be injected.
'A flu jab?' Dlamini asks.
'No,' his guards tell him.
'What for? For flu?' he asks.
No clear answer can be heard.
'No! I don't want it,' he says. 'I am not a donkey.'

As the Ninjas place their gloved hands on his shoulders, Dlamini keeps repeating: 'I am not an animal. I am not an animal.'

'Bring him!' André orders, and the Ninjas press down on his shoulders while they push his arms up. Half bent down, Dlamini is marched through the hospital, past other prisoners, who hurriedly move their chairs out of the way. Dlamini can be heard yelling 'No! No! No!' as they lead him into a room. As they forced him, belly down, onto the bed, he says: 'I will see you in court.'

The Ninjas are then heard yelling for the nurse to come.

I've been searching for evidence of forced medication, of electroshocking. My bosses have been getting impatient – they want some output after a year of investigating.

I instantly know this video means I can finally go to print.

Several weeks later, late July 2013, I meet with Oswald at a greasy café in downtown Bloemfontein. He has just seen Dlamini and has agreed to represent him in a civil case, aimed at receiving compensation from G4S and Faranani Healthcare for the forced medication.

'He was complaining about the quality of the food they served. Lunch consisted of Vienna sausages, and Dlamini demanded "real meat",' Egon relates before updating me on the details of the injections. 'He says he has no record of mental illness and hasn't, before or after that incident, ever been injected again.'

This could be seen as evidence that the medication was administered not to treat illness – because then it would have had to continue – but for other purposes.

Dlamini's case seems promising. But in court, G4S claims the date on the video does not correspond with its medical records.

Oswald, who works on a contingent fee arrangement, lacks the funds to further pursue the case.

At the end of October 2013, the Bheki Dlamini video footage is posted alongside the online articles I'd written for the *Mail & Guardian*[44] and the British *Guardian*.[45] It is also screened by the BBC[46] and the

South African investigative journalism show *Carte Blanche*[47] at the same time. The video then travels the world via CNN, Reuters and a host of other international media.

G4S categorically denies any wrongdoing. 'We do not use any form of torture or shock treatment,' Andy Baker, G4S Africa president, tells Andrew Harding of the BBC in a television interview that airs in October 2013. 'It's difficult in an environment with so many people and so many moving parts to categorically state that there has never been somebody stepping over the line. To my knowledge, there has never been an abuse of this type of nature.' He adds: 'It is important to note that the G4S people do not make the decision to medicate. The medical staff do not work for G4S. They are a completely independent entity.'

Theoretically speaking, he's right. Medication has to be prescribed by medical professionals; Faranani employees in this case. But the video clearly shows G4S personnel fetching a prisoner from his cell, informing him that the 'injection has been approved', and then holding him down for the medication to be administered.

Who approved it? Who is deciding that people like Dlamini, who claims to have no record of mental illness, should be injected, while he's clearly objecting?

Warders, inmates, nurses and admin staff working at the hospital tell me that the 'prison management' approves injections.

I know the names of some of those employed by G4S to manage the prison. I know the prison director is called Johan Theron and the G4S compliance manager is Tertius du Toit. I have also heard of deputy director of operations Derrick de Klerk, campus director Esandran Naidoo, the centre director Joseph Moyante and assistant director Xander Snijders, who left DCS's employment shortly after a suspicious death at the facility led to an inquest. I have no idea, however, if any of these people are ordering the injections.

Officially, G4S keeps shifting the blame to Faranani and later to Life Esidemini, when that company took over the prison hospital. The people ordering and enabling the use of antipsychotic drugs remain faceless and invisible.[48]

Following the media reports, two investigations are commissioned, one by Minister of Correctional Services Sbu Ndebele, and a separate one by the Judicial Inspectorate of Correctional Services (JICS), a semi-governmental prison watchdog.

Previously the Inspectorate had been firm when it challenged G4S about unlawful isolation, and I expect equal treatment with the forced injections investigation.

But my expectations are not to be met. In early November 2013, Umesh Raga, JICS's legal services manager, is called to parliament to answer questions about the situation at Mangaung.[49] In his answer, he indicates that, 'The head of the medical section [at Mangaung prison] had been asked whether injections took place. He had answered that it was done, and that it was necessary in his professional opinion. The medical section had provided a list of names of inmates who had been injected. The medical staff had opined that it was indeed necessary.'

And that is that in terms of the JICS investigation.

In 2019, I write to JICS, asking them to elaborate on their seemingly very brief investigation into these serious allegations. Their press officer writes to me by email: 'JICS does not possess the scientific/medical knowledge nor the financial resources required to evaluate the said medical evidence. This matter also falls into the jurisdiction of the contractual relationship between DCS and G4S. A committee evaluates and determines whether G4S breaches/has breached any law in relation to the associated duties between DCS and inmates relative to the provision of health care.'

It baffles me that a watchdog like JICS would deem the issue of forced medication with antipsychotic drugs as a contractual, not a constitutional, matter.

The DCS releases an interim report in June 2014, and one of my sources leaks it to me. The report contains the response from Bloemfontein Correctional Contracts (BCC) – the legal entity comprising G4S and four other shareholders – that is party to the prison contract.[50]

In its response, BCC denies any knowledge of forced administration of antipsychotic medication to Aubrey Buthelezi.

In the case of Willem Boetie Vis, the report claims that BCC was not in possession of his medical files and asked the DCS to provide these documents. I find this a bizarre claim from BCC, given that G4S, the company actually running Mangaung prison, is one of its shareholders. How can the people managing the prison not have access to medical records of those being held there?

The report then lists the documents that *are* in BCC's possession. There's a document from a clinical psychologist, dated 28 September 2011, that notes that Vis 'refused to come to the clinic' and that she 'will ask the [doctor] to write [a] repeat script and that the [prescription] should be given by force'. However: 'There is no corresponding prescription from a medical practitioner [...] indicating that any medication should be administered to Mr. Vis.' Clearly, medical procedures are not being adhered to.

The wall of silence around the forced injections is near perfect: the DCS, BCC and even the JICS, the watchdog intended to hold everyone accountable – they all keep their mouths shut.

The G4S business

G4S has three business divisions.

The company's (rather ironically named) Care and Justice division provides prison- and immigration-related services – transport, detention, healthcare and electronic monitoring – and has a presence in the UK, Australia and South Africa.[51] While Care and Justice comprises only 7 per cent of G4S's entire business, it is lucrative. An investigation by the South African National Treasury in 2003 revealed that Mangaung Prison earned BCC a whopping 30 per cent return on equity.[52] Mangaung is G4S's only African prison. G4S also runs four prisons, two immigration detention centres and one juvenile detention centre in the UK, and two prisons in Australia.

G4S Cash Solutions[53] offers cash-in-transit services and has a presence in 44 countries. It comprises 14 per cent of the total business. It recently announced it was going to sell its cash business. American security company Brinks is considering a $1.23 billion takeover of that part of the company.[54]

Security Solutions[55] is the biggest division within G4S. It provides security services for the oil and gas industry, for international organisations such as the UN and the European Union and for the private sector. It provides security services, such as transport and technology, at big events and in war zones.

The execution of G4S's services appears too often to be carried out with little attention to the necessary care, insight, training or oversight. This, it can be argued, leads to poor contract compliance[56] and pervasive labour unrest[57] in many countries where they operate.

An aggressive acquisition strategy,[58] which is deeply rooted in G4S's DNA, leads to wide risk margins. This means that risks to the company, such as labour unrest and lawsuits, are often interpreted in purely financial terms. And when the risk outweighs the profits, the company simply sells off the problematic part of the business.[59]

While G4S's aggressive acquisition strategy has yielded impressive profits for the company, it has also created a trail of chaos, abuse and irregularities on the ground.

6

Death in the dark room

WHEN I WAS A PRETEEN I joined the Young Investigators, a kids' club in a neighbouring town. I was a bit of a nerd girl. The aim of the club was to foster a love of all things scientific in our young minds. I was drawn to their photography lab. I would wander around the town, in its parks and markets, taking pictures of people, animals, buildings, anything really. Later in the dark room I would inhale the acrid smell of photo chemicals, peer at the gleaming white sheets by the light of a safelight and marvel at the image slowly emerging as the sheets floated around in a chemical bath. That process was magical to observe, the gradual appearance of a slice of life. The memory came alive and was forever arrested in its movement.

In the dark room in Mangaung prison, there is no safelight. It is said that in this pitch-dark, soundproof cell in Broadway, brutal reckonings take place. 'EST members would bring inmates here, strip them naked, pour water over them and electroshock them,' a Broadway guard told me. 'It was awful.' Once you're in the dark room, there's no way out, and no one hears your screams. G4S calls it the 'quiet' room. Most of the people I interviewed over the years have preferred the term 'dark' and spoke of this room with notable urgency, and they seemed desperate to let the world know this place exists, to bring the dark room into the light.

Isaac Nelani is the name that comes up most often – in conversations with prisoners and warders alike – whenever the dark room is mentioned. His name first came up for me on Lwazi's list of the dead. Nelani died in the dark room on 18 May 2005.

The dead have no voice, and they cannot look you in the eye. Nelani, the protagonist of this story, cannot relate what happened to him on that fateful night in Broadway. He has no lines. His absence means I have to piece his story together from the different versions of the event: eyewitness accounts, documents. Stories about the dead are different from the stories about the living. The absoluteness of Nelani's absence permeates the heart of the story, leaving an unforgiving silence behind.

My investigation into Nelani's death materialised much like the discovery process that mesmerised me as a young girl. From darkness, a picture of what happened that night slowly emerged, as its constituent parts became exposed to my scrutiny, and ultimately, public scrutiny.

Many stories are told about how Nelani died. Some say he died after being brutally assaulted by the Ninjas. Others say he committed suicide, that he hanged himself.

The unfolding story of how Nelani died and who was responsible for his death takes many turns, morphs into different versions and has many holes. One thing is clear though: while G4S registered it as a suicide, there is reasonable doubt about the cause of death.

Dan tells me G4S designed one of the cells on Broadway as a suicide-prevention unit. The cell's temperature is kept intentionally low, so prisoners could cool down. Everything in the cell – the bed, basin, toilet and chairs – are fixed. 'That dark room is like a police holding cell. You can't move anything. The bench is made out of concrete. There is just one light bulb and no windows,' a prisoner who was held in the cell opposite the dark room tells me. It is so dark in this cell, it's impossible to distinguish physical features – or tell one person from another.

On a printout from the prison's administration system I get from Dan, there's a grainy headshot of Nelani in the top left corner. He has a beard and looks like he's in his forties. He stares straight into the camera in a calm, determined – yet also defeated – way. Like he had seen it all but is not done seeing yet. He was convicted of an armed robbery and culpable homicide in 2002.

Then, Isaac Nelani, the man, is summarised in a few details. Race: black. Gender: male. Nationality: South Sotho. Date of birth: 20/05/1957.

His address is registered as Sasolburg in the Free State, despite several sources calling him 'that Zulu guy from Newcastle', a city in KwaZulu-Natal. Maybe it's because he's a Shembe man. Also known as the Nazareth Baptist Church, which is given as Nelani's religion on the printout, Shembe has a large Zulu support base.

Nelani was 1.79 metres tall. He was right-handed, his complexion was captured as 'dark', his speech 'normal', his teeth 'good' and his birthplace 'Parys'. His weight was just below 74 kilograms. Under 'specialty' is listed: 'aggression'. He was HIV positive, and his marital status was 'widowed'. Lastly, there was a list of scarred body parts: head, face, right arm, right leg and chest.

Next, the possessions he had on him on the day of his arrival: 'Face cloth, underpants, pants, jean, 2 T-shirts, yellow container, spoon, white container, socks, 3 toothbrushes, comb, books, belt, gloves, pjamas [sic], shoes. Nokia 5110, battery, charger and yellow Omega men's watch, spectacles, ring.'

In the pictures the police took before Nelani's body was transported to the pathologist, he's lying on his back on the floor, one eye closed, the other half open, his light-blue prison jacket open. It seems to be torn. Underneath, he's wearing a black shirt. His palms are turned up. I try to glimpse a trace, an emotion, a last word, on his lifeless face. But it's vacant.

While I'm trying to piece together the story of Nelani's death, the first inconsistency that comes up is what he used to hang himself. In his affidavit in the inquest report,[60] Dr Robert Gene Book, the state pathologist who received the body at the morgue and who also conducted the autopsy, reported that the police told him that Nelani hanged himself with a leather jacket. Inmates don't get to keep their leather jackets, or any item of clothing. There was no leather jacket presented to the pathologist.

G4S, on the other hand, alleged that Nelani hanged himself with strips of his prison jacket. But Dr Book received the body naked.

There are police pictures of the knotted strips of material, slung over the back of the padded door to the cell, with which Nelani apparently hanged himself. But no one knows where those knotted strips are – they have disappeared. Forensically speaking, clothing needs to remain untouched if a suspected crime has been committed, as it is considered evidence.

DCS investigators inspected the cell in 2014, when the department investigated various allegations of abuse at Mangaung prison, including Nelani's death. This inspection was not part of the inquest. The investigators, who spoke to me off the record, also claimed it is impossible to hang oneself from the door, as the knotted strips would slip off the door, there was nothing to tie the knotted strips onto. If it had indeed been built as a suicide-prevention cell, as Dan claimed, this would make a lot of sense.

In the pictures Dr Book took in the morgue, Nelani is unclothed and lying on his back on a metal surface. He has a few scars below his collarbone. Both his eyes are closed. A piece of paper with the SAPS docket number is on his chest.

Nelani the man has now been reduced to a docket number of a botched police investigation.

I start putting together a timeline of that fateful day: 18 May 2005.

At around 3 pm, Nelani is moved from cell 09 to cell 34 in Broadway. Gerard van Staden – known in the prison by his nickname 'Sewende Laan' after the popular Afrikaans TV soapie – is the duty operations supervisor on the day, in charge of prison operations. From Van Staden's affidavit in the inquest docket it's clear he made the decision to move Nelani to the dark room, which he describes as a cell designated for '*oproerige*' prisoners, the 'riotous' and the 'high risk'. Nelani is deemed *oproerig* and high risk because he had allegedly damaged the window in cell 09.

At 4:40 pm, Vuyo David, who worked as a DSO in Broadway, looks 'through the hole in the door that serves as a window' and finds that everything is 'in order' in Nelani's cell. But then, just 23 minutes later, he gets called to Nelani's cell again, by his colleague Power Maluleke, the supervisor who appears frequently in the Bheki Dlamini video, the one who tells Dlamini that he's going to get an injection.

He sees 'through the hole in the door that inmate Isaac Nelani had hung [sic] himself', David writes. He claims he then got a knife from the kitchen, which he slid through the hole in the door to cut Nelani loose. He went over to the control panel at the workstation and opened the door to the cell. The nurses are called, and they pronounce Nelani dead.

My next lead is a prisoner who – so I'd been told – made two conflicting statements about Nelani's death: one to G4S and one to the DCS. Neither of these statements are included in the inquest. The only name I have for him is Madondo. He worked in the Broadway unit, serving meals. He was on dinner duty that day and he claims it was him, not David, who saw Nelani's dead body through the food hatch when he arrived to deliver his dinner. Why Madondo's statement is not part of the inquest is unclear to me, especially seeing as he claims he was pressured by both the company and the department to draft a statement on what he saw.

Dan and Lwazi both mention Madondo. 'He works a taxi in Soweto,' Lwazi says as he slips me his phone number.

I take one of my WJP colleagues along as an English-isiZulu interpreter to my meeting with Madondo outside one of the hostels in Mapetla, Soweto in May 2013.

Madondo is sitting at a wooden table outside a spaza shop selling beer and cooldrinks on a little windswept square flanked by hostels. He's in his forties or fifties. His morose expression doesn't change when he sees us. With a nod of his head, he invites us to sit down. I shake his hand before I sit down and try to look him in the eye, but he just keeps peering at his Coke. I thank him for meeting with us. I then try a smile, but he does not reciprocate. I sense this is going to be a short interview. So, I get straight to the point.

Madondo says he was the one who found Nelani, around 5 pm, when he looked through the food hatch in the cell door. The police statements in the inquest list David as the one who found the body at 5 pm.

Madondo says he saw Nelani's lifeless body, slumped against the door. When the DSO opened the door, they saw Nelani was dead. They tried to resuscitate him, Madondo claims, but he was gone.

'In my statement to G4S, I wrote that Nelani had committed suicide. I could see him through the hatch in the door.' He says that once the cell door was open, he 'went inside, I saw he was dead, but there was no blood in the cell. He hanged himself with a prison jacket.'

In the same week that he wrote this statement for G4S, the DCS asked him to draft a second statement, he claims. 'DCS instructed me to write that he died because he was beaten up,' he says. 'A man working at the DCS controllers' office, Xander Snijders, and the DCS controller himself, Clement Motsapi, both told me to write that.' Madondo looks at us briefly, then looks away and takes a sip of his Coke.

Some said G4S bribed Madondo with a promise of a transfer if he claimed Nelani committed suicide. I ask him if that's true.

'I was moved to Grootvlei prison and then transferred to

Groenpunt prison in Vereeniging, and then they moved me to Sun City in Johannesburg,' he says.

I ask him why he made two different statements.

'I don't believe in lies. This is what I saw,' he says.

He gets up quickly and walks away.

When an incarcerated person is a victim or perpetrator of a crime while he is in prison, the eyewitnesses to the crime are most likely other inmates. But because these men are considered criminals with very little respect for the law, their eyewitness testimony is often ignored or discredited.

In their press statements, G4S repeats again and again that Mangaung prison houses the most hardened criminals in the country.

I find and then interview three eyewitnesses who were in an isolation cell at Broadway on the night Isaac Nelani died. I speak to Oupa Mabalane, Mxolisi Ndaba and Papi Maruping. The police never asked them what they saw and heard.

Sometimes the living compensate for the silence left behind by the dead. Oupa Mabalane is angry. I observe him through the glass partition in the visitors' section of Kokstad prison, officially known as the Ebongweni Centre of Excellence, in KwaZulu-Natal.

Mabalane's face and arms are covered in gang tattoos and when he speaks he shouts and makes urgent gestures with his hands. I sense it doesn't take much to upset him.

During my visit with Mabalane at the beginning of 2014, he gives me his account of Nelani's death. He was being held in the cell opposite cell 09, where Nelani was before being moved.

'Nelani turned on the taps in the toilet. He was angry,' Mabalane remembers. 'It was winter, and he was cold. He was HIV positive. He asked for an extra blanket, and the warders refused. Then I heard Nelani screaming. He was tortured to death. The EST came back after he died and hung him up by his clothes.'

Mxolisi Ndaba was in the cell next to Oupa's. 'I saw Isaac Nelani being taken to the shower. He was still clothed and cuffed. The Ninjas put him inside the shower cage and using a broom stick turned the shower on. Once he was wet, they took him out of the shower and brought him along the corridor. The ninjas were shocking him around the body with their shields. They put him inside a room known as the dark room which I could see from my cell. They closed the door. I don't know what happened next. We all thought he would be attacked in there.

'I heard Nelani scream,' he says. 'The Ninjas electroshocked him. They tortured him to death.'

I travel to Kroonstad in the Free State, about halfway between Johannesburg and Bloemfontein, to speak to Papi Maruping. Mostly medium security, Kroonstad Prison is probably the most welcoming one I visit in South Africa. The vibe is much more retirement complex than correctional facility. The prisoners sweep their stoeps, and some huddle for a smoke in the courtyard in front of the warder's office. They chat and joke around with their guards, who seem jovial and laidback.

The staff at the prison are accommodating. They quickly create a consultation corner for me to have my interview. Maruping ambles in and takes his seat opposite me. I don't really want anyone to eavesdrop on our conversation, so I ask a warder to turn the volume on the radio up. Maruping has to lean in to make himself heard over the babbling from the radio. 'Nelani got into an argument with Power Maluleke, who was at the time the supervisor at the Broadway unit,' he says. 'Nelani wanted an extra blanket, and Power refused to give him one. Power then phoned the EST. They arrived around three o'clock in the afternoon. The team of Ninjas was led by a guy called Van Staden. His nickname was Sewende Laan.'

Maruping was in cell 39 above cell 09. From his cell, Maruping could see the area around the workstation and the showers – and also the door across from him, marked SO 27. That door led to two others, to cell 33 on the left, and to cell 34 – the dark room – to the right. Maruping says he saw Nelani outside the showers when the EST arrived.

'They twisted his arms behind his back, and he fought back. Van Staden then ordered them to take Nelani to the showers. They stripped him first. They pushed him into the showers, and then I couldn't see him, but I heard him screaming. I think they put him under a cold shower, in the middle of winter, and they left him there for at least five minutes.'

Maruping then heard Van Staden ordering Nelani to get dressed again. He must have been out of the shower. 'Nelani was still arguing with them, and then I heard Van Staden say, "Take him to the dark room."'

There they were, those terrible words. Yet, G4S keeps denying the very existence of this cell.

Did Nelani know that the dark room was a harbinger of pain and suffering? Is that why he resisted when the EST men tried to push him inside?

'His feet were still wet from the shower, and the floor was slippery, so he fell when the Ninjas grabbed him,' Maruping continues. 'They grabbed him, beat him and then pushed him into cell 34.'

Through the slit in the door, Maruping could see into cell 34, as the two doors were left open. 'The doctor had arrived, and he stood with Power, watching the six Ninjas cuff Nelani, place him on his stomach on the floor. And then they started kicking, hitting and electroshocking him with their shields. It went on for about 15 to 20 minutes and I saw that Nelani was bleeding from the mouth. I heard him screaming. The Ninjas yelled at him and insulted him, calling him a sissy and a bitch.'

Then the doctor was called, and he entered the cell. Maruping says he injected Nelani in the neck. Maruping saw Nelani lying on the floor, face down, unconscious. Then the doors were closed.

Madondo, the prisoner on dinner duty that evening, told me he saw Nelani's body through the hatch, but Maruping says the door of cell 34 was open and Madondo even touched Nelani's body. Madondo 'asked Power to open cell 34 for him,' Maruping explains, describing how Madondo might have thought Nelani was asleep. 'He bent down and started shaking him. He then went back to Power and started whispering to him and pointing at Nelani's body.'

Maruping saw Maluleke walk over to Nelani's body and also shaking him. He claims Maluleke phoned prison management. The G4S security manager and EST supervisor appeared within minutes. He didn't touch Nelani but made another phone call. Some minutes later, several prison managers appeared. Papi saw them walk out of his line of sight. He knew there was an interview room in that direction. He heard a door close. Then three men returned, all wearing rubber gloves. They entered cell 34 and closed the door.

'When they opened the door again, they had uncuffed Nelani, and they had taken a bedsheet and torn it into a thin piece. They tied that around his neck and attached it to the door, making it look like a suicide,' Maruping says.

He thinks the police were informed around 6 pm, and they arrived around 7 pm. 'The police came and lifted the body, cut it loose from the sheet and placed him on a stretcher,' Maruping concludes his memories of the night.

The three men who claim to have witnessed Nelani's death do not have identical recollections. Mxolisi remembers the police carrying Nelani out of Broadway on a stretcher and says his hands were still cuffed. Papi says Nelani went into the dark room handcuffed yet was transported out of the unit uncuffed.

But they all heard his blood-curdling screams.

In court, Dr Book, the pathologist who carried out the autopsy on Nelani, observed there was severe bruising to the posterior of his heart and concluded that 'blunt force had been applied to the heart'.

Bruising of the heart can arise when CPR is administered, but then the bruising would not be at the back of his heart.

The position of the bruising seems to support Maruping's observation that the Ninjas assaulted Nelani while he was face down on the floor.

In his autopsy report, Dr Book notes that strangulation is the most probable cause of death, but he also concludes that the force that produced the bruising could have caused the death. He deems the bruising to the heart suspicious: 'it is never seen in suicidal hanging by the neck,' he states in his report.

Dr Book's report notes some inconsistencies in the police investigation. He was not called to the scene of death and so had no first-hand impressions of the material Nelani had allegedly used to hang himself or any other possibly pertinent evidence. Dr Book's frustration is palpable when he writes: 'In civilized countries throughout the world, the Forensic Pathologist is called to the scenes of deaths in custody; it never happens here in Bloemfontein. Never.'

There is no mention of a head wound in Dr Book's report. But then in April 2014, Dan sends me a picture of a laptop screen shot showing part of a document that states 'In respect of Isaac Nelani a discrepancy exists between MCC [Mangaung Correctional Centre] report and pathologist's records: MCC records the death as a suicide whilst pathologist records it as a head wound.'

After I badger Dan for months and months, he finally hands me the document that mentions the head wound. It is the DCS interim report with responses by BCC,[61] that was issued following an investigation in 2013 into alleged wide-ranging abuse at Mangaung, including past incidents such as Nelani's death. The disciplinary task team conducting the investigations consisted of doctors, lawyers and government officials. Dan assists the team, and he tells me the doctor on the team claims he has X-rays showing that Nelani suffered substantial head injuries.

'Isaac Nelani did commit suicide in the quiet room in 2005,' the report states. 'This incident was investigated by the Supervisory Committee and was resolved in 2011.' The supervisory committee had the mandate to impose fines and penalties for violations of the terms of the prison contract. Its members worked for G4S and DCS. The committee was supposed to make sure the prison was run in a humane and orderly fashion.

Did the committee read Dr Book's report? What did they make of the 'suspicious' bit? Did they not wonder what happened to the strips of material with which Nelani allegedly hanged himself? And what about the head wound – where did they get that from? Where was the X-ray showing the substantial head injuries? And did they not think to perhaps follow up on the 'discrepancy'?

The interim report concludes its assessment of Nelani's death: 'The Contractor is not required, as part of its obligations to keep a record or report of all deaths, or to obtain or retain a copy of an autopsy report.'

This is a wildly incorrect statement that is not even compliant with G4S's *own* internal policy guidelines. 'Deaths in Custody', a G4S policy document,[62] stipulates that: 'the name, date and time as well as the number of the member of the SAPS [investigating the death] must be recorded' when a prisoner dies in custody. Further obligations are also noted: the prison director needs to notify the SAPS, a medico-legal post-mortem and investigation must be conducted, the prison director must order an investigation, and the death of a prisoner must be registered with Home Affairs and the SA Criminal Records Centre. Most importantly though, the policy document also clearly states that a register must be kept – in prison – that contains all the documents of the legal investigation and autopsy.

DCS officials revisited the dark room, with Dr Book, to determine if it was at all possible to hang oneself from the back of the door of what was supposed to be a suicide-prevention cell.

'I spoke to Book, the pathologist, and he told me that it would be impossible to hang yourself with a bruised heart,' one of the DCS officials explains to me. 'Bruised hearts are mostly lethal, and if you manage to stay alive, you will not be able to move, because it is a very serious injury. There is no way to bruise a heart after you've hanged yourself, unless the EST men kicked and thrashed a dead body. And how could you get a bruised heart first, and then hang yourself? That's also impossible. Nothing makes sense.'

Logan Maistry, a DCS spokesperson, denies in August 2015, when I write about Nelani's death for the *Mail & Guardian*, any knowledge of a head wound. 'DCS is not aware of any reference to a head wound with regard to Isaac Nelani. We request that such information be provided to DCS for investigation.' This comment is strange, because DCS put forward that very allegation to BCC in their interim report.

The report contains another worrying observation by the department on how G4S handles inmates dying: 'death investigation reports are either not available, signed or include an autopsy report.'

In responding to my questions, Maistry discloses that Zach Modise, the then national commissioner of correctional services, has decided to appoint: 'a task team to look into all unnatural deaths at Mangaung Prison.' Their main obstacle, Maistry writes, is the 'non-availability of documentation' provided for by the contractor.

This DCS task team never release any findings, which means Nelani's death remains shrouded in darkness.

G4S CEOs

In the UK, where the company is headquartered, a never-ending cascade of G4S-related scandals has dominated headlines for more than a decade. The one scandal that perhaps still angers most Brits is G4S's failure to provide effective security during the Olympic Games in London in 2012.[63] The British army had to step in at the last minute. It was a very public humiliation.

A serious fraud case involving an electronic monitoring contract followed hot on the heels of the Olympics debacle. G4S was charging the British government for about 3 000 electronic ankle bracelets of 'phantom' prisoners who had returned to prison, moved abroad or were dead. A criminal case was opened with the British Serious Fraud Office (SFO) in 2013.[64] In 2014, the company agreed to pay back £108.9 million plus tax to the UK government.[65] While the investigation was still ongoing, the British Ministry of Justice awarded G4S another contract, worth £25 million, again for electronic monitoring.[66] In 2019, the company had a contract for electronic monitoring extended for another few years in Australia.[67] However, the SFO has, at the time of writing, still not completed its fraud investigation into G4S.

G4S's London Olympics scandal also shone a light on the salary of the man who led the company. CEO Nick Buckles stepped down in 2013, but not after he had accepted a £16 million golden handshake.[68] He had continued the company's expansion strategy, including forays into sectors where the company arguably had limited experience or skills. Shareholders – mostly comprising major asset managers and financial investment companies such as BlackRock and Ivesco – opposed Buckles's plans of acquiring ISS, a large Danish security and cleaning company.[69] At the peak of his reign, Buckles led a company that had a presence in 125 countries and employed close to 700 000 people.

Buckles's successor and current CEO of the company, Ashley Almanza, is a South African. He completed his undergraduate accounting studies at the University of Natal and holds an MBA from the London Business School. He worked in the oil, gas and offshore drilling sector before he joined the security behemoth.[70]

Unlike the flamboyant Buckles, Almanza is publicity shy. In corporate videos, he exhibits very little emotion, appearing detached and watchful.[71]

In 2015, after he steered the company back to profit, Almanza's annual package increased by 73 per cent.[72] It's been reported that in 2017, Almanza took home £3.8 million. In 2018, when he only earned £2.9 million as he failed to make targets, Corporate Watch calculated that his salary is 403 times the average G4S pay.[73] In 2019, concerns were also raised about contributions to his pension being a quarter of his base pay, which substantially exceeds the pension contributions earned by the majority of G4S staff members.[74]

Where Buckles pursued acquisitions, Almanza is focused on consolidation, shedding problematic businesses and contracts. Most prominently, G4S pulled out of Israel, and Almanza also started the process of selling troubled juvenile detention services in the United States and the United Kingdom. The Guardian *has described Almanza's vision as: 'a decluttering exercise to restore G4S to its security roots' following 'Buckles's disjointed vision of G4S as a jack-of-all-trades outsourcer'.[75]*

G4S is still huge: it retains a presence in 90 countries and employs close to 550 000 people.

7

Dust to dust – Tebogo Bereng

ANNA, DIKILEDI AND Bassie Bereng drive around Bloemfontein's South Park Cemetery looking for the grave of their son and brother Tebogo. It is April 2017. They struggle to remember where they had buried him. Four years have passed since they were last at his grave on the day of his funeral.

Tebogo's grave is easy to miss. With its simple metal plate in lieu of a tombstone, the mound of red-brown earth that is his final resting place is at the far end of the cemetery. It is but one mound in a row dotted with the odd bunch of withered flowers and empty bottles planted head down. Litter spirals up into the air in mini tornadoes. The forgotten and the poor are buried here.

The graves closer to the entrance of the cemetery are better maintained. They're clearly demarcated, the headstones are properly engraved ones, and here and there you find fresh flowers and other decorations.

South Park is opposite Universitas, the neighbourhood built around the University of the Free State's campus. The university's main building perches atop an elevation, seemingly untouchable, overlooking the sprawling collection of graves.

'My son, mother is here. Tebogo, my son, who I love,' says Anna. She's 89 years old. Reddish-brown dust slips through her gnarled fingers and onto her son's grave. A small dust cloud dissipates into the air. Tebogo's sister Dikiledi wipes her tears with the sleeve of her woolly cardigan. Bassie keeps his head down as he heaps dry dusty earth onto the mound with a spade. According to biological kinship ties, Tebogo was his uncle, but they grew up like brothers.

Anna gave birth to seven children. But Dikiledi – a woman with a moon-shaped, light-skinned face, deep wrinkles around her eyes and a few missing front teeth – is Anna's only surviving child. Dikiledi's siblings all passed away, disease and crime claiming their lives. Now, Anna's orphaned grandchildren all look to her for motherly support, referring to her as 'Mom' or 'Ma'. They all call each other brother and sister.

Anna's face is wrinkled and worn, and her back stooped, but, leaning on her stick and with surprising strength, she grabs the spade and starts piling earth onto her son's grave. She spits on a small rock in her hand and then places it on the grave. Bassie and Dikiledi follow her example. They clasp their hands together and start praying. They speak to him, reassuring him that his family is taking care of him.

When the ceremony is finished, Anna clutches my arm.

'*Baie dankie*,' she says, because I had suggested the idea of revisiting her son's grave. I see tears brimming in her old eyes.

'Have you forgiven him?' I ask in my best Afrikaans.

'Yes, I love him. He is my son. He will always be my son,' Anna says as she looks at the dusty heap that is now decorated with a colourful small plastic guitar, and many small stones covered in fresh spit.

Tebogo's death certificate[76] states that he died of natural causes. But mere days after his passing on 31 March 2013, both Bassie and Robert, another of Tebogo's nephews, call me to tell me they're convinced Tebogo had been murdered.

Robert says two guys who worked for G4S during that time came to his house and said that Tebogo had been killed in the prison, and that it was not a natural death.

I go and see Robert at his house down the road from Anna's in April 2013. A mechanic, Robert is a healthy-looking forty-something man with bulging arm muscles and a generous smile, revealing a set of gleaming white teeth.

Robert and Tebogo differed only a year in age and, as children, they used to play. They would roam the veld and catch rats and rabbits, which they grilled over a fire and then ate. 'He was the bravest of all of us,' Robert remembers. 'I looked up to him and got to wear all his clothes when he grew out of them. He was my brother. He was my very good friend.' Robert is the only family member who visited Tebogo in jail after he was convicted for statutory rape – of a 16-year-old girl with developmental challenges – in 2010. The rest of the Bereng family refused to visit Tebogo because it was too serious an infraction. What's more, he'd physically hurt Anna – he'd hit his own mother. The family had taken him to the police station and reported Tebogo and his crime.

'He was always in trouble, in and out of prison,' Robert says, with a brotherly smile. 'He was a thief and a thug before he was arrested for having sex with that girl.'

He tells me he implored the G4S guys who came to see him following Tebogo's death to give him details.

'I asked them, please talk to us, to lawyers, talk to journalists, give us names. But they ran off. They feared they would lose their jobs,' Robert says. Anna sits next to him, her beady eyes peering over her glasses. She's wrapped in a red towel that's gathered at her chest with a huge safety pin.

'They, the G4S people, they told us that Tebogo had passed away and that his body was at the government mortuary,' Robert continues as Anna clutches her towel. Sunlight filters in through the lace curtains, deepening the leafy green colour of her headscarf.

'I want my son to rest,' she says. But she still has too many questions, about Tebogo's death. And his life.

Tebogo wrote to the Wits Justice Project shortly before he died. In spikey handwriting, that looked like print-out of an ECG film of the heart, he told us about the expired epilepsy medication he was given at Grootvlei prison, a medium-security state-run prison. He had been transferred from Grootvlei to Mangaung two months before his death. He wrote that he suffered from seizures and blackouts and he feared the expired medication might have lost its potency. He asked us for help or advice on how to sue the department for negligence. Looking back, it seems a minor worry, compared to the fate that awaited him.

'Did you know Tebogo had epilepsy?' I ask Anna.

She looks at me, and her voice croaks in her throat, like an old engine suddenly jolting back to life. She raises her hand.

'No! I knew nothing,' she says.

'They told us that he died on the way to hospital,' Robert says, protectively wrapping his arm around Anna.

'The day after he died, I went to the mortuary with a family friend. They turned us away, told us the body was still under control of G4S. Then we drove to the prison. A guard gave us his clothes. She said he had fainted,' Robert tells me. 'Already in those first few days, we heard different stories about how he died.'

JR, the nurse who gave me the names of the medication with which prisoners were being injected, was working at Mangaung prison the night Tebogo died. I arrange to see him again, at the Wimpy in Mimosa Mall in May 2013.

He grabs my notebook, just like the previous time, and starts drawing the last route he thinks Tebogo took in prison. In erratic, pointy handwriting, JR scrawls 'Port Phillip' in my notebook – this is the unit where Tebogo was held.

'He was here, in this cell,' he says, drawing a circle around a square.

'He complained to the supervisor that he was cold. It was around midnight.'

The supervisor became angry and started accusing Rasta, as Tebogo was known, of spoiling for a fight. Tebogo was swearing, JR remembers.

Then the Ninjas were called in.

'The EST took him to the hospital unit, where he was checked for injuries,' JR says. 'I saw him. He was foaming at the mouth but still walking.'

JR's shift finished shortly thereafter. The next day another nurse told him that Tebogo had passed away. After hospital he was apparently taken to Wolds, and when the guards checked on him an hour later, they found him dead.

'He had a convulsion in his cell [in Wolds]. His cellmate pressed the panic button, but no one came,' JR says.

JR finishes drawing Tebogo's final route through the prison complex. He looks at me with watery eyes.

'Epilim. That's Bereng's medication. He had epilepsy. They never should have used those shields on him,' he says, revealing what he thinks happened when the Ninjas stepped in. 'That would trigger an attack.'

'That's it. I have to go,' JR says, and he's on his feet. I also stand, failing to think of something to say, something that would keep him here, so I could ask more questions about that fateful night.

Lawrence Sehonka, who shared a cell with Tebogo in Port Phillip, writes to us shortly after the death, confirming JR's account.

'He had a conversation about his inner duvet cover [...] and the DSO didn't want to change the inner. The supervisor arrived [...] and he told Tebogo Bereng to pack his clothes [...] and things from the cell.' The EST promptly arrived, and they took Tebogo away. After about 30 minutes or an hour later, Sehonka writes, the supervisor came back and told him that Tebogo had fallen down and died in the hospital.

In a second letter sent to the WJP, another eyewitness writes that he saw Tebogo and the Ninjas as they went in and later left the hospital. 'I saw them handcuffing his wrists. [...] I saw him coming from hospital [...] It looked like he was fitting.'

Hlello Mbatyazwa was also in the hospital unit when Tebogo arrived. I speak with him at Kokstad prison, in early 2014. 'Four or five Ninjas electroshocked him with their shields in the corridor at the entrance of the hospital, where there are no cameras. Tebogo was screaming and trying to protect himself.'

The Bereng family give me a copy of the pathologist's report,[77] which states that 'no injuries' were noted when Tebogo's body was examined in the state morgue.

In May 2013, I visit Chantelle Liebenberg, the state pathologist who wrote the pathologist's report on Tebogo's death, which states that a cellmate saw the 42-year-old feeling unwell and then collapsing.

'When we receive bodies from prison, we follow the prison doctor's suggested cause of death, unless there are clear marks of injuries not consistent with the stated cause of death,' Dr Liebenberg explains. She's young and blonde, with a smile permanently plastered across her face. 'There were no visible injuries, so I followed the DCS's notes.'

I can't help but think back to what Robert told me about his visit to the funeral parlour before they buried Tebogo. He was the one who washed the body, and he said the funeral was a blur because he was still reeling from what he saw. 'There was a scratch on his head, dried-up blood under his lips. There were big greenish bruises on his sides. There was a brown, cream-like substance applied to his sides. It came off and onto my hands,' he told me, holding up his hands, as if the brown stuff was still there. Did Dr Liebenberg not see this? Did the bruises only appear after her examination?

No internal post-mortem was conducted, as it was not requested, Dr Liebenberg tells me. She was unaware of his epilepsy. She also didn't check for any marks that correspond with electroshocking or other forms of torture. Electroshocking leaves behind welts and red marks on the skin, which will disappear after a few days.

She listens as I tell her about my research at the prison, specifically mentioning the torture allegations. 'Yoh,' she says, softly.

That electrified riot shields can kill is something the producer of this equipment once acknowledged. A Johannesburg-based company called Force Products, which recently rebranded as Security Focus Africa,[78] sells them to the Department of Correctional Services. In 2014, Force Products advertised its 'Force Electrified Riot Shield'[79] on its website as follows 'The product has its own defensive and tactical application and can prevent an incident escalating from basic confrontation at the low end of the scale to the use of lethal force at the high end.' They quickly take it down after I email them questions about the word lethal, but not before I took a screen shot of the page.

In the same year (2014) Tienie Labuschagne, the then manager of Force Products, is called to testify on behalf of the state in the case of 231 inmates at St Albans prison who were brutally attacked, electroshocked in 2005.[80] His affidavit[81] makes for interesting reading. Labuschagne makes a strange claim about the use of water when applying the shields. He says water has no effect on the severity of the shock because 'Normal tap water is not a good enough conductor to make a significant difference on increasing the level of shock experienced.'

He recommends 2–3 second bursts with the shock shield. This, he claims will make 'the local pain dissipate after approximately 45 seconds and there are no further physical effects.' I wonder if Labuschagne knows how his products are used in practice.

Tebogo's death was as lonely and forbidding as the dustbowl cemetery where he is buried. He represents the nearly forgotten among the bones and skulls of the forgotten, the poor and the downtrodden.

There are conflicting narratives of how and where he died: in his cell, on his way to the hospital or simply 'he fainted'.

From the eyewitness accounts and other evidence, I think he most probably died in his cell following an epileptic fit, brought on by the use of electrified shields and possibly expired medication. His death was never investigated or followed up, and no internal post-mortem was requested.

Like the brown dust whirling aimlessly above the graves of the souls in the corner of the cemetery where Tebogo lies, his death got swept away by lies and fear, and it nearly dissolved into nothingness.

G4S's list of the dead

Isaac Nelani and Tebogo Bereng are not the only people who died while placed in the care of G4S. The company has a long track record of people dying on their watch.

In February 2014, Reza Baharti, an Iranian asylum seeker, died during protests at an offshore Australian detention centre mainly run by G4S on Papua New Guinea's Manus Island. The death was used as evidence of general dangerous and damaging conditions at the centre in a class action that resulted in a ruling in 2017 ordering compensation to the tune of Australian $70 million be paid to those held there. The centre was officially closed at the end of October 2017.[82]

In November 2012, Clive Carter, a guard employed by G4S, beat a delegate at an HIV conference in Glasgow in the UK to death with a fire extinguisher.[83] Part of a G4S team providing security services at the conference, Carter's GP, had apparently earlier referred him for anger management counselling.[84] He assaulted and killed Khanokporn Satjawat, a pharmaceutical worker from Thailand, allegedly because he did not like her attitude. He was found guilty of murder and was given a life sentence.

In October 2010, Angolan deportee Jimmy Mubenga died after being restrained by three G4S security guards – Stuart Tribelnig, Terrence Hughes and Colin Kaler – on an aeroplane at Heathrow Airport in the UK.[85] The 2013 inquest concluded that he had been 'unlawfully' killed.[86] It transpired Tribelnig had written racist text messages: 'Fuck off and go home you free-loading, benefit grabbing, kid producing, violent, non-English speaking cock suckers and take those hairy faced, sandal wearing, bomb making, goat fucking, smelly rag head bastards with you.'[87] A further 76 racist texts were found on the phone of another guard. However, the judge deemed the racist text messages as 'not having any relevance'. The three guards were charged with manslaughter. In the court case, fellow passengers testified how they heard the Angolan shouting 'I can't breathe' while the guards held him down. They later claimed they did not hear his pleas. The three men were acquitted in 2014. Clare Sambrook from the UK-based investigative journalism project Shine a Light notes that G4S was among the security service providers that were explicitly 'warned about the dangers of excessive force and guards' racist abuse [...] more than two years before the killing of Jimmy Mubenga'.[88]

In 2009 – shortly after arriving in Iraq to provide security services for his employer, ArmorGroup, now part of G4S – former British soldier Danny Fitzsimons shot and killed Paul McGuigan and Darren Hoare, two of his colleagues.[89] He also injured an Iraqi security guard. It was subsequently revealed that on the eve of the deployment to Iraq, a whistleblower also working for G4S had warned the employer about Fitzsimons having a violent past.[90] Not only did he allegedly have a criminal record and firearm and assault offences to his name at the time of his appointment with G4S, Fitzsimons was apparently also previously diagnosed with post-traumatic stress disorder. G4S later seemed to acknowledge that its vetting process was problematic in this case. The company was vague in its response to receiving the whistleblower's warning. In 2011, Fitzsimons was sentenced to 20 years in prison and was set to serve his sentence in Iraq. In 2019, however, he was extradited to the UK to serve the rest of his sentence.[91]

Eleven illegal immigrants burned to death at a detention centre run by Securicor (which merged with G4S in 2009 in the Netherlands) at Schiphol Airport in the Netherlands in October 2005.[92] G4S is still the biggest security contractor in the Netherlands, according to G4S's Dutch website.[93]

In April 2004, 15-year-old Gareth Myatt died from asphyxia after being restrained by three officers at the Rainsbrook Training Centre, a G4S-run prison for children and teenagers in the UK.[94] The inquest reveals[95] that when Gareth complained that he couldn't breathe while being restrained, David Beadnall, one of the officers, responded: 'If you can talk, then you can breathe.' The boy then warned that he was going to soil himself and was told 'you are going to have to shit yourself'. The restraint continued despite him defecating and later also vomiting. Beadnall (who had the nickname 'Clubber' in Rainsbrook) later became a health and safety manager at G4S children's homes.[96]

G4S's competence in vetting its employees has been widely called into question. 'These tragedies have happened too many times in too many different situations in too many countries to not believe that G4S has a systemic problem. Is it systemically racist or systemically incompetent?'

Simon Hattenstone and Eric Allison ask in an article for the Guardian. *'Perhaps it is only when G4S knows that it will be charged with corporate manslaughter if somebody in their care dies unnecessarily, that they will ensure they recruit responsibly and learn how to look after people in their care without killing them'.*[97]

8

Don't call me farm boy

THERE IS A GENDERED difference in how people respond to trauma. Women often repeat childhood trauma by placing themselves in the same position, revictimising themselves. Men, on the other hand, often repeat the original offender's behaviour, switching from victim to perpetrator, re-enacting the trauma.

Sigmund Freud called this 'traumatic neurosis' or 'repetition compulsion', and he posited that it is actually a way of remembering. Victims of childhood abuse repeat the same behaviour later in life because they don't or can't consciously remember the original traumatising event. They repeat the repressed memory, so it becomes a contemporary experience.

The repetition of traumatic events has everything to do with language, or more precisely the lack thereof. When a traumatic event – be it domestic or sexual violence, a natural disaster or war – happens, there is often very little the victim can say or put into words. The feelings of helplessness mostly manifest in nonverbal images and sensations. The repetition of the trauma later in life is an attempt to give words to the experience. 'Give sorrow words,' Shakespeare's Macbeth already observed centuries ago.

'Being unable to protect oneself from hurts inflicted by others was a source of shame,' author bell hooks writes about how she viewed and processed her experiences of domestic violence as a young girl.

'shame is the most disturbing emotion we ever experience directly about ourselves, for in the moment of shame we feel deeply divided from ourselves. (…) shame divides us from ourselves just as it divides us from others, and because we still yearn for reunion, shame is deeply disturbing.'[98]

The power of language has the potential to break through the walls of silence and shame. This power is palpable in the conversations I have with the imprisoned men. Many tell me it is the first time they are offered a space to talk about their experiences of abuse and violence.

The men I interview – almost all prisoners and some guards – had terrible childhoods, filled with poverty, violence and abuse. They validate the theory that men often process childhood trauma by becoming the perpetuator, as most of them are in Mangaung for committing violent crimes. Locked up behind walls, these men were then subjected to the kind of terror they might have inflicted upon their own victims.

Ishmael

'There, that's one of them,' Ishmael Mohlomi nods his head at a big guy standing at the palisade fence. He's an EST member who worked in Mangaung during Ishmael's time there. The man is nervously eyeing us. He walks to the road and starts phoning. He jumps into a car that stops at the kerb. It speeds off.

The sun is beating down. It's the summer of 2016, and I'm waiting with Ishmael at the Bloemfontein Magistrate's Court. His arson case is about to start.

In 2009, Ishmael set fire to his cell in Mangaung. Prison authorities had for months ignored his complaints about his reclassification, and he felt arson was his last resort.

Ishmael was arrested for a murder in 2009 and sentenced to 15 years' imprisonment. In 2014, he had become a free man again after a judge acquitted him.[99]

We find some shade under a tree.

Four more big men arrive in quick succession. One after the other they park their cars, get out and mill around, chatting to each other.

I lean back against the wall. Ishmael walks towards the men, who all look vaguely familiar to me, but I can't put names to their faces. He shakes hands with one of them.

'Bra Shakes.'

'Sho' bra.'

They keep their hands entwined as they continue the banter, shaking at intervals, as if to underline an important point. They smile, chat, nod their heads. They could have been neighbours or friends. But they are not.

When the men are done, Bra Shakes looks at me and waves. I wave back, feeling like I should know him. My mind races through memories, but it draws a blank. He starts walking towards me, determinedly. He is still smiling when he says, 'Hi, Ruth. Ruth Hopkins.' He announces my name in a loud voice. The other guys are now looking at us. He grabs my hand and starts shaking it, vigorously. 'I'm Shakes,' he says. 'Finally, we meet. You know, *mos*, you're famous in Bloemfontein.' The other men smile and nod in agreement.

Then it hits me. I had never met this man before, but I put two and two together and realise that this must be the Ninja who slipped Dan the video clips of incidents during which the EST used force – with the approval of prison authorities – in Mangaung. In and among this series of videos, I found the damning evidence of Bheki Dlamini being injected against his will.

As I'm sifting through my memories of the Ninjas, a court official appears and tells us that Ishmael's case will be postponed. I watch as a prisoner, who had earlier been brought to court in shackles, is bundled into a G4S van and driven away.

Shakes was part of the EST that was called in after Ishmael set his cell on fire. That day they beat him up so badly that he would never be able to see from his left eye. The police ignored his complaint about the damaged eye and added his name to a two-year backlog of prisoners' cases. His complaints following the incident generally went nowhere.

Ishmael lives in Senekal, making a living off his car-wash business. He's in Bloemfontein for the court case and invites me to the shack where he lives when he's in town. It's at the far edge of Bloemfontein's Freedom Square township.

As I enter, a lorry drives by on one of the dirt roads, leaving a diaphanous cloud of dust behind. It creates a misty lens through which the tin roofs, long-drop toilets and open fires make the place look a bit fairylike. But when the dust settles, it's desolate: dry, windy and unforgiving.

The wind keeps on lifting the roof of the corrugated-iron shack, which belongs to Ishmael's uncle. He's sitting on the bed, which takes up most of the space inside. There's also a fridge, which can't be working as there's no electricity. Stacked on top of the microwave is a battered radio and some plates. The heat is suffocating.

Ishmael looks uneasy in his temporary home. He's clasping his hands in his lap.

I ask him why he chatted with Shakes at the courthouse that day, while this very man was responsible for his damaged eye. I wonder why he seemed to temporarily suspend the anger, the outrage, the excruciating injustice of it all.

'It's better to act friendly around those guys. I know Shakes from the hood. I see him around. If I challenge him, what will happen to me?' he asks. 'They're not humans, they're monsters.'

Monsters. That word stays with me. What does it mean? For Ishmael, monster and human seem to be mutually exclusive identities – you can't be both at the same time. I didn't think he is saying Shakes is Frankenstein's creation, a physically deformed monster described in fairy tales and novels. Shakes's physical traits are not monster-like, he's just a normal guy. The perceived monstrosity is to be found in his morals, or the lack thereof. What I think Ishmael is trying to say is that Shakes is morally corrupt and therefore incapable of doing any good.

Shakes

At some point in Shakes's life, a chord was struck that awakened a ruthless, violent side in an otherwise quiet, introverted man. I meet with him several times in 2016 and 2017 in order to try to understand these two competing sides in him, to find the monster hiding in the shadows, softly growling at his kinder more compassionate inclinations. I want to understand the Shakes who carried out torture, but I also want to see the Shakes who decided these atrocities had to see the light of day. I need to see the Shakes who had risked his livelihood when he smuggled video footage out of the prison, the Shakes who eventually admitted: 'What we did was wrong.'

Shakes has worked for G4S since Mangaung opened its doors in 2001, and over the time we meet he's still working for them. He was present when violence was meted out: he struck the blows, broke arms and ankles, he poured water on naked men bound to metal bedframes, and he took out his electrified shock shield with an output of 6 000 volts. He placed the shield on genitals, heads, backs and chests – and pressed the trigger. Until the screaming was too much to bear.

In one of our conversations, he tells me about the nightmares he has, of rivers of blood spilling onto the floor. 'I think back to the things I did,' he says, 'and it haunts me. I have tried explaining it to my wife, but she just says, "Don't talk to me about your traumatic prison work. I don't want to know."'

Shakes was feared. He belonged to the rank of men who *should* be feared. But the more I talk to him, the more I realise that on the inside, he's still very much the quiet, introverted farm boy who grew up hungry.

Shakes was used to going to school on an empty stomach. His parents were poor farm workers who could barely feed their brood of 10. They lived on farmland near Kroonstad.

Growing up, Audick, as his parents named him, played soccer, earning him his nickname, after Ephraim 'Shakes' Mashaba, a legendary player and manager of the national team.

But he also had another nickname – farm boy. 'Don't listen to him. He's a dumb farm boy.' For years, Shakes would wince when he heard the school bullies refer to him in this way.

'What they said confirmed what I felt,' he explains. 'I had an inferiority complex.'

He also saw his own elders being denigrated. 'I saw my father come home with a bruised face, time and again. He was a stubborn man and would get into fights with the farmers, who would beat and fire him,' he says. 'Why did they have to humiliate my father?' he asks.

The farmers referred to his family as 'kaffirs', but he would see them together, this white tribe, extremely protective of and caring for their next of kin. He says he always wondered what made them different.

As a teenager, Shakes had something of a political awakening. 'My parents had no idea who Mandela was. They didn't read. They are simple people,' he says.

'My teacher started telling me about our history, the role white people played. Our land. That it was taken away from us. I read about Black Power. Then one day, I saw youngsters in the centre of town throw rocks at the police. All my life, I had been taught to run away from policemen, and now I saw my peers throwing rocks *at* them. I thought they were crazy.'

But the seed had been planted.

He realised that the history of his country was intimately linked to his father's humiliation. A deep-seated rage welled up. 'I developed an absolute hatred of white people. I vowed never to work for a white *baas*, like my father.'

He was no longer going to take the school bullying lying down. Amplified by a newfound consciousness of the violence of colonialism, racism, land grabs and apartheid, his repository of rage was punctured the next time he was called a 'farm boy'. Ignoring a teacher's advice to avoid confrontation, he locked the bullies in the schoolyard one day and beat them up, one by one.

He was also determined to finish matric. No one else in his family had ever done so before. He still remembers how proud his mother was when his results came out.

He then moved to Bloemfontein. He survived on piece jobs and slept on friends' couches. For a while he lived with a childhood friend and his mom in a shack. He says he was grateful for the surprising kindness of the people around him.

He often went to bed hungry, but he was never tempted by crime, even when he lived with a petty criminal for a while.

'My father taught us never to take something that didn't belong to us,' he says. 'He was an authoritarian. All I wanted was to make him proud – to find a job.'

When he picked up a glossy G4S recruitment brochure at a library, he didn't think he had a chance. But he went for an interview and made it to the second round.

'I didn't even know what the word "contract" meant when they offered it to me. I felt, wow, now I finally belong somewhere,' he says. 'It was a huge turning point in my life. I had been offered an opportunity to escape the life my father led.'

During his training with G4S, he was taught that the EST was always to be in charge. 'You tell the inmates what to do, not the other way around – that is what we were taught,' he says. He also learned how to use 'minimum force' when restraining a violent man.

They tried out the electric shields on each other during training, so they would know how it felt. 'You know, it can knock out a cow. Do you know how big a cow is?' he asks, looking at me incredulously. 'It's like you're hit with an iron rod.'

When he started his job, he was taught some other tricks. Shakes says that it was the deputy director of operations at Mangaung – the main person in charge of security – who taught him about the water during his first few months on the job. 'You know, *mos*, if you mix electricity and water – it hurts,' he explains.

The deputy director also taught him that electroshocking hurts even more when one is naked. 'Shocks hurt a lot more if they're applied directly to the skin,' Shakes says.

I ask Shakes if humiliation was part of the plan, thinking back to what Wits psychology professor Malose Langa told me about nudity in front of warders being way more traumatising than any physical pain since it's profoundly emasculating for the prisoners. But Shakes keeps saying that electricity hurts more when it's applied directly to the skin. Maybe he doesn't want to consider the idea of humiliation, or maybe it's too painful or shameful to acknowledge.

He does describe endless cruelty. How the 'dark room' was exactly that – dark – but that you would see the victim when you pushed the trigger on the electrified shield, as little sparks would throw some light on the prostrate, often naked man who was about to get beaten up. The aim, Shakes says, was to teach the men some respect. To get them to give up information or to just stop complaining. But first and foremost: respect.

I ask him if any of these memories were exceptionally atrocious to him. 'There was this one guy – a big guy, a general who ruled with an iron fist over the other men. He was known for his strength and violent disposition. We had taken him to the dark room and were beating him, kicking him, electroshocking him. He begged us to stop. To hear a big man like that beg so desperately – that stayed with me,' he says.

I think of Ishmael and how he shook Shakes's hand, despite these acts of violence. At the courtroom that day, they looked like buddies at a bar, cracking jokes. But this was the very man who had beaten Ishmael in the face, cracking the socket of his left eye and ruining the optic nerves forever.

'When we heard about the fires, I was furious,' he recalls when I ask him about the incident with Ishmael. 'I thought, "Who would do this? Which adult would ever behave like this? *How dare they* treat us with such disrespect?" So, we beat the shit out of them.'

On the day Ishmael was assaulted, the EST members were responding to many acts of defiance within Mangaung, including fires and the hostage situation. 'It was total chaos,' Shakes says. 'The cells were on fire. We had to unlock them and douse the fire. Then we tortured and beat them up. Inmates were lying everywhere. Ninjas were all over the place, shocking, kicking, *klapping*. I saw blood on the floor. Those prisoners had to *feel* who was boss. We made them feel. They were going to realise they could never do this again. We were boss – not them.'

Outside the prison walls – once they'd left the arena where the muscled, armed Ninjas fought unarmed men who felt they had nothing left in their lives but rage – prisoners and warders assume 'public' roles. They are guys 'from the hood'. They come close, shake hands and laugh. They plaster over the past with small talk.

The mostly white management, meanwhile, sit in their sleek offices. They recline in swivel chairs. And they watch, observing the wounds, squirting blood, hair-raising cries of agony and despair. It is not always clear who is going to win. Usually the prisoners, clad in light blue uniforms, lose, while the Ninjas, the men in black, walk away victorious. But sometimes the enraged men nearly win. In 2017, a prison guard ended up in ICU with a punctured lung. The inmate had aimed for his heart and he had nearly died.

The EST men are untouchable, especially compared to their unarmed colleagues in the units. Shakes sends me the Ninjas' conversations they have been having on their WhatsApp group. They gloat when an inmate has been assaulted. "You gents are my heros [sic]. Warriors are never trained to quit or give up. What we all witnessed today was character. EST won the fight. Period." Bennie van Aardt, the security manager at the prison writes. "I'm sweating it out at the gym while he is licking his wounds like a little bitch that he is. Little did he know what he was attacking. But now he knows about the beast that I am." "He got it," another EST member writes.

When I drive out to see Shakes in early 2017, I get lost. My sense of direction is comparable to that of a duck in a thunderstorm, so despite having been at his house before, I can't find it. My GPS fails, and there are barely any road signs. I take a picture of a spaza shop and send it to him to check if I'm close. 'I can see you,' he responds.

The setting sun is spreading its orange yolk across the sky in a big fatty blob. I see his silhouette in his front yard: short with a sizable belly. Shakes and I are the same age: 43. He still plays soccer, but life seems to have caught up with him and the circumference of his waist.

'You don't remember where I live, hey?' he asks, laughingly, as I get out of my car. Shakes is in shorts, a long-sleeved T-shirt and slippers.

He walks ahead of me, across the small dusty yard and past a skinny Boxer chained to a pole next to a wooden doghouse. The dog gets up, ears pointing. His eyes follow me as I enter the house. He sits down again.

We enter the house through the kitchen. I smell dinner and hear a television blasting away. Kedibone, his wife, is doing the dishes. She's small, with curly black hair framing her very round pretty face. She smiles, and a few golden teeth glitter back at me. She never leaves the kitchen during my visit. But she's so quiet that I forget she's there.

We go to the small lounge. The enormous television takes up nearly the entire wall. Shakes sits down on the couch, his legs bent to the side. We start chatting: about prison politics, soccer, his two young daughters, Paballo and Rethabile, who dart in and out of the room as we talk. They both inherited their parents' round features. The older one keeps to herself, but the three-year-old interrupts us to show me things: her dinner, clothes, earrings and a book.

Our conversation drifts to the men Shakes interacts with every day at Mangaung.

'I remember one inmate. He was one of those guys who had raped and murdered a lesbian. Her death was horrible. He had smashed her head to a pulp with a big rock after raping her.'

The man was younger than him, but Shakes knew him from Kroonstad. They both grew up there, around the same people and families. The Ninja and the prisoner chatted about all the friends and acquaintances they had in common. 'I had a long conversation with him,' Shakes tells me. 'He opened up about his crime, how he felt about it – his guilt. I just listened to his grief, his pain. And after a while, I started to feel for this guy. He was so young, and he had made a horrible mistake, but he was still a human. There is humanity in all of us. Inmates are paying for their mistakes, and they should be given a second chance.'

His voice is soft, and he chooses his words carefully, sometimes halting as he searches for the right one.

It's clear this conversation was a critical moment for him. 'This prison work has changed me,' he says. 'I feel angry a lot of the time. I have horrible nightmares. The terrible things I have done …' His voice trails off. 'And I bring it home. I take it out here.' He later tells me he'd once hit Kedibone.

While her dad talks about nightmares and anger, three-year-old Rethabile climbs into my chair and squeezes her bum into the seat next to mine. We just about fit.

'I realised what we were doing was wrong,' Shakes says, and I'm surprised by this sudden admission. 'I tried talking to inmates, asking them why they behaved the way they did. I found that talking to them was more effective than all the violence. I explained this to my colleagues, and they agreed that we were going overboard. When I raised it with my boss, all he said was, "Are you questioning my authority?" It felt like a threat.'

'You vowed never to work for a "white *baas*",' I remind him.

'I ended up in the same situation as my father. Sure, I'm getting paid a lot more than him, but a white man is running that prison. A few years ago, I realised that they enable the violence to maximise their profits. As long as there is violence and chaos, there is also a need for security. They don't give a damn about us. And instead of taking them on, we were beating down our brothers. And that is wrong.'

Shakes had asserted his need to be respected, stemming from generations of racially charged disrespect and humiliation, by assaulting black men. The bullies would never call him farm boy again, and the prisoners would never think of disrespecting him again. But the white people remain out of reach, unreckoned with.

'Apartheid is still alive in that prison,' Shakes says, when I draw the comparison between the schoolyard bullies and the prisoners. 'To them, we are all disposable. But they are in charge. They call the shots.'

On my way out, Kedibone confesses: 'I'm scared. This is not going to get him fired?' She's smiling, but I see the fear in her eyes. She rests her hand on my arm.

'I protect my sources,' I try, feebly, smiling back at her. What could

I say? Shakes has risked his job before. It was his choice to leak those videos. It's his choice to talk to me. He could be fired, possibly sued. But at his house that night, I try my best to reassure Kedibone that he would be fine.

When I leave Shakes's house that night, darkness has fallen. I scan the street for other cars. The road is empty, the dust of the day has settled, and the sun has withdrawn its orange rays.

G4S prisons and detention centres

Are the terrible conditions in Mangaung prison a product of a G4S culture or are they simply part and parcel of a broken South African prison system? The answer to that question is not clear cut. Prisons in South Africa are in a bad state: There is systemic overcrowding,[100] uncontrolled spread of communicable diseases and high levels of violence. However, looking at G4S's track record in the field of the prisons and detention centres they run, there seems to be a systemic problem in how they run their incarceration business.

Most recently, in August 2018, the British government had to take control of G4S-run Birmingham Prison. G4S was awarded a 15-year contract to operate the formerly public prison in 2011.[101]

Newspapers ran lengthy descriptions of the conditions that led to the government takeover in Birmingham such as 'a prisoner who returned to a blood-spattered cell after his fellow inmate had been assaulted'. Rory Stewart, the Tory prison minister who visited the prison, observed: 'there were prisoners leaning on the gallery, openly smoking, which they are not supposed to do be doing under the rules. Cell toilets with no screen, broken showers and "ever present" cockroaches contributed to the "unfit" living conditions.'

He rounded off his observations in a very British manner: 'It just wasn't decent, clean, orderly, and well run.'[102] Like Mangaung prison, Birmingham prison saw extremely high levels of reported violence.

The UK government takeover of the prison reminded me of DCS's ten-month reign at Mangaung prison, a similarity no British journalist picked up on. However, the company has been forced to hand back control of two private prisons to the state on two different continents due to utter mismanagement, unacceptable levels of lawlessness and violence.

Stewart criticised the company: 'I am absolutely convinced that G4S was not going to be able to turn this round on their own.'[103] But he quickly reassured the world: 'the crisis at the prison was not linked to it being privately run. We have good, privately-run prisons across the country and while Birmingham faces its own particular set of challenges, I am absolutely clear that it must start to live up to the standards seen elsewhere.' He even tied his political future in with a set of goals: If drug use in prisons hadn't decreased within a year, he would step down.[104]

In 2016, British children placed in a juvenile detention centre run by G4S, Medway secure training centre endured abusive treatment.[105] This was followed by a similar scandal at G4S's UK Brook House immigration detention facility in 2017.[106] Guards were caught on camera abusing the people placed in their care, with allegations of racism and misuse of physical force. The Brook House contract was extended last year for another two years.[107] The National Audit Office determined that: 'G4S has made £14.3 million in profit from Brook House immigration removal centre between 2012 and 2018.'[108] In June 2019, a judge ordered an inquest into the treatment of two men who were held in Brook House.[109]

'A public inquiry was required, the judge continued, because the "full extent of the discreditable behaviour has not been exposed to public view" and that having open hearings would be necessary "to maintain public confidence in the rule of law"', according to the Guardian.[110]

In Israel, the company provided technology for the wall separating Israel from Palestine[111] and equipped prisons where political prisoners were being held.[112] International legal norms were flouted. Due to a hugely successful human rights and divestment campaign, the company was forced to withdraw from the country, but it still runs a police training academy there.[113]

The company had a $70-million contract to supply 'detainee hospital work' for another notorious prison: Guantanamo Bay.[114] UK human rights organisation Reprieve alleged the company profited off human rights violations committed in Guantanamo Bay, such as the force feeding of detainees, for which G4S should be held criminally liable.[115]

G4S's public detention failures provide a glimpse of a company that is otherwise highly secretive, protected by corporate confidentiality clauses and cooperative governments. And what is even more striking about G4S's public sector failures across the globe is their Teflon quality. Nothing seems to really stick; no lawsuit is big enough or damaging enough and governments are not brave enough to hold the multinational responsible. Quite the contrary, G4S is often awarded new contracts following public scandals and poor contract compliance. During the presentation of their 2018 financial results, Almanza reported new contract wins worth £1.4 billion.[116]

9

The strike

'Please save us from this private monster'

About two weeks later, Shakes is dismissed, together with seven other EST members. Not because he's talking to me, but allegedly for failing to comply with one of Derrick de Klerk's orders.

During the winter of 2013, Dan, the Madiba clansman, is taunting a profitmaking prison from the Old Empire. He becomes the informal leader of the biggest prison strike to ever take place in South Africa.

The strike does not happen overnight. The DSOs had previously stayed home, in 2009 and again in 2010. Wage negotiations between G4S and POPCRU had been declared a dispute in October 2012. The workers demanded pay and benefits in line with their colleagues working in state prisons.

'We demanded a housing allowance, a danger allowance. But our safety concerns came first though. Because what use is a R900 housing allowance if you're crippled or dead?' Dan says when we meet in Bloemfontein in September 2013.

A few months previously, in March 2013, the Commission for Conciliation, Mediation and Arbitration (CCMA) rules that G4S is 'reasonable' in its employment and remuneration policies. The guards' most important demand is not related to money though. Rather, they fear for their lives and ask for improved safety and security measures.

One of the big demands is for the ceramic toilets to be replaced with steel – and unbreakable – ones. Ceramic shards are often used to stab the guards.

Barring a court application, the workers have now exhausted the procedural route for challenging their working conditions, because the CCMA had ruled in the company's favour. A strike is imminent.

POPCRU shop steward Dan is part of the team trying to negotiate with G4S. But he's also planning to bring the entire prison operation to a grinding halt.

Around this time, in early 2013, he starts organising the prisoners. He calls a council with the gang leaders. Through them, he develops an operation much like a military underground network of cells. The generals have soldiers in every one of the seven units of the prison. Dan's own army of prison guards – his soldiers, who often accompany him when we meet – are also present in every unit, and they report to him on a daily basis.

He's also getting to know a growing number of disgruntled EST members.

'The EST was the integral part of my plans to destroy the system. Because if they are not on duty the inmates can destabilise the prison and the only way to clip the wings of G4S was through the [...] EST,' Dan writes in 'My unionist and activist life since 2010',[117] an essay he wrote in 2016.

He wins the trust of the Ninjas and, during lunch breaks, they gather around his car in the parking lot.

'During these lunch breaks,' Dan writes, 'we planned the downfall of G4S.'

On a sweltering hot day in March 2013, I get to see how Dan organises his men.

After interviewing several inmates in the morning, I exit the prison around noon for a lunch break. Fusi Mofokeng, who had joined me as

The strike

a translator, is with me. Fusi is in his late forties and has spent a large chunk of his life behind bars. In 1992, he was arrested and convicted for the death of a policeman in Bethlehem. He served 19 years in prison for a murder he claims he didn't commit and was released in 2011 on early parole. Currently, he is trying to get his conviction and sentence overturned.[118] In 2002, Fusi tells me, he requested a transfer to Mangaung prison, where he stayed for two years. He says he requested the transfer because it was advertised as a modern prison with ample educational opportunities, which seemed attractive to Fusi. 'It was the worst prison I ever stayed in,' he says now.

During lunch I use the bonnet of my Mercedes as a table and unpack food and a tea flask. Fusi looks uneasy. I think it might be because of the figs, hummus and crackers that I arrange on the bonnet.

'They're looking at us,' Fusi says.

I look around and see several Ninjas leave the prison.

'Are they?' I answer as I crack open a bag with mixed nuts and dried fruit.

'They've never seen a white woman and a black man eat lunch together,' Fusi continues. I take a bite of a fig and observe the men as they walk to the far end of the parking lot, their bulletproof vests strapped around their torsos.

They crowd around a car. I wander out of the parking lot to get a better view. A man wearing the dark blue G4S uniform gets out of the car. He's wearing reflective sunglasses. I recognise Dan, but I don't call out to him, honouring the agreement between us not to publicly interact in any way within the prison complex.

The guards are drawn to Dan and his prophetic announcements about orchestrating the downfall of a huge company. Dan tells me he convinces them of his strategy: the outcome of any strike would be dismissal – that's a given. But, so he tells me, their skills and knowledge of the private prison system are irreplaceable. The prison would be completely gridlocked if they all stay away. They'd be dismissed but that would create the leverage to reinstate them on their *own* terms and conditions.

I travel back and forth to Bloemfontein during the strike and I watch as Dan moves to the helm of a workers' movement that is swelling and gathering speed every day. He instructs the workers to stand up to those running the prison. And then he shows them how to do it, in a confrontation with HR Director Stephen Page, the man who noticed Dan the young G4S trainee back in 2008 and encouraged him to lead his class.

During one of the strained wage negotiation sessions, Dan loses his cool when he sees Page refusing to acknowledge that warders are being stabbed and assaulted nearly every month.

'In that meeting, I stood up,' Dan tells me later. 'I waved my finger at Page and said: "Listen, Page, you might think that we are stupid, but you just wait: one day I will outsmart you." Then I walked off.'

Dan promised himself he would never be a shadow of a man.

Nearly every DSO I interview has experienced terrible violence. They show me their medical files that document injuries for which they'd been hospitalised, others pull up their sleeves or shirts and show me living proof: bruises and scars covering their bodies. None of them are apparently offered any significant counselling.

Not even the woman I spot always wearing sunglasses that cover nearly half her face. Her colleagues tell me a prisoner apparently kicked her in the face and injured her eye, which became sensitive to light, hence the sunglasses.

According to South African labour law, prison guards – and police officers, air-traffic controllers and those providing blood-transfusion services – are not allowed to strike because their work is classified as 'essential'.

The G4S prison guards circumvent this by taking collective sick leave on Monday, 12 August 2013.

This is the moment, Dan tells me, for every black man and woman working at or living in the prison to 'stake their rightful claim'. Like his icon Steve Biko, Dan believes white domination will crumble in the face of black unity.

Dan tells me that the sick leave is all about 'testing the system' – and it does just that. Inside the prison walls, chaos erupts. Not anticipating the stay-away, G4S is unprepared and scrambles to find staff to run the prison. Admin staff, vocational trainers, IT workers – the mostly white part of the workforce that was still working – people not qualified to be prison guards – are hastily sent into the 'streets', as the corridors with cells on each side are called.

Most white staff are accommodated in the building that houses management offices, which was later dubbed 'Nkandla', referencing the previous president Jacob Zuma's private homestead, which had been built with money siphoned off state coffers.[119] Although 'Nkandla' is adjacent to the entrance of the prison, the people in that building barely interact with prisoners during the course of their work.

And now management has to deal with the unspooling of order. Inmates riot and set fire to three cells in Port Phillip and Wolds. A workstation where guards log in and out is torched. Two non-striking Ninjas who come in to deal with the fires are stabbed with broken glass: one in the nose, the other on his hand.[120]

'I am scared,' a non-striking warder tells me. 'I fear for my life. Warders are getting stabbed, and there are only two emergency security team members on duty.' He alleges the company is paying uncertified admin staff to feed the prisoners who are being kept in their cells for 23, sometimes 24, hours a day.

'They're hungry,' Sajeedah Coutts tells me when she phones me in a panic. Gershwin, her fiancé, is a prisoner being held in Wolds. She contacted me on a previous occasion, after the prison apparently refused to investigate an assault or allow Gershwin Coutts to lay a charge with the police. 'He says he is missing meals and is being locked up for 24 hours,' she tells me.

G4S sends the absent workers an SMS, warning them that their collective sick leave amounts to an 'unlawful strike' and that they should return to work – or else. When the 158 striking guards ignore the ultimatum, G4S takes the case to the Labour Court and is granted an interdict. The collective sick leave is declared 'unprotected'. The workers are ordered to return to work. Not one of them does.

The spreading unrest coincides with Dan's uncle, a father figure in his life, passing away. In his essay, Dan writes: 'In the month of August I lost my uncle, who was like a father to me. I cried for the first time after a decade, after I had lost my brother in 2002. I felt the same pain, and I still feel that pain. He was going to be proud of me, for being a true leader like he was, a Unionist, a father, an uncle, [...] a unifier and a comforter to all of us in the family.'

The day after the Labour Court rules that the stay-away amounts to an unprotected strike, Dan writes a letter to Mangaung management, on a POPCRU letterhead, detailing the main grievance of the striking workforce – victimisation. 'Our working conditions are unbearable and unfavourable,' he writes, noting that they have 'raised this numerous times' and that G4S is 'hell bent' on dismissing them. 'We will put forward more during our grievance hearing, to expose the company,' the letter concludes.[121]

Shortly thereafter, he pens another two letters, again on POPCRU letterheads. The first one deals with the 'Rye Hill Grievance'.[122]

Two white DSOs had neglected, as protocol prescribes, to check for weapons or sharp objects on a newly arrived prisoner. The prisoner used a hand-made knife he was carrying to stab a black guard in Rye Hill.

G4S appointed Rudi Mathee, whose job it was to gather intelligence on impending gang warfare and other disruptions in the prison, to investigate the case. He was also instructed to recommend action in the Rye Hill case. According to Dan's letter, Mathee recommended that the black warder should be suspended, whereas the two white DSOs who had neglected to carry out their duties should not be disciplined.

Dan concludes in this letter to management: 'Whites will protect whites. We have raised racist tendencies in MCC [Mangaung

Correctional Centre] and our cries are falling on deaf ears and we are starting to see that racism is tolerated at the prison.'

He writes a second letter of complaint on 19 August, accusing G4S of trying to win over the activity officers, who work with the prisoners in vocational training and other programmes, by discussing their employment offer behind the backs of union officials. 'We are not attacking your credibility,' Dan writes. 'We are stating the facts.'

Not surprisingly, Dan is suspended, along with four others. The announcement is made on 9 September.

'I slept very well the day they suspended me. It was a beautiful day in my life,' Dan says when I meet him several weeks after the strike. We are at the Wimpy again. I'm sipping the weak coffee, and Dan is sucking Coke through a straw. He looks rested. He opens up about the emotional toll prison work has had on him.

'There was this one prison general in my unit, he was called Nagel. I had a very serious confrontation with him. He asked an inmate to send me a message: he was going to call me to order. A few months later, the inmate messenger stabbed a warder in the Wolds unit, with razors. And I knew that could have been me.'

In the fabled hierarchy of prison gangs, stabbing a warder is related to honour: a warder's blood on the floor elevates the status of a member.

'I had this awful nightmare, where inmates were pushing us into a corner, and then the warders turned on me as well,' he remembers, his forehead a brief tangle of wrinkles.

'You know when an African man talks about having emotional problems, it is not accepted. In our culture they would say this person is bewitched. But I speak about it, because I realise I am not the only one.'

Dan's suspension doesn't neutralise him, as the company hopes. Rather, it catapults him into an even more significant leadership role. Now that he no longer has to show up at the prison every day, he works for the union fulltime, with a newfound focus.

'We would get together around a braai at someone's place, we'd sit and drink beers and talk about everything. Revolution, Black

Consciousness and communism. We felt strength in unity. We were hopeful,' he remembers.

Emboldened by Dan's leadership and in the wake of the Marikana massacre that had taken place a year before near Rustenburg, the G4S workers start gathering at the Koppie: a garbage-strewn field in Rocklands, one of Bloemfontein's oldest townships. They sing struggle songs and plan to march to the prison.

The prison guards' unity grows by the day, and when Dan's suspension is announced, they protest by organising another strike. This time, they don't hide behind collective sick leave. This strike includes 331 people – representing two-thirds of the workforce.

On 11 September 2013, hundreds of striking prison workers march 3 km from the Koppie to the gate of Mangaung prison. Their placards read: 'We are not Slaves. Stop Treating us Like Rubbish!' 'Please save us from this Private Monster.' 'There's no safety in this centre of Frustration. Our Lives are Gambled with.' Other signs call for the resignation of Stephen Page and HR Director Thabang Molise, another G4S leader who noticed Dan's talent way back in 2008 when Dan was a trainee – and Molise was POPCRU's secretary before being recruited by G4S.

Clad in their G4S uniforms, the strikers arrive at the prison gates, where they intend to hand over a memorandum with their demands: improved safety and security for the warders is at the top of the list, followed by the removal of Page and other management officials, and the reinstatement of Dan and the other four workers who were suspended.

They run into a wall of riot police officers who don't allow them to enter the premises because it would amount to 'trespassing'. The management refuses to appear or accept the memorandum, and the strikers dance and sing their way back to the Koppie.

Initially, POPCRU has Dan's back. The reinstatement of the five suspended guards – Dan specifically – is incorporated into their list of demands during negotiations. The union also demands G4S leave the country.[123]

G4S accuses Dan of 'inciting violence, labour unrest, gross intimidation and victimisation, amongst others'.[124]

The Labour Court rules in G4S's favour on 13 September.[125] 'The respondents are interdicted from engaging in intimidatory, threatening and violent conduct and inciting unrest and industrial action at the prison,' the court instructs Dan and his co-defendants.

⁂

During the run-up to the strike and while the strike is raging, G4S goes into damage-control mode and tries to convince the world that the company is conducting 'business as usual'.

On 16 September 2013, Andy Baker, the company's clean-shaven 'Africa president' addresses a press conference at OR Tambo International.

According to the company's website, Baker 'will leave you with two impressions – his great energy levels and his infectious enthusiasm for his [...] role with G4S'.[126] His main assignment in Africa is in line with G4S's global business strategy – to expand the business.

I'm on my way there when Kirsten van der Nest, G4S head of marketing and communication for Africa, calls.

'Are you still coming?' she asks while I try to navigate Johannesburg's rush hour traffic.

'Yes, I am actually on my way.'

'Good, because we would like to offer you the chance to have a one-on-one interview with Andy Baker.'

This takes me by surprise, as all I have received from G4S up to this point are frosty replies that the company is contractually bound to refer all media inquiries to the DCS.

'Okay,' I answer.

'There is one condition. You may not ask any questions during the press conference.'

When I arrive, Baker's already behind the microphone. His voice is soft and sibilant. I can barely make out what he's saying and start walking down the aisle to move closer. A hand lands on my arm. Another arm points at the place where I'm supposed to sit – right at the back. I'm amused at the thought that one of the world's biggest and most powerful security companies is trying to contain me, a one-woman show on a shoestring budget.

From my allocated seat at the back, I try to follow.

The company, so Baker claims, 'has an exemplary record in prisons'.

'They,' he says, referring to the striking workers, 'want a dismissed shop steward [Dan] reinstated.' The strikers have been ordered back to work, he continues, moving the conversation from the suspension of Dan and the others to unfolding industrial action involving two-thirds of the workforce at Mangaung. 'The deadline came and went, and we regrettably saw no other option than to "remove" the 331 staff members.'

Two cameras have been set up. Baker keeps talking, one smart, polished, concise sentence after another.

'What about the spate of stabbings in the prison?' someone asks.

'We think that they are motivated by financial motives,' Baker responds. 'We have affidavits from some inmates that payments have been made. Payments for attacking a warder. Forces outside the prison are influencing events, and they are leading to criminal actions. We are a fair organisation with fair human resources practices.'

Baker is like a man reassuring his family all is fine, while the family home is burning down to the ground behind them. He appears stubbornly blind to the chaos erupting around him.

In the one-on-one interview after everyone else has left, I ask Baker about the woman who'd just been held hostage in Mangaung.[127] I heard that the prisoner who took her hostage tried to rape her. I also heard that she wasn't a certified prison guard and that she never should have been allowed in close quarters with prisoners in the first place.

He shifts in his seat and draws the chair closer to the table. Then he smiles at me.

'We're extremely upset by what happened,' he says, briefly looking upset. 'We're very relieved that she was not hurt or molested. She loves working for G4S.'

'So, was she a qualified warder?' I ask.

'She was not an admin assistant, but she was more advanced than the role of warder. She worked in vocational programmes.'

'So not a qualified warder?'

'She has skills. She has worked with us for years. She worked all over the prison.'

'Not a qualified prison guard then?'

Baker ignores my question and returns to his sales pitch: 'We have an exceptional management team. We have an exemplary record in health and safety and have won several awards in this field. We were elected top employer in 2012 and 2013.'

I realise that this interview won't add much to the evidence I've gathered. So, 10 minutes in, I let Baker know that I'm grateful for his time and the opportunity to speak to him personally and start gathering my belongings to take my leave.

'But you seem a bit angry?' he says, questioningly.

'Not at all.' I smile and leave the room.

On the same day that Baker is busy fielding questions at OR Tambo International, Boxer Maphikisa, Captain Rampa, Sandile Dastile and Patrick Rakhetsi – four prisoners being held in the Buckley Hall unit – take advantage of the industrial action by setting fire to their mattresses and also smashing toilets.

The arson and vandalism follow long-standing dissatisfaction with the prison mismanagement's maladministration. The complaints and requests they'd submitted to management, for reclassification among other things, had been ignored for months, if not years, they say. They also allege they're being locked up for entire days, and that some days pass without showers or sufficient food.

The EST is called in to deal with the situation and they enter Buckley Hall at around 11 am. 'They entered firing at us,' Rampa writes in an account of the events of the day that he later sends to the WJP. When they tried to run away, he writes, the 'G4S EST followed us and [started] firing at us again'.

Rampa then names one of the Ninjas, G4S security manager Bennie van Aardt, as the man who shot 'one of my fellow inmates Boxer Maphikisa on the left eye'. Van Aardt's close-range shot with a rubber bullet leads to blindness in Maphikisa's left eye.[128]

Van Aardt had previously gloated in a Whatsapp group about another assault: 'I'm sweating it out at the gym while he is licking his wounds like a little bitch that he is,' reinforcing the idea that he was a strong man and the inmates were feminine and therefore weak and despicable.

Rampa also claims Van Aardt was carrying a needle and that he said to him: 'I hope you know this injection. You have to cooperate with us.'

Rampa and Maphikisa tried to flee the barrage of rubber bullets by scaling the fence in the exercise yard before they finally surrendered to the EST. Rampa claims they grabbed him, poured water on him and shocked him with their electric shields before beating him up. He and Maphikisa were then escorted to the prison hospital, from where the latter was immediately transported to Pelonomi, a hospital in Bloemfontein. Medical records from the hospital reflect that Maphikisa's left ear was also lacerated.

The doctor, registered as CA Loubser in the files, who discharges Maphikisa from Pelonomi two days later notes that his 'left eye still has no light perception'.

The medical records from the prison hospital reflect that Rampa[129] sustained a 'wound on the right leg and swollen right eye'. Later, when I meet him face to face and ask him about his injuries, he lifts up his orange prison uniform to show me the scar of about 5 cm on his right shin. 'This is where Bennie van Aardt hit me with the butt of his gun,' he says.

Rampa and Maphikisa's medical records are included in the docket that's opened at the Bloemspruit police station following the incident.

Maphikisa's 'facial injury' is specified in a controller's report on the incident that DCS controller Clement Motsapi sent to Johan Theron, Mangaung executive prison director. The report, that is leaked to me, makes no mention of Rampa's injuries.[130]

But the DCS controller's office starts asking questions. 'Is the injury of [Maphikisa] consistent with Minimum Use of Force?' the email asks. 'Investigations must indicate the extent of the injury: will the inmate be able to see again? Did Contractor comply with the Firearms Act?'[131]

About a week later, Van Aardt is suspended for the assault and resulting injuries. Prison operations director Derrick de Klerk and security manager Anneke la Grange are also suspended.

The day after their suspension, Kobus Fourie, G4S managing director for South Africa, sends a letter of complaint about the suspensions to Nontsikelelo Jolingana, acting DCS commissioner. In the letter, Fourie claims that neither Captain Rampa nor Boxer Maphikisa 'were injured in the manner prescribed'. Fourie admits that 20 rounds of rubber bullets were fired that day at the prisoners. He also concedes that a firearm – one that released real deadly bullets – had been discharged: "The firearm was discharged once, into the ground, as a warning shot to certain inmates who failed to heed a verbal instruction to stop fleeing towards the fence."[132]

Van Aardt, De Klerk and La Grange are arrested for the assault of Maphikisa and causing the grievous bodily harm that he sustained, but five days later the prosecutor entered '*nolle prosequi*' on the docket, which meant there would be no prosecution for the crimes. No reasons are provided for why the charges were dropped.[133]

Rampa and Maphikisa are later found guilty of malicious damage to property and are each sentenced to an additional 18 months in prison. When Maphikisa asks if his J88 form – reflecting his injuries – can be included as evidence, Rampa says the judge tells him that it is 'not why we're here today'.

When attorney Egon Oswald tries to consult with inmate Boxer Maphikisa – who alleged prison employees had shot at him, blinding him in one eye – in November 2014, management and the Department of Correctional Services deny access. They claim that Maphikisa is not Oswald's client.[134]

When I meet him later, Rampa tells me that following the incident on 16 September 2013, a unit supervisor came into his cell 'with an affidavit he said I should sign, because if I didn't, he would inject me. He was holding a needle.' There was a threat, but also an incentive – if he cooperated, so Rampa claims, they said they would pay money into his prison account.

Rampa is not the first prisoner to claim that he was threatened with an injection if he did not cooperate with the prison authorities. 'I reasoned it was better to sign than to end up a cripple or dead. I thought I was going to die,' he tells me. So, he signed the affidavit that stated Dan 'influenced inmates to burn the prison'.

I remember Baker mentioning during his press conference that prisoners had signed affidavits implicating Dan in several offences.

The Labour Court reiterates again, in a ruling on 19 September, that the strike is unprotected and orders the 331 workers to return to work – or face suspension.[135]

During this time, most of my sources no longer feel bound by the confidentiality clauses in their contracts, and they speak freely to me. I'm in and around Bloemfontein a lot and speak to as many people as possible.

But not everyone wants to talk. A black female manager, who did not partake in the strike, practically throws the phone down. 'I can't talk. My house was stoned and nearly burnt down,' is all she says before disconnecting.

It's clear there's intimidation happening to those who are not part of the strike.

'I don't want to stop working,' says JR the prison nurse who is not a POPCRU member. 'I need the money. But I'm scared to go back. They will burn our houses.'

I ask Dan about the rumours of Molotov cocktails being tossed at a manager's house. 'Threw them where? Stephen Page's house?' I ask.

'No, the lower-level managers, the men and women who live with us in the townships,' he answers.

Burning down a white man's house was obviously a step too far.

In the end, the strike does not bring the company to its knees, as the disgruntled workers had hoped. Instead, the DCS takes control of the prison, for almost a year – from October 2013 to August 2014.[136]

DCS Free State commissioner Zacharia Modise is appointed the temporary head of the prison, and one of the first things he does is reverse the suspensions of De Klerk, Van Aardt and La Grange. A DCS spokesperson explained: 'The suspension of the said officials by the DCS Controller was not a suspension per se, due to the fact that they were not wholly suspended from duty but only suspended from operational duties (...). They reported for duty then, and continue to report for duty now, but were only allowed to perform administrative functions. During preparations for the handing over of MCC back to G4S, and based on information at the time, the said officials were requested to return to their operational duties. However, based on further investigations, a decision has been taken to uphold their suspension from operational duties.'

During this time, POPCRU negotiations are successful, and the dismissed workers, except for Dan and his small cabal of soldiers, are reinstated. The return of the workers means G4S and BCC can retain the prison contract.[137]

POPCRU suspends Dan in early 2014, accusing him of organising 'side meetings' and ignoring instructions from the leadership. POPCRU gets an interdict barring him from 'trying to control POPCRU members, organising, demobilising and discouraging members to accept settlement agreements'.[138]

'We are closing this chapter,' Lawrence Msinto, POPCRU's Free State secretary, tells me. 'The workers were without pay for ten months. We have made sure they have an income again. We hope G4S will show competence going forward.' His position is the complete opposite to POPCRU's stance during the strike, when the union demanded the company leave the country.

In August 2014, the guards return to work. They soon find out that their grievances have not been addressed at all. Instead, the prison has returned to 'business as usual'. It leads to a mass exodus from POPCRU. The disgruntled guards are angry that nothing has changed; the salaries remain the same; the toilet pots are still ceramic; the inmates still violent and the prison management still indifferent to their complaints.

G4S workers unite

Strife and unrest within G4S's workforce is a staple ingredient of the global security giant's operation. The cost of labour is the biggest expense for most companies, usually taking up around 70 per cent of the budget. G4S, subject as it is to the approval of its shareholders and investors, will aim to bring down labour costs in order to increase profits. G4S's corporate strategy over the past ten years has seen the company retreat from wealthy European countries, while expanding into countries in the Global South, where wages are low and union regulations flexible.

G4S guards in several countries have gone on strike and have sued the company for unfair working conditions.[139] Most recently, in January 2019, 13 500 G4S guards in the US sued the company for withholding meal breaks during working hours.[140] A court ordered the company to pay the workers $130 million in compensation.

A 2004 transnational labour union campaign aimed at G4S produced an effective narrative of labour rights' violations and poor working conditions in countries in the Global South. This argument ultimately swayed some of G4S's investors and shareholders from the Global North to withdraw their investments in the company. It provided the much-needed pressure to get the company to sign a Global Framework Agreement, which it finally did in 2008.[141]

The US-based Service Employees International Union (SEIU) and the Switzerland-based Union Network International (UNI) officially started their global campaign advocating for better working conditions for G4S workers in 2004, on the day G4S started trading on the stock exchanges in the UK and Denmark. Countries such as Poland, Nepal, Zimbabwe, Uganda, Mozambique, South Africa, India, Malawi and the Democratic Republic of the Congo (DRC) joined the fight. G4S workers from the US were also involved and later Ghana and Morocco joined.

The global campaign has its roots in an American union campaign to improve working conditions of janitors and guards.

In 2001, the union federation SEIU organised workers from a company called Argenbright, a subsidiary of Securicor. This was the security provider that merged with the Danish group Falck in 2004 and it thus became part of the G4S family. Argenbright workers secured airports around the US and they had not picked up on the men who flew the 9/11 planes into the twin towers in 2001. The union used this oversight in their campaign and linked air passenger safety slippages to the poor working conditions of the guards. Airport security was nationalised in the wake of the attacks.

SEIU also organised workers at Wackenhut, an American company that merged with G4S in 2008. The company fought a dirty war: They instructed employees to take pictures of union workers' vehicle number plates so they could threaten them at their homes.

The American G4S labour union campaign did not cause even a dent in G4S's resolve to expand across the globe. The company kept bidding for and winning contracts throughout the world. This intransigence is the main reason SEIU decided to start a global campaign against G4S.

After the two organisations announced the global campaign in 2004, it remained an online campaign for some months. But in April 2005, that changed. Hundreds of former full-time G4S Indonesian guards were converted to part-time guards without prior notice, following a local merger of two companies. This sparked a 15-month-long strike, making Indonesia the first battleground for the global campaign outside rich countries. Now the unions had a 'ground' war that would complement their 'air' war aimed at the top-level executives with the ultimate goal of creating reputational damage to the company and its shareholders.

The company fought back with death threats to unionists and they laid criminal charges against union leaders. This is also what had happened to Dan during the 2013 strike in Bloemfontein. After he led the marches to the prison, the company reported him to the police and, so he claims, had his phone bugged.

As the Indonesian strike unfolded, SEIU started working closely with UNI. They widened the campaign to G4S guards and their unions in Poland, Nepal, Zimbabwe, Uganda, Mozambique, South Africa, India, Malawi and the DRC.

In 2006, SEIU and UNI announced the creation of the 'G4S Alliance' that would serve as the organisational body of the campaign. This also ushered in a strategic change in the campaign: a refocus on human rights issues in the Global South.

In March 2006, South Africa's most violent protest since 1994 broke out.[142] Approximately 100 000 security guards went on strike and they waged battles with police and rival unions. Around 60 people died. According to Jamie McCallum's book Global Unions, Local Power, *Nick Buckles was meeting with shareholders on a yacht during these protests and he accused UNI of causing these deaths, because the union had prolonged the strike unnecessarily.*

That same year UNI filed a complaint against G4S with the UK national contact point for the Organisation for Economic Cooperation and Development (OECD)[143] citing violations of its guidelines on multinationals in 11 countries, 'including blacklisting of unionists, wage theft, union recognition and access to bathrooms on the job'. The company replied with a letter pleading with the OECD to recognise it as a 'people business'.[144]

UNI published a report in 2007 on working conditions of G4S guards in Mozambique, Malawi and South Africa titled Who Protects the Guards?[145] *It detailed poverty wages, poor working conditions and widespread racism in South Africa. South African G4S workers alleged in the report that they were called 'kaffirs' and 'monkeys'. And that there were 'whites only' toilets in a G4S location in Pretoria where a manager provided only white guards with keys to the company toilet.*

In Blantyre, Malawi, guards' salaries were so low that they were forced to live in places without electricity or water. They couldn't feed themselves or their families. In 2007 the workers went on strike. The often volatile and violent campaign resulted in a 16 per cent wage increase for the workers. This still meant the workers earned just above the one-dollar-a-day standard and they were still forced to work 12-hour shifts.

The 2007 UNI report was instrumental in a Moroccan G4S campaign aimed at securing a holiday bonus while Ugandan G4S workers signed their first collective bargaining agreement with the company after using the report to shame the company in the local media.

By early 2008, G4S labour campaigns were underway in Poland, Nepal and the DRC.

In December 2008, the company finally capitulated to a Global Framework Agreement.[146] The agreement required the company to respect four important international labour conventions; there were provisions included against child labour and discrimination as well as provisions protecting freedom of association. It also included a formal dispute resolution mechanism.

While many heralded the deal as a successful example of a transnational labour rights campaign aimed at a powerful multinational, its implementation has been haphazard. A representative working at UNI told me, off the record, that working conditions are still abominable. In India, for example, G4S provides security for a trade free zone in Ahmedabad for pharmaceutical and car manufacturing companies. Because many guards live miles away from their work, the company provided accommodation. 'G4S guards sleep in shifts on thin matrasses on the floor. No water. No sanitation and no electricity. They are kept like cattle.'

The company has not been able to get away with its labour practices in first world countries. In 2018, former detainees and G4S guards at the Manus Island detention centre successfully sued the company in what has become the biggest class action human rights litigation case in Australia.[147] The government and the company were forced to pay Australian $70 million in compensation. In 2019, the company had to pay a staggering $130 million in compensation to 13 500 guards in California who had been denied a meal break during work.[148] Also in 2019, it had to settle a £35 million charge for equalising benefits for historical pension obligations between men and women in the UK.[149] In June 2019, the company was ordered to pay a young mother €52 000 in compensation because it had given her job to someone else after she had taken maternity leave. It was the second time the company had been fined for this behaviour in Ireland.[150]

10

Keeping it tight: The Department of Correctional Services

ON 8 OCTOBER 2013, following G4S's attempt to replace the 331 dismissed guards at the prison, Nontsikelelo Jolingana, acting DCS national commissioner, writes in a press statement that there is 'a worrying deterioration of safety and security' at the centre. 'The contractor has lost effective control of the facility,' Jolingana argues. 'The contractor continues to use uncertified staff to perform custodial duties.'[151]

In terms of the Correctional Services Act, it is unlawful to employ uncertified staff in prisons. Invoking section 112 of the Act, which provides a legal basis for the state to take over a private prison if the contractor has lost control, the DCS sends 246 officials to Bloemfontein to restore order and security at Mangaung. At first, the team is led by Zach Modise, Free State DCS commissioner, who is appointed as temporary prison head. G4S workers are to remain at the prison, to run the food and educational programmes.

Two weeks later, the *Mail & Guardian*[152] and the British *Guardian*[153] run my article on the investigation. At roughly the same time, the BBC[154] and *Carte Blanche*[155] both broadcast shows based on my investigation. After the exposé, my phone rings non-stop with enquiries from international news networks and media from all corners of the world wishing to cover the stories of the abuse of imprisoned men at the hands of one of the biggest companies on earth. Video footage of Bheki Dlamini shouting 'No! I am not a donkey!' travels the world during this brief but intense media coverage.

While all of this is still in full swing, S'bu Ndebele, the minister of correctional services, tells parliament, on 5 November 2013, that the privatisation of prisons has 'failed'. He explains that government entered into a public-private partnership to construct, maintain and manage the Mangaung facility in 2000 and that this partnership 'experiment seems to be showing that the desired results are not being realised'.[156]

Minister Ndebele instructs a DCS task team to investigate allegations of abuse at the prison and compile a report. Ndebele's astute assessment of the situation comes as a surprise; never before had I heard a Correctional Services minister or official stating anything this unequivocal and damning.

Ndebele tells parliament: 'The Department would strive to ensure compliance in terms of the law and the concession contract between the DCS and the Bloemfontein Corrections Consortium.'[157] A meeting was to take place, he announced, on 12 November. My sources have alleged that the shareholders are 'summoned' to this meeting, which allegedly takes place at President Jacob Zuma's homestead near Nkandla in KwaZulu-Natal not long after Ndebele's address to parliament.

It's not clear if this meeting took place or what was discussed, but afterwards, the pieces on the chessboard are rearranged. Minister Ndebele is replaced by Michael Masutha and national commissioner Jolingana by Zacharia Modise, who moves into this position five months after being appointed head of prison at Mangaung.

Minister Masutha is full of praise for the 'state-of-the-art' prison when he later visits the facility.[158]

Following Minister Ndebele's address, I expect the DCS to take a hard line. But that doesn't happen.

I'm told that, by early 2014, the task team has collected a 'bakkie-full of evidence' on the abuse at Mangaung. A law firm is appointed to write the report.

In June 2014, a draft 'preliminary investigation findings report' is leaked to me. It is a document drawn up by the lawyers. It includes the findings of the DCS task team and BCC's responses to the allegations. DCS flagged evidence of unauthorised use of force, unlawful segregation of prisoners, unnecessary use of violence, suspicious deaths and forced injections with antipsychotic drugs, mostly reaffirming the findings in my investigation. BCC's response contains explanations for the medication, the force and various other issues. It mostly denies any responsibility.

In the same month, G4S's (international) Director of Investor Relations, Helen Parris, reassures potential investors,[159] that it had 'been informally told that the DCS investigation found no evidence to support the allegations in the media' and that the company 'had been cleared'. The statement also includes a blatant lie: 'we put in place a number of short-term plans which included requesting support from the Department of Correctional Services,' Parris writes. The 'requested support' was not that at all: DCS invoked section 112 of the Correctional Services Act. The letter to investors goes on to deny any wrongdoings.

I also receive a leaked email,[160] sent around the same time by Pappie Mokoena, the chair of Bloemfontein Correctional Contracts (BCC), to the other four BCC shareholders. In the email Mokoena explains that Zach Modise has promised the prison will soon be returned to BCC. Mokoena writes that Modise made the promise in a phone call to him earlier that month, mere days before the DCS sends BCC the preliminary report detailing abuse at Mangaung on G4S's watch, the report that is never finalised.

In other words, Modise assured BCC shareholders that Mangaung prison would be returned to them, despite the investigation into abuse and corruption at Mangaung prison not having been finalised.

After the prison has been returned to G4S and BCC in August 2014, the investigation stalls indefinitely. The 'bakkie-full' of evidence goes 'missing'. The preliminary report is never finalised, and nothing ever gets to parliament, as Minister Ndebele promised.

In 2014, lawyers from Wits' Centre for Applied Legal Studies (CALS) request access through the courts to the preliminary and final report under the Promotion of Access to Information Act (PAIA), but the DCS – and G4S, which applies to be a co-defendant in the matter – continues, to this day, to obstruct the release of the report.

Nearly six years later, on 7 February 2020, the High Court in Pretoria finally renders judgment on the case. Judge Pierre Rabie instructs the department to release the unredacted report within 15 days. At the time of writing, the Department of Correctional Services had not yet responded to the judgment.[161]

I hear rumours that the DCS officials are divided on who should control the prison: G4S or the DCS. 'There are basically two camps: those DCS people who want to take over the prison and others who want G4S in charge,' Dan tells me.

Many of the G4S employees apparently think they'll get better treatment as DCS guards, so they also support a DCS-run facility.

Michael Masutha replaces Ndebele as Minister of Correctional Services, and the acting national commissioner of correctional services, Nontsikelelo Jolingana, is moved to another unit in the department. During these months one person rises through the ranks quite spectacularly. His son works at the prison and he is a Bloemfontein local. His name is Zacharia Modise, the temporary head of prison, who is promoted to National Commissioner of Correctional Services halfway through his stint in Bloemfontein, a position that is later confirmed as permanent. While Modise promises insiders he wants the British company gone, he evolves into one of their staunchest allies.

Sources involved in the investigation tell me some officials working for the departmental controller want the DCS to terminate the contract with G4S, because the levels of abuse and corruption are unacceptably high. The controllers' office starts issuing regular warnings of non-performance by G4S, in an attempt to build a case to terminate the contract.

In 2019, a source tells me all these notifications of non-performance have no impact, because of a 2005 DCS letter,[162] which I have in my possession. In the letter, the then director of contract management at DCS's head office, Joseph Maako, writes: 'Kindly be informed that [...] breach of policies and procedures cannot constitute a breach of contract and therefore give rise to penalties.' The company and the department use this letter to ensure no penalties or fines are imposed. According to the source, to this day, the instruction contained in the letter is referenced when serious issues in Mangaung prison are brought to the attention of the department. It effectively neutralises any report of abuse of malfeasance from the controller to head office.

And then there are the allegations that DCS officials – notably Errol Korabie, the man who takes over as acting prison head from Modise in February 2014 – are bringing in men from other prisons to stir things up when G4S returns to the helm.

I receive an affidavit written in July 2014 by Thembekile Sane Buso, claiming that, earlier that month, Korabie visited the notorious St Albans Correctional Services prison in Port Elizabeth where Buso, a gang leader, was being held.

'Director Korabie had addressed us that he had came [sic] from Mangaung Prison, which was currently administered by him and EST,' Buso writes.[163] 'He had realized that through our resistance we can stand ground to face tough challenges. He informed us that his department wanted to take over the centre from G4S but there are business politicians with big influence who stood in a way of them.' Korabie then confided in Buso and the other gang leaders that he was transferring them – prisoners with known disciplinary records – to Mangaung 'in order to affect a timeous collapsing of the security control in Mangaung Prison, as soon as he and his ETS team hand over the centre back to G4S'.

In the early hours of 11 July 2014, Buso writes, they were shoved into DCS bakkies and driven to Grootvlei and after three days were taken to Mangaung next door. When they arrived, Buso claims, the EST men welcomed them as 'heroes'. He writes that they met with other senior DCS officials who all confirmed this plan to return Mangaung to the state once and for all.

'I believe we have been set up as a sacrifice in the process of getting this prison,' Buso concludes. 'People will die here and others get really hurt in this situation.'

Buso signs a second affidavit on 30 October 2015,[164] this time with 29 others incarcerated at Mangaung. Listing the Minister of Justice and the G4S prison director as first and second respondents, the affidavit asks about the reason for the alleged recruitment at St Albans Prison: What motivated the first respondent (the Minister of Justice) to send the head of Mangaung to St Albans 'to recruit, select and/or to conscript violent prison gangs with explicitly and implicitly instigatory instructions to cause mayhem in Mangaung […] as soon as the 1st Respondent's Emergency Security Team and its officials leave it, when G4S returned it to normal operation?'

Buso and the other prison-gang leaders transferred from St Albans might have had a hero's welcome, but by all accounts, conditions didn't really improve for the Mangaung prisoners under the DCS.

The department allegedly deprives all privileges, locking prisoners up for 23, sometimes 24, hours per day and only allowing them out for a quick shower and food. There are allegations of prisoners going hungry. Warders I speak to confirm that the prison is 'under lockdown'. It remains this way until the end of the DCS's time at the prison in August 2014, leaving behind a hugely frustrated prison population.

Modise orders most of the troublemakers to be transferred to the super-maximum correctional facility in Kokstad.

I track down six of these men who'd been transferred from Mangaung to Kokstad shortly after the DCS's arrival. In the interview notes taken by the lawyers from CALS, who visit them on 31 July 2014, the prisoners in Kokstad sound bewildered.[165]

Mduduzi Felepe, a man in his sixties with high blood pressure, only arrived at Mangaung a day or two before being transferred to Kokstad. The lawyers write: 'He was never told why he was transferred but did not ask because "they will beat you". Felepe appeared very nervous and indicated that, "I just keep quiet in my cell. I don't want trouble."'

Like Felepe, most of the others were also not given reasons for the transfer. Some mention allegations of starting riots and taking hostages, but they deny involvement in any such activities.

Most say they were beaten and electroshocked by the DCS EST before being pushed into vans that transported them to Kokstad.

Troublemakers who stay behind at Mangaung during this time are also disciplined with brute force.

Tebogo Meje claims to have been assaulted and electroshocked by the DCS EST, before being placed in isolation in Broadway for six weeks. Tebogo was charged with armed robbery and murder and was sentenced to 15 years in 2008, but he's acquitted on appeal in 2014.[166]

Tebogo first writes to the WJP in August 2013. His letter details his struggle to complete his information technology course through the distance-learning University of South Africa. He'd paid and registered, yet was not provided with internet access in Mangaung, which made his remote studies impossible. When he protested, he was classified as 'high risk', a semantic term used by the company to place inmates in isolation cells for lengthy periods, without having to comply with legal requirements around segregation.

I meet Tebogo one dry, hot summer's day in the Bloem Plaza Mall in the bustling downtown area. It's November 2014. We sit down in a greasy snack bar, with used coffee cups and chicken bones strewn across the table. A pretty young girl, who looks to be in her early twenties, accompanies Tebogo. She sits at the table next to ours and stares at me with a bored, vacant look. After introductions, Tebogo grabs my phone and tells me to put it in my bag, while scanning those coming and going. 'It's not safe,' he says. Tebogo is a handsome man, with a soft, gentle face and a naughty glint in his eye. He's wearing squeaky-clean tekkies, and a pair of trendy sunglasses are perched on his head.

When the DCS team arrived, Tebogo says he sighed a breath of relief. Now at least the Ninjas would be kept in check, he thought.

But the reverse was true. On 17 December 2013, DCS members of the EST dragged him out of his cell in Buckley Hall. There were riots in the prison, with inmates protesting the lockdown regime. A warder was stabbed, and the EST had found handmade weapons in Tebogo's cellblock. They took him and his cellmate to the office of the unit manager, where there are no cameras.

'When we arrived there, they took off my shirt and my trousers. I was only left with my underwear,' he says. DCS men crowded around him. 'Then they handcuffed my hands behind my back. They were using this language of "*sak*!" and "*chaf op*!" They made me lie on my stomach, poured water on me and then electroshocked me and kicked me.

'There were 10 DCS warders present in the room when my cellmate and I were electroshocked and kicked. I saw their DCS badges. They shouted at us: "Now you must confess!" and "Tell us what happened." They nearly broke my knee. It was as if the DCS guys were trying to teach the G4S Ninjas how it should be done.'[167]

Tebogo reaches under the table to produce something I'd seen countless times before. He starts emptying the contents from a weathered plastic bag on the grubby table.

'Here – this is my J88 form,' he says. 'And this, the eyewitness statement. A letter to the prosecutor.'

Although I'd seen many prisoners with bags stuffed with every grimy scrap of paper they ever received, Tebogo's is different. His papers are ordered. It's clear he knows his rights.

He knew he had to see a doctor to document his bruises before they disappeared. He also knew that an eyewitness statement – from his cellmate – would help his case.

Somehow, he manages to circumvent the ineffective prison complaints system and contacts the police. An officer visits the prison a few days later. But after seeing one of the warders who was part of the assault meet the police officer at the prison entrance, his cellmate no doubt feels intimidated and refuses to give his eyewitness account. The police officer then visits the prison hospital, where the doctor on duty says he knows nothing about Tebogo's J88 form.

Tebogo perseveres, and with the help of the police officer, the J88 form is eventually found. It documents bruises, swelling and lacerations to his head. But it does not help him one bit.

Following his 2014 acquittal and release from Mangaung, and armed with his J88 form, Tebogo pursues the assault case against the DCS warders. But it's dismissed because the prosecutor finds there is a 'lack of evidence'.

The prosecutor is also not swayed by my subsequent phone call to point out that Tebogo's cellmate is still willing to sign an eyewitness affidavit.

And so Tebogo's complaint ends up on the ever-growing pile of dismissed assault, torture and death cases coming from Mangaung.

Manelisi Wolela, the then spokesperson for the department, responds to the allegations: 'The department will investigate all assault and torture allegations made against [Correctional Services] officials deployed at the Mangaung Correctional Centre and will deal with anyone found to have violated the legislation and policies of safe and human custody.'[168]

In 2015, the department publishes *Team Mangaung: Keeping it Tight*, a glossy magazine dedicated solely to DCS's ten-month stint at the prison and focusing on 'the successes and challenges of a team of correctional officials that were deployed at Mangaung [...] to re-establish the safe and secure incarceration of inmates at the Centre'.

The cover of the magazine folds out and features a large group shot of the operational team: dozens of men and women, some standing, others sitting on chairs or cross-legged on the ground, all clad in brown DCS uniforms and with brown beanies or caps on their heads. Their coats look warm and padded. In the background, the prison looms. Bursts of light radiate from the bright security lights in and around the prison like yellow stars, their halos evenly expanding against the backdrop of an orange sky. Judging by the angle of the light on their faces, the photograph must have been taken at dawn or dusk. Most people in the picture are smiling.

Prison director Korabie, positioned in the middle of the picture, has the biggest smile. He's a physically imposing man, and he grins widely, his cap shading the left side of his face. He looks like a mix of friendly neighbour and proud dad.

The magazine is filled with managerial pep talk. According to the editorial, the world should 'take note of what can be achieved' when 'one does the basics' and does 'them right; one builds a team through quality leadership and quality management; team members allow themselves to be led by a common purpose; the organisation acknowledges your contribution.' The editorial closes with: 'This publication is filled with good news stories.'

A profile on Korabie mentions his daily *scumba* (isiZulu for 'gathering') around 7 am, where he would ask the officials, 'How do we keep it?', to which they would respond: 'We keep it tight!' A picture alongside shows some DCS officials, batons attached to their waists, one of them holding an orange in one hand and an apple in the other.

While my name doesn't pop up anywhere in the magazine, the 'media exposé' is constantly mentioned as playing a key part in the DCS's decision to intervene and investigate allegations of abuse at the prison.

An article entitled 'Official investigated medical malpractice' introduces Masilo Moshoeshoe, a nurse from a prison in Wepener who joined the Mangaung team 'under the primary instruction to investigate medically-related allegations'. A picture of a laughing Moshoeshoe accompanies the article. A microphone is strapped to his shirt, and he is looking to the side. He seems to be in mid-laugh, baring his teeth, his eyes narrowed, cheeks bulging. The caption reads: 'Masilo Moshoeshoe has become an ace investigator.' There's a rather mundane list of his achievements: he encouraged medical staff to hold meetings, called out nurses who were moonlighting, helped an offender with an oozing head wound and another offender with an infected catheter wound. Then, there is this bit: 'A peculiar situation existed at the mental health clinic [at Mangaung], which was staffed by a psychiatrist and a psychologist. The rate of administering antipsychotic drugs at the clinic seemed odd and this matter was also investigated.'

Clearly, the DCS investigators had come across irregularities at the 'mental health clinic', and the fact that this was the term chosen to refer to the prison hospital is also quite revealing. One could only guess what Moshoeshoe meant by the 'odd' rate of antipsychotic drug administration.

Heinrich Veloen, an EST member who was put in charge of the isolation unit during the time the DCS ran Mangaung, is profiled next. 'Broadway is no stage for shows', the headline reads. In the picture, prison gang expert Veloen has pepper spray strapped to his chest. With its prisoners set to stay for long periods of time, a maximum-security facility is fertile ground for gang activity. He claims to be interested in what's important to the prisoners, and the men often confide in him about family matters. Once he's gained their trust in this way, 'the ground has been laid for getting information about gang activities', his profile states.

The first profile to appear in the magazine is that of Modise. In the full-page photograph that accompanies his profile, Modise – who does not appear in the group cover photo – is in uniform and stands in front of a chain-link fence, looking away from the camera, seemingly in mid-sentence. Modise is of the opinion that security was slack at the prison when his team intervened: 'Offenders would walk to wherever they pleased.' Throughout my years-long investigation into Mangaung prison, I'd never heard a guard or prisoner ever mention the fact that prisoners could walk wherever they wanted, as the entire system of doors and locks was operated remotely from the central control room. However, Modise praises his team for re-establishing order by implementing a lockdown system, where the prisoners are only allowed out of their cells an hour a day, for both exercise and a shower.

Modise's profile contains a list of practical recommendations: the official-to-prisoner ratio should be brought to one guard to every 30 prisoners, instead of the prevailing 1:64 ratio; the equipment should be bolted to the floor; and nurses should be appointed on permanent contracts.

I become interested in Modise, the DCS man who's initially in charge of the intervention at Mangaung. While G4S has remained relatively impassive after my exposés – meekly threatening legal action once but never taking any steps – Modise, and the DCS, on the other hand, are not as unresponsive. Once I start digging into his past, I catch a glimpse of the game that might have been played behind closed doors at Mangaung.

And then the man who once promised to 'root out all whistle-blowers' in the department has a go at me.

It's certainly not the first time a man has a go at me. But by this time, I had taken up boxing.

G4S's vetting of employees

The company's disregard for employees and the people placed in their care starts before they are hired.

G4S claims in a corporate brochure that: 'A robust employee screening programme helps organisations minimise the risk of making inappropriate recruitment decisions. We have a wealth of experience in developing and implementing background checks and security clearance for companies in the private and public sector.'[169] However, there is not much evidence of this practice on the ground.

The downward pressure on corporate labour costs means the company usually employs under-educated and unskilled labourers on the ground.[170] They are often overworked and underpaid and this can have terrible consequences.

In 2016, it seemed the company still hadn't learned a lesson from their past. Omar Mateen, a G4S guard, committed the worst massacre in the history of the US. He walked into the Pulse nightclub in Florida and shot dead 49 people. Mateen had passed G4S screenings and background checks. The reason he passed the psychological testing was revealed in a subsequent lawsuit: the company had 'falsely listed psychological testing information on more than 1 500 forms that allowed employees to carry guns.'[171] Mateen was one of those 1 500 employees. The psychologist who had supposedly screened him had retired and moved out of the state two years before the screening supposedly took place.

The American publication **USA Today** spent a year investigating G4S's screening and vetting procedures, following the Mateen massacre. They established that at least 300 guards had questionable records. 'Some went on to rape, assault, or shoot people – including while on duty.'[172] The investigation also revealed that more than 600 G4S-issued guns had disappeared or been lost.[173]

11

Zach 'No blood on the ground' Modise

I SPEAK TO SEVERAL DCS officials working at Mangaung during the time the DCS holds the fort there. Most of them want to remain anonymous because they fear losing their jobs or other repercussions.

Modise expects his team at Mangaung to hit the ground running. 'No blood on the ground,' Modise instructs the guards going into the 'streets'. 'No blood on the ground.'

Modise's leadership during his time at the helm receives mixed reviews.

Some say his tactics are Machiavellian and accuse him of nepotism and corruption. His son Tumi Modise also works at the prison, and some view this as a conflict of interest.

But one source says he's 'the last person to get into self-enrichment. Can't put my head on a block,' this source tells me, 'but Modise is not that kind of a guy.'

According to all my sources, Modise is initially eager to hold G4S accountable. Dan tells me that, in meetings, Modise expressed his confidence that they would 'nail' G4S.

'He hated them,' a DCS official who'd worked closely with Modise for years tells me about the G4S managers they dealt with. 'They were extremely arrogant. They spoke down to him. Modise hated them.'

Another source confirms that, 'Zach wanted G4S out, but he never said a bad thing about BCC. He cares about officials, not inmates. He has certain loyalties – and he doesn't forget or forgive.'

In 2014, shortly after being promoted from Mangaung head to acting national DCS commissioner, Modise is called in to testify at the sentencing hearing of Oscar Pistorius.[174]

The Paralympian had just been convicted of culpable homicide for shooting and killing his girlfriend, Reeva Steenkamp, on 14 February 2013 – Valentine's Day.

At the sentencing hearing, Modise speaks about the conditions in South African prisons, and I watch the live stream from the courtroom closely from my office at the WJP. He isn't wearing his uniform, opting instead for a casual look: a dark-green suit, white shirt, no tie. His eyes are slits behind his thick glasses. He speaks confidently, neither faltering nor pausing. Everything is uttered in the same intonation, with barely any emotion registering on his face.

He answers prosecutor Gerrie Nel's questions about the state of prisons and prisoners in the country, mentioning 243 prisons and the prison population. He claims South Africa has the best jails on the continent. In short jabs, he explains the details of the 'complaints and request forms for prisoners'. He sums up all the courses one can do while in prison. He speaks about the 'humane treatment of offenders' and 'sentence planning'.

Then Barry Roux, Oscar's defence attorney, asks him about the DCS coming 'under fire in parliament' – at a portfolio committee meeting on correctional services held the previous day – where an 'increase in torture cases' was discussed. This portfolio committee meeting was attended by my colleagues Nooshin Erfani-Ghadimi, who ran the WJP, and Robyn Leslie, our legal researcher. They asked Modise why the department still hadn't released the DCS investigation report, more than a year after the minister had promised to release it in 30 days.[175]

When Roux suggests that the WJP and other non-governmental organisations (NGOs) who attended this meeting are 'basically good people', Modise responds with 'it depends'. Roux then takes it further: 'Who of them are not good?'

Modise's answer astounds us all. 'There are these NGOs who operate in our environment,' he says. 'They come and do research and without verifying their findings. That is why I'm saying it depends who the NGO is. WJP, no [...] WJP is being led by two journalists, who are writing articles for the *Mail & Guardian*, one of them being Ruth Hopkins. Their objective [...] is to write anything that is negative that they have sourced by themselves. For instance [...] what happens is, they make the point that they provide two officials that are unscrupulous of the department to take pictures of scenes in a centre and also provide that to offenders.'

One of the 'unscrupulous officials' is obviously Dan.

Modise continues: 'So [...] from time to time you will find articles in the media space about correctional services that have not been verified but that have been taken at a particular time so as to depict DCS in a negative light.'

When Roux confronts him again about the NGOs telling members of parliament 'about a serious complaint about torture of inmates by prison officials', Modise answers: '[...] that was the allegation that was received yesterday by ourselves and the portfolio committee.'[176]

In the building, every single member of our small team is tethered to their computer with headphones on. Modise is speaking at length on the state of prisons – our area of work. As he criticises our methods and basically accuses us of practising unethical journalism, I hear cries coming from the other offices. When he's finished, we run outside and start yelling in the corridor.

'What did he actually say!?!!'

'This is bullshit!'
'For fuck's sake!'
'Uncorroborated??!!?'
'Unscrupulous?!!?'
'What the …?'

Following Modise's allegations, I'm invited to explain his outburst on the radio and on the television channel dedicated to broadcasting the Pistorius trial. We politely decline several requests from Pistorius's defence team to be included in their arguments.

I struggle to understand why Modise chooses this platform to make this statement. I think back to the source who told me that the commissioner does not 'forget or forgive'. I start looking into his past.

Moleko Zacharia Isaac Modise is a disciplined soldier. He joins the DCS in 1979, at the age of 22, and retires from the department at the end of 2017. He does his basic training in Klerksdorp, and then serves at prisons first in Gauteng and later in the Free State: Grootvlei in Bloemfontein, and nine years at a prison in Boshof, his hometown. In 1994, when the new dispensation is still fresh, Modise is appointed 'senior official in external and internal custody' at a prison in Kimberley. There's a brief period as prisons inspector at DCS head office, after which he's sent back to Kimberley.[177]

In 1997, he gets his first career break; he's promoted to the level of director when he is appointed as a regional commissioner, of the Northern Cape and the Free State and also in the Eastern Cape. When widespread corruption and 'inhumane treatment of offenders' in South African prisons is exposed in 2001, Modise is one of the DCS officials who's expected to address the matter on a provincial level.

From 2001, he represents the Northern and Eastern Cape and the Free State during an inquiry under Judge Thabane Jali into alleged incidents of corruption, maladministration, violence and intimidation at the DCS. Modise testifies before the Jali Commission that he was taken hostage during Operation Quiet Storm,[178] a strategy allegedly designed by POPCRU, that was aimed at making prisons ungovernable and ultimately unseating prison managers who were not considered progressive.

He evidently does not have much time for 'hard-to-please' union shop stewards. 'The emergence of the labour movements and the fact that outspoken and hard-to-please shop stewards were appointed into senior positions brought about the misconception that one must fight management to be promoted,' he tells the Commission.[179]

As for whistle-blowers, Modise is recorded, at a meeting, as vowing to 'root them out' from the department.[180]

He certainly tries to remove DCS whistle-blower Tatolo Setlai on more than one occasion. Following Setlai's late 2010 report on unlawful isolation practices in Mangaung, Modise reports him to the minister of correctional services and transfers him to another position within the department. Setlai is later vindicated by the minister, and the criminal charges brought against him on this occasion are dropped.

Almost a decade earlier, Setlai is also transferred, this time from Grootvlei prison he heads up at the time after he allows prisoners to take a camera inside the building and record warders incriminating themselves on various counts. The recorded footage is broadcast on national television and also included as evidence before the Jali Commission. On this occasion, Modise claims Setlai had intentionally incited prisoners to riot in the footage and reports him to the police. The 14 counts of corruption against Setlai are later dropped.[181]

An email also reveals that he plans to take legal action against Setlai, and others in the department, in 2008. 'I have registered with my attorney a request that action be taken against [...] the Minister for [...] labeling me as corrupt and degrading my reputation. This would also include action against Mr. T.A. Setlai [...]'[182]

The email is sent in response to Modise's six-month suspension for maladministration and malpractice, following several complaints against him. In the internal disciplinary process, Modise is accused of seven instances of nepotism while stationed in Bloemfontein, where he lives. His removal and appointment of people to various positions – ranging from the post of deputy director to regional coordinator and manager: spiritual care – are described as 'irregular'.

A stint at head office and another one as regional commissioner of Gauteng precede his appointment as temporary head of Mangaung in 2013. By this time, he has worked for the DCS for close to 40 years. Modise worked his way up from the trenches. He understands the stress and pressure prison officials are under – he has walked in their boots. His name comes up when candidates for the post of national commissioner are discussed, but he is passed over at first.

I wonder if his appointment as head at Mangaung comes as a disappointment to the DCS careerist. The move from regional commissioner to prison director could be seen as a demotion, as he went from overseeing a large geographical area to running one prison.

His time at Mangaung, however, turns out to be a springboard to the highest attainable post within the department: he's appointed acting national commissioner, a post that later becomes permanent. His appointment is well received in DCS circles. Warders trust him because of his correctional services background. In post after post on a Facebook group for prison guards called 'Prison Matters',[183] DCS officials sing his praises. Finally, there's a man in charge who would deal with their issues and protect their interests.

This is Tebogo Bereng's football team, which he joined before he was sent to prison. Tebogo is standing in the middle of the back row in a green outfit. (photo courtesy of Bassie Bereng)

Dan Mbelwane, former Mangaung prison guard, former shop steward for the Police and Prisons Civil Rights Union (POPCRU). Dan led the strikes at Mangaung prison in 2013. (still from Prison for Profit *by Femke and Ilse van Velzen)*

Thabo Godfrey Botsane was incarcerated in Mangaung prison for eight years. He was allegedly electroshocked, injected and assaulted in 2009 by the emergency security team (EST). Following his release, Thabo grew into a community leader, advocating for unemployed and formerly incarcerated people. (still from Prison for Profit *by Femke and Ilse van Velzen)*

Striking guards at Mangaung prison designed this placard in 2013. The strike brought the prison to a standstill. G4S dismissed two-thirds of the workforce and replaced them with unqualified workers. (still from Prison for Profit *by Femke and Ilse van Velzen)*

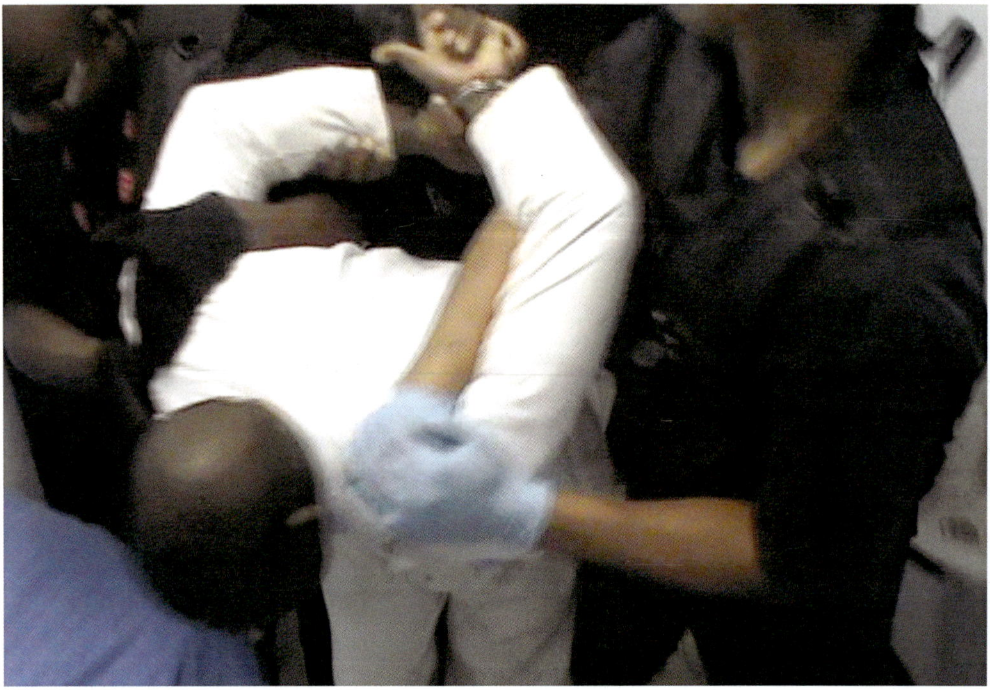

Bheki Dlamini was forcibly injected with anti-psychotic drugs in 2013. He is seen here arguing with the guards, telling them: 'I am not an animal.' (still from Prison for Profit *by Femke and Ilse van Velzen)*

Audick "Shakes" Letsoara was a member of the EST at Mangaung prison, until he was sacked in 2018. Shakes admitted his team was involved in torturing inmates and he conceded: 'What we did was wrong.' (still from Prison for Profit *by Femke and Ilse van Velzen)*

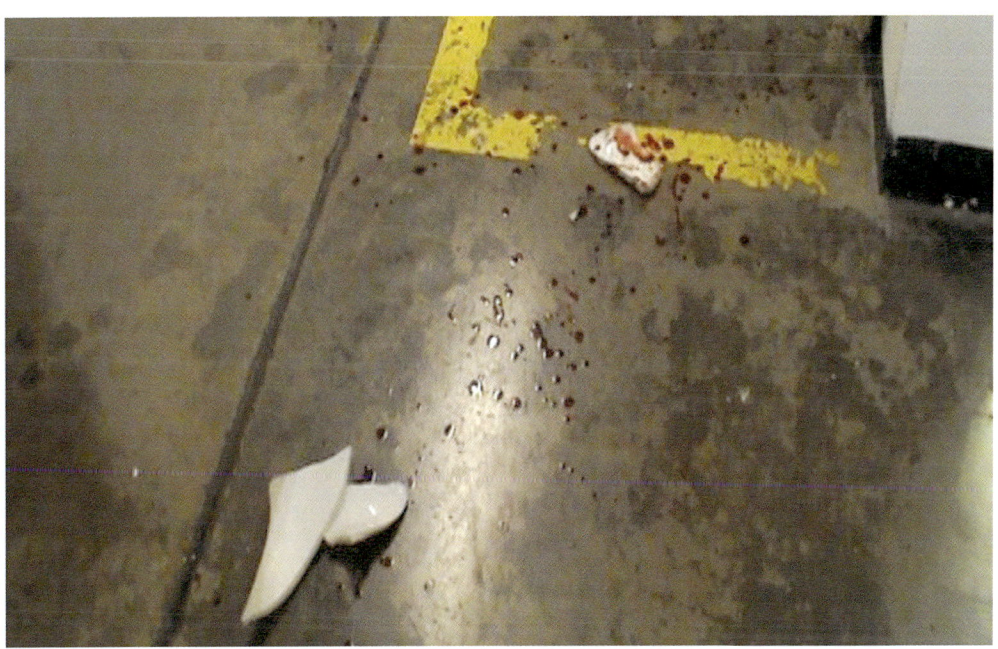

Ceramic toilet pots are smashed and used as weapons in the prison. G4S did not replace the ceramic with steel toilet pots, despite repeated requests from prison guards. To this day, guards and inmates are being stabbed with the broken pieces of toilet pots. (still from Prison for Profit *by Femke and Ilse van Velzen)*

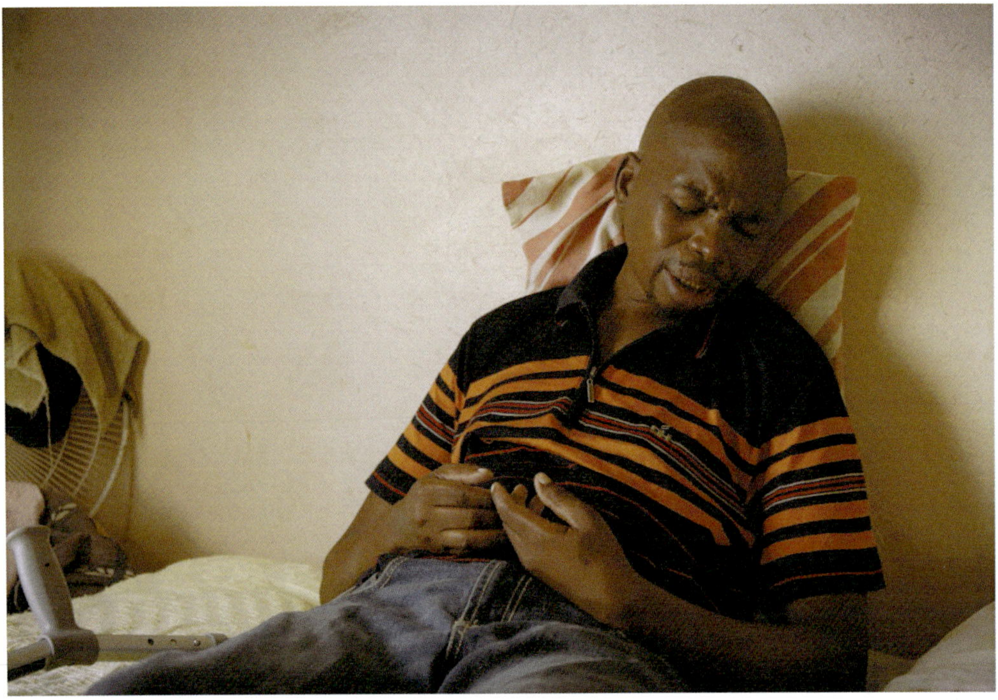

Francis was awarded medical parole in 2013, after a DCS doctor established he would die soon. Francis ended up in a wheelchair, following a brutal attack by the EST that damaged his spinal cord. (still from Prison for Profit *by Femke and Ilse van Velzen)*

Anna and Dikiledi Bereng tend the grave of their son and brother Tebogo Bereng, who died in 2013 in Mangaung prison, following an alleged assault by the EST. Tebogo had epilepsy and the electrified riot shields might have brought on his final and fatal epilepsy fit. (still from Prison for Profit *by Femke and Ilse van Velzen)*

This man suddenly appeared at the door of my room in a guest house one night, telling me he was looking for 'someone who looks like me'. The staff of the guesthouse provided the image of the man from their CCTV footage. He was not a guest yet did manage to enter the highly secured premises.

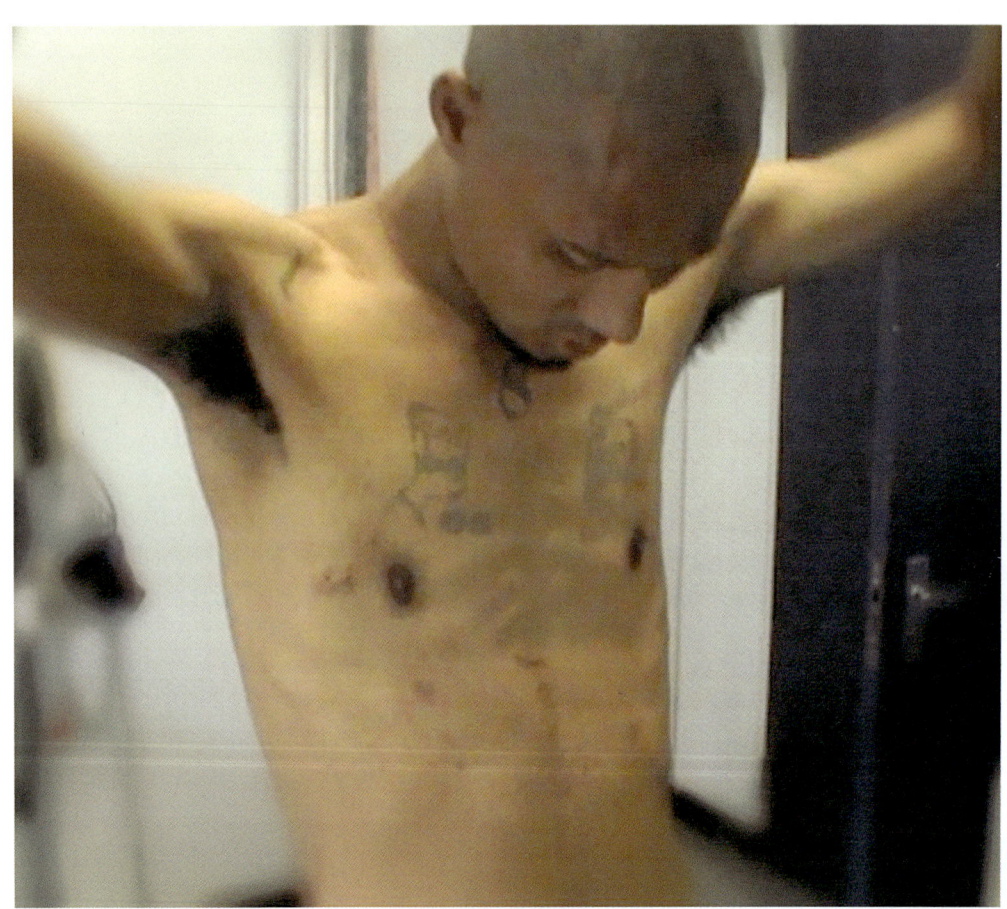
Gershwin Coutts alleges he was assaulted and electroshocked by G4S guards in 2013. (still from Prison for Profit *by Femke and Ilse van Velzen)*

Early in 2015, shortly after G4S is again running Mangaung, Britta Rotmann, the head of legal services at DCS, requests a meeting. It is not our first, as I'd met with her before to discuss my investigation. She and I have a similar background in common: we both studied international law and human rights. Possibly because of that, I trusted her up until then.

But things change. I meet Rotmann in the Wits Journalism Department's boardroom. In her beige DCS uniform, Rotmann looks out of place. Stuck onto the glass façade on one side of the boardroom are the names of South African journalists who have paved the way for us: Henry Nxumalo, Bloke Modisane, Ruth First and many others. Like they are watching over us.

'I've been sent today by Zach …' she tells me. I sit up in my chair. I'd been surprised by her request for a meeting. She wanted to come and see me at my office. It was usually the other way around.

'To tell you to stop talking to Clement Motsapi,' she adds.

From 2009 to 2014, Motsapi had been the DCS controller at Mangaung. Following the DCS investigation of abuse at Mangaung prison, Motsapi becomes the scapegoat: he is first suspended and later dismissed.

'I can't confirm or deny I'm speaking to Motsapi,' I say to her, and I try to wrap my head around what I'd just heard.

'I find it strange that you would instruct a journalist not to speak with a source,' I add.

'He is not to be trusted – and you should know that.'

'Who told you I was speaking to Motsapi?' I ask.

'Ah, you know Mangaung prison, it's a rumour mill,' she answers.

I quickly end the conversation. My head is spinning. Why had Modise officially dispatched Rotmann, a senior DCS official, to my office to tell me to stop talking to a source? Rotmann is her usual polite self, she doesn't see anything wrong with telling a journalist not to speak to a source.

There are further attempts from the DCS to frustrate my investigation during the period Modise is national commissioner.

Not long after my meeting with Rotmann, in February 2015, I interview a by-then retired Tatolo Setlai, the whistle-blower who has an axe to grind with Modise. We speak about the time DCS controlled Mangaung. Setlai is convinced Modise is corrupt, he alleges Modise unlawfully enriched himself while DCS ran Mangaung prison.

As per my agreement with Setlai, I email him the article I write based on our interview. He apparently prints it out at an internet café and gets a friend to type up his feedback – a document entitled 'Amendmend', which is printed out and faxed back to the Wits journalism department.

Several days later, it becomes clear that the communication between Setlai and myself had been intercepted by the DCS. I receive an email to this effect from DCS spokesperson Logan Maistry. 'Our sources have provided us with a copy of the article, regarding the said matter, that you intend to publish, which we have perused,' he writes. 'We have also perused the comments made by Mr. Setlai, entitled "AMENDMEND," where you afforded Mr. Setlai an opportunity to comment on the article you intend to publish.'[184]

Maistry's email also accuses me of bias: 'Based on this modus operandi, it is clear that you, and your sources, have a certain agenda, and have already taken a subjective stance, and made up your mind/s, on this matter.'

I'd asked the DCS for comment, but, writes Maistry, 'It is also clear that your request for comment [...] is merely a formality for the record.' He refuses to answer any questions.

This email sends us into a tailspin at the WJP. It's the second time the department tries to interfere with my meeting with a DSC source. How had the department found out I was meeting with Setlai? Had they followed me? Had Setlai told them? Had they bugged our offices? All these questions buzz through my head. I knew they had the fax, because Maistry repeats the spelling error: Amendmend.

Briefly, everything and everyone at the office seems suspicious. When a colleague mentions seeing two strange men at Wits, my paranoia kicks in. I change the locks and pour over CCTV footage, but the two strangers are never identified.

All of this doesn't stop the article from getting published, both in the UK and South Africa.[185] It details the many ways in which DCS had done nothing to hold G4S accountable, following credible evidence of very serious abuse.

Wits's legal department sends the DCS a letter demanding they 'cease and desist' intercepting my communication. A sweep of our offices for bugging devices comes up empty. Most likely, someone had intercepted my communication and handed it to the DCS.

The audacity of the department, to intercept my communication with a source and then confront me with it as if there were not a worry in the world, unsettles me, but it also spurs me on. An old journalistic adage seems to apply: if officials hate your guts, you're doing something right.

Then, in October 2015, the DCS files a complaint against me with the Press Ombudsman.[186] Maistry pens the rambling grievance, accusing me of 'intentional and negligent departure from the facts' before referring to a September 2015 article I wrote about Isaac Nelani and Tebogo Bereng, the two men who had died while being held at Mangaung. It was published in the *Mail & Guardian* in South Africa and the *Daily Telegraph* in the UK.[187] According to the complaint, I'd omitted information that was part of the DCS's three-page response to my questions about the deaths. It specifically wanted me to include more information on why the department hadn't produced a final report on abuse in Mangaung under G4S management. The Ombudsman ruled that the complaint against me was unfounded.

Nelani's death had been on my radar from the day I started the investigation into Mangaung. His story was so important, I felt I couldn't write it up without having all the evidence. I worked on the story for three years. Only after I finally received the post-mortem that mentioned his bruised heart I felt I could finally write the story on his and many other suspicious deaths in this maximum-security prison.

The department couldn't have selected a more well-researched story to use as evidence in the first-ever Press Ombudsman complaint against me.

The attempts to obstruct my investigation baffle me. It starts to feel like Modise has a beef with me personally.

Then, as allegations of tender corruption and collusion start emerging in the media, I begin to realise he probably has a lot to hide.

In June 2017, Modise is called to explain his department's irregular expenditure before the Parliamentary Monitoring Group's Standing Committee on Public Accounts (SCOPA)[188] and face allegations of colluding with security solutions providers SASSTEC. DCS officials had allegedly worked with SASSTEC to draw up favourable contract specifications worth R378 million.[189] Fence and Gates, one of SASSTEC's subsidiaries, also holds contracts with Mangaung. An official working for the company had alerted SCOPA. According to the Parliamentary Monitoring Group's summary of the meeting, Modise is 'closely questioned [...] which at times became heated – to explain why his car was parked outside the house of the director of a company that does business worth R2bn with the Department and whether he has a personal relationship with SASSTEC directors.' Modise does not provide any satisfactory answers to questions posed by the members of parliament. Modise had previously defied Treasury, who had ordered him to cancel the contract with SASSTEC, because the tender process was so irregular. Timothy Brauteseth, a Democratic Alliance member of parliament, accuses Modise of 'flagrant corruption'.

Two weeks after he appears at SCOPA, despite his bid to have his term in office extended, Modise's retirement is announced.[190]

Then in 2018, at the Commission of Inquiry into State Capture, Modise is named as one of the DCS officials who 'allegedly benefitted unduly' in their personal capacity from contracts between the DCS and Bosasa, a local company providing prison and other services to government. Former Bosasa director turned whistle-blower Angelo Agrizzi lists the wide range of benefits allegedly enjoyed by Modise and others: 'cash or cars, travel and accommodation, sponsorships for their children's studies or in one case, a matric dance, the arrangement of concession for a relative's stay at a retirement village as well as security and maintenance and repairs at their homes'.[191] According to Agrizzi, Modise received R1 million in kickbacks over the years,[192] in instalments of R20 000 a month.[193]

He describes how Modise would receive a 'grey security packet wrapped in a newspaper' from Bosasa director Papa Leshabane.[194]

Agrizzi's version is yet to be tested under cross examination at the Zondo Commission or in a civil or criminal trial.

Setlai phones me out of the blue in February 2019 to tell me that he'd gone to the Hawks to report that Modise and several other senior DCS officials unlawfully enriched themselves while they were running the prison from 2013 to 2014. After noticing an overwhelming number of financial irregularities relating to Mangaung while the DCS team was stationed there, Elias Jacobs, a DCS official working in administration at Grootvlei prison had alerted Setlai.

I contact Jacobs. Apparently, the DCS allocated R120 million for Mangaung operation under Modise. 'I came across claims for R60 000 for subsistence and travel allowances when the officials in question hadn't been travelling at all. The men and women of the DCS team stayed at the Protea Hotel in Bloemfontein,' Jacobs tells me. He also says officials received overtime remunerations, in some cases up to R50 000 a month. In addition, they charged the department for accommodation and meals at the hotel when they weren't even in town. He also uncovered some personal purchases made on the DCS's tab.

In other words, on Modise's watch the DCS officials allegedly milked the system. Jacobs claims Modise instructed him not to report the irregularities.

Not surprisingly though, Modise immediately reports Jacobs to the police. In turn, Setlai and Jacobs put pressure on the Hawks, the country's Directorate for Priority Crime Investigation, to investigate the claims laid out in Jacobs's affidavit, to no avail.[195] My subsequent questions to the Hawks and the police remain unanswered.

Modise is like a Tefal frying pan: nothing seems to stick.

Modise's obsession with me takes an even stranger and more personal turn, when he starts communicating with me through seemingly rather unhinged text messages.

In August 2017 I receive a bizarre anonymous text about Katie Hopkins. Hopkins is a British right-wing columnist who, towards the end of 2017, had written a degrading blog about South African intersex athlete Caster Semenya,[196] questioning her gender.

'Birds of the sa.e [sic] feathers flock together. The British journalist Katie Hopkins aka Caster Semanya and Ruth Hopkins aka G4S/Correctional Services. Hooray!!!!', the message reads.

I ask the writer to reveal himself, which he doesn't and so I forget about the bizarre text. I am reminded of it when on 5 December 2018, I receive another message from the same number, but this time 'Uncle Zach' signs off.

'Good morning CSO Lucky Mthethwa. Please note that your inmates are complaining about water and generally poor and abusive treatment in KZN, especially Martizburg, Westville and Qalakabusha. For your attention, regards, Uncle Zach.'

Lucky Mthethwa was at the time Chief Security Officer (CSO) and Deputy National Commissioner of Correctional Services. Clearly, Uncle Zach is getting his phone numbers mixed up.

This is followed by an even more bizarre message on 28 January

2019, when the Zondo Commission's investigation into state capture is in full swing. Angelo Agrizzi is spilling the beans on Modise, alleging that the national commissioner received R1 million worth of bribes from Bosasa.

'Good afternoon Natcom Fraser, I sent you an email yesterday and further requested Ms Carol Strydom who I ccd to provide you with said email as the one I sent could not be delivered. Please confirm. Regards. Zach Modise.'

Now this piques my interest! The former national commissioner of correctional services, Zach Modise, thinks he is texting the current national commissioner of correctional services, Arthur Fraser, but in actual fact he is sending me these texts.

I write back and ask him what this email is all about and he replies that it is about his possible appearance before the Zondo Commission. This presents an interesting dilemma. On the one hand, I have Uncle Zach eating out of my hand because he thinks I am the national commissioner. On the other hand, is it unethical to continue this conversation?

I can't help myself and I continue the conversation, asking Modise where the Mangaung files have gone. That 'bakkie' full of evidence that went missing. Modise masterfully evades the question and after a few messages he stops replying altogether, possibly realising he is texting his nemesis.

Nevertheless, in an often-stressful investigation, these lighter moments are the comic relief I need to lighten my mood.

12

Power in numbers

'The Rolls Royce that should have been a Toyota'

WHILE MODERN PRIVATE prisons were only introduced into political discourse in South Africa in the 1990s, privatised prisons were built as early as 1885. Diamond mining company De Beers employed convicts – many serving a sentence for violation of pass laws – in its mining operation, after gold and diamonds were discovered. 'The mining company paid the expenses to incarcerate their labourers and also paid the state for the use of their prison labour. By the end of the 19th century, the De Beers Diamond Mining Company was using over 10,000 prison labourers daily,' KC Goyer of the Institute for Security Studies (ISS) writes.[197] Privately enlisted convict labour in the mines was only abolished in South Africa in the early 1950s.

South African poet and academic Gabeba Baderoon writes in her ground-breaking essay *The Creation of Black Criminality in South Africa*,[198] about the exploitation of prison labour in South Africa. '(…) after the South African war ended in 1902, the state and the mining industry became increasingly reliant on the labour of incarcerated Africans. There was a direct correlation between laws that increased levels of imprisonment and the labour needs of the state and the agricultural and mining industries.' Prison labour became central to the economy of the state and thus the number of laws that criminalised Africans shot up.

That legacy is still felt today. South Africa currently has one of the highest incarceration rates (rates of inmates per 100 000 people) on the continent.

Pre-1994, South Africa had a strong economy based on 'state-supported industrialisation, the strength of gold as the foundation of the economy and the state's overall success in maintaining an ultra-cheap black labour system', Stephen Greenberg writes in his 2006 book *The State, Privatisation and the Public Sector in South Africa*.[199]

The devaluation of gold in the '80s heralded the end of this economic model. The apartheid state looked to the market for reinforcement. It started selling state-owned enterprises. The iron and steel giant ISCOR was privatised in 1989, retaining the state as a majority shareholder.

Steeped in struggle and socialism, the ANC has embraced a different economic vision. 'All [...] industry and trade shall be controlled to assist the well-being of the people,' reads the Freedom Charter, one of the key documents outlining the principles of the ruling party. And, 'The mineral wealth [...], the Banks and monopoly industry shall be transferred to the ownership of the people as a whole.' The ANC believed the apartheid government was championing privatisation as a way to preserve and retain white wealth. This is why they were against it. Initially.

In the early '90s things started to shift within the ANC, as the idea of a 'mixed economy' gained ground, paving the way for public-private partnerships, or PPPs. The post-apartheid state inherited approximately 350 state enterprises. The idea that these enterprises could be privatised was broadly accepted, initially on a pragmatic, case-by-case basis.

The fall of the Soviet Union and with it the sustainability of a centralised, state-led economy, the rise and success of emerging markets in Asia, as well as the prescriptive deregulation and liberalisation agenda of the International Monetary Fund and the World Bank were all factors that pushed the historically socialist ANC-led government in a more liberal direction.

Privatisation became official policy in 1996, with the Growth, Employment and Redistribution (GEAR)[200] strategy. The central idea behind GEAR, Greenberg writes, is that capitalist growth would lead to poverty reduction.

Privatisation was accepted as many believed that, compared to state bodies, commercial companies would get the job done swiftly and affordably, as competition fuels efficiency and affordability. State departments worked within allocated budgets and were not subject to the laws of supply and demand, which meant dysfunctional units or departments could often continue to exist. The private market would make that a thing of the past, proponents of privatisation preached. It would be better, for less money.

Formally, Greenberg writes, the process of privatisation has three goals: to reduce national debt, redistribute infrastructure and services and, lastly, to improve the efficiency of the economy.

Black economic empowerment (BEE) is only later added as a goal to privatisation policy. BEE becomes institutionalised when the National Empowerment Fund is established in 1998. The Fund receives stakes in recently privatised companies. With that money, black entrepreneurs and investors can start up new businesses or buy shares. Through the Fund, the ANC-led government hopes to achieve redistribution of wealth and to fast-track black entrepreneurs through the system.

What it does in practice, though, is strengthen the ANC's control over business, with senior managers of the so-called parastatals earning exorbitant salaries. The masses enjoy little to no benefits from BEE policies. A small group of politically connected businesspeople see their fortunes grow. It creates a protective wall of business patronage around the government.

The privatisation of South Africa's former state-run companies is not subjected to many democratic checks and balances.[201] The elite, pressured by international financial institutions, decides this is a good idea. The laws enabling the privatisation are tabled in parliament but a discussion around the necessity, desirability and utility of privatisation is not held. Should a state outsource one of its more interventionist powers – the monopoly on restricting or withholding freedom of movement and the monopoly on violence – to a company that is part of and subject to pressure of financial markets? That question is not discussed.

The Correctional Services Amendment Act 102 of 1997, which provides for the minister to contract out the design, construction, finance and management (DCFM) of any prison or part of any prison, is hastily pushed through parliament in the middle of 1997, amid rafts and rafts of other new post-1994 legislative proposals.[202] Treasury regulations for the procurement for PPPs were not in place.[203] 'This lack of regulation meant that no feasibility study was conducted to test affordability, risk transfer and value-for-money,' writes Tim Prussing, a researcher at the Department of Finance & Tax, University of Cape Town in a 2016 article.[204]

'[T]he government wanted to clamp down on the fear,' Gideon Morris, director of the JICS, a semi-independent government watchdog for prisoners, says of that time. He's quoted in Sarah Massey's master's dissertation on the experience of privatisation in South Africa's PPP prisons.[205] Morris continues to opine that government 'also said [...], "let's outsource the risk of keeping the worst of the worst, let's send those baddies then to the private prisons, so when they escape, it's not us".'

This outsourcing of political risk in times of rising crime rates in an otherwise volatile society is an obvious attraction for governments. When something goes wrong, they can blame the company and the company can hide behind corporate confidentiality. In effect, there will be no one to blame.

Sipo Mzimela is the New South Africa's first Minister of Correctional Services and the man who pushes the privatisation of prisons in South Africa through in record time. His plans are announced in April 1997; by July 1997 five different consortiums have been shortlisted to tender for four prisons. In 2001, Mangaung opens its doors, followed by Kutama Sinthumule Correctional Centre, run by American GEO group in Louis Trichardt, Limpopo.

Mzimela spent some of his time in exile in the United States, where he was ordained as a priest. As a prison chaplain, he got to know the US correctional system from the inside. In his view, privatised prisons are beacons of modernity and efficiency. In 1997, Mzimela returns to the US with a group of high-level DCS officials to gather further evidence of the success of privatised prisons.[206]

'Wherever the private sector got involved, they have delivered a better service, and have done it at less cost to the taxpayer,' he says upon their return. 'What I have seen in the United States is very good. The prisons that are run by the private companies are far more efficient in every sense because they are run by businesspeople, unlike those in the Department of Correctional Services who are not necessarily trained to run businesses.'[207]

The government's formal political rationale to delegate the constitutional duty to provide humane incarceration to inmates is that privatised prisons will help combat severe prison overcrowding. At the time, some of the country's prisons are up to 300 per cent overcrowded. This causes a vicious cycle of malnutrition, scarce or non-existent medical care, violence and abuse. This in turn leads to sickness, suicide and the deaths of inmates who are warehoused in often old and dilapidated buildings.

Mzimela wants to build 15 more prisons throughout the country to address the acute overcrowding problem fast and head-on. In the US, Mzimela saw private prisons being built in 15 months, much quicker than the eight or nine years the Public Works Department was known to take to build a new facility. He could achieve results soon.

His conviction that private commercial companies are best suited to the task also hinges on the belief that it would save the government and the taxpayer. Both outcomes – a speedy solution to overcrowding and savings – would serve the dignified treatment of prisoners. It is a win-win situation, he feels.[208]

The state will not incur any initial construction costs. The private partner raises the capital and builds the prison, and the government repays the company over the however many years the contract stipulates. The kind of capital required to build and maintain a prison from scratch, especially a maximum-security facility, is no small amount; it costs R400 million just to build Mangaung. Hence big private companies – often foreign ones – being part of the tender contracts.

It is often impossible for government departments to raise this kind of capital swiftly. Government bonds would have to be sold, which parliament would need to approve. In other words, the delaying force of democracy can get in the way.

The tender process is extremely detailed and lengthy. The bidders are directed through an investigation process, where they have to answer many questions about their funding, socio-economic achievements, economic empowerment and other criteria. Their compliance with the strict tender conditions is scrutinised.

It's hard work for BCC, the consortium that eventually wins the tender for Mangaung. Beside G4S, BCC has four other equal shareholders including Old Mutual and three empowerment companies: Fikile Mangaung, Ten Alliance Mangaung and Ikhwezi Community Trust; all three are registered at the same address as G4S South Africa.

BCC negotiates on three levels, Massey writes, after interviewing several BCC board members: 'with the bankers, in order to secure funding, with the lawyers, in order to draw up the tendering document, and with the government, in order to win the bid'.[209]

In 1998, the prison tender is discussed before the tender board, comprising officials from three different government departments. The board guidelines do not allow for tenders of this magnitude, but Mzimela lobbies for it and pushes through approval. In 1999, the tender for the construction, maintenance and operation of Mangaung prison is awarded to BCC. The contract is signed in 2000.

The prison contract

According to the lease-purchase contract between BCC and the DCS, government pays rent and an annual fee for the services the private consortium provides. 'The lease payments include not only a day-to-day fee per prisoner but also repayment for capital expenditure over the long term (25 years) to ensure that, by the expiry of the contract term, the government has repaid (with interest) those costs,' law professor Julia Sloth-Nielsen explained in a 2003 article.[210] After 25 years, once all the payments have been made, the title for the facility returns to the government.

The contract sets out the legal framework for the DCFM of the prison. BCC, the main contractor, is allowed to subcontract. The construction of the prison is subcontracted to FMR, a joint venture between construction company Murray & Roberts Buildings and BCC empowerment shareholder Fikile. FMR completes the construction three months earlier than planned. In July 2001, the first prisoners arrive, and the prison reaches its capacity of just under 3 000 in January the following year. Later, Murray & Roberts sell their shares to Old Mutual.

The operation agreement is subcontracted to Group 4, which becomes GLS, and when it acquires Securicor in 2004 it becomes G4S.

BCC provides only 10 per cent of the funding required for the project, ABSA and Investec loan the remaining 90 per cent.[211] Their loans are placed in the Bloemfontein Prison Trust, represented by Hendrik Beukes Oppermann, a senior banker with ABSA. Because the Bloemfontein Prison Trust provides the funding for the project, security is ceded to them. BCC provided security to the Prison Trust for the loan, by offering the Trust rights to 'project documents, the project revenue, all the accounts of the borrower (BCC), as well as all amounts held in those accounts'. In other words, the Bloemfontein Prison Trust, which holds money secured from ABSA and Investec, ultimately controlled the prison operation in Bloemfontein.

The high costs of their own debt is one of the reasons private prison contractors often charge high fees, and increase them over the years, argues Tim Prussing in his master's dissertation on public-private financing in South Africa.[212]

It is the banks who are ultimately in control, they make decisions about appointing a new private partner, should there be operational failure. '[U]nder the terms of a PFI [private finance initiative] prison contract, in the event of operational failure it is the project's financiers – the banks – not the state authority that decide whether a new private operator should be brought in or whether the state can buy out the contracts and take over,' researcher Stephen Nathan explains in a report for the Open Society Foundation on prison privatisation.[213]

It is close to impossible for the government to terminate the contract without incurring crippling debts. If the contract is terminated, the DCS will be responsible for paying off the full capital cost of the prison, in addition to what it had already spent on the prison.

'In effect, BCC can hold the Department of Correctional Services to ransom for the full capital cost of the new prison in Bloemfontein. Since the South African government does not have sufficient funds to pay that ransom, the government and the South African public is at the mercy of BCC,' Goyer writes in 2001.[214]

The long-term costs of the privatisation project become obvious quite soon. G4S specifies their services in units – education, meals, gardening, vocational training, religious classes, and so forth – and they can add items to the bill, as the contract does not prohibit that.[215]

In Mangaung, the price per inmate per day – made up of an operation and construction fee – increases from R154 in 1998, when the conditions in the contract are negotiated, to R215 in 2002, when a National Treasury task team on PPPs investigates the costs and affordability of the prison contracts.[216] In 2018, the cost per prisoner per day increases to R365.88. Because the contract was drafted to the benefit of the shareholders, by allowing for endless additions, the total annual amount DCS had to pay ended up being even more than what the per inmate fee should indicate.

In 2002, the National Treasury orders an investigation into if and how the government can renegotiate the contracts with the consortia and the answer was a firm no. The contracts are inflexible and do not permit any wriggling room. The shareholders, meanwhile, earn a 30 per cent return on their equity, which translates into a handsome profit.

The private prisons turn out to be much more expensive than government had initially thought, and contractually there is nothing much they can do about that. 'We ordered a Rolls-Royce, but we should have ordered a Toyota,' Sue Lund, the government's advisor on PPPs, comments at a 2003 conference on private prisons.[217]

The prisons prove so expensive that the government announces a recruitment freeze on all public servants in 2002/2003.[218]

In 2014, it is calculated that the DCS had already paid BCC more than R1.7 billion in fees. Roughly 6 per cent of DCS's budget is spent on the two private prisons.[219]

Very few people actually understand the 2 300-page contract, which is written in dense legalese. In parliament, this is highlighted as a possible obstacle to understanding the obligations of the consortium and those of the state.

'None of the DCS officials working at the prison had been trained in compliance with the prison contract,' one of my sources tells me. Case in point is the 'supervisory committee' – comprised of DCS, G4S and independent members – that is mandated, as per the contract, to impose penalties and fines on BCC for breaches of contract. 'The decisions of that body were shocking,' my source continues. 'Most decisions were in favour of G4S.'

Privatisation of prisons might happen in record time initially, but it does eventually meet with resistance. There's opposition in parliament, with members citing moral arguments on the one hand – the state should never outsource safety and security – and cost inefficiency on the other.

In 2011, under pressure from Parliament, Minister of Correctional Services Nosiwiwe Mapisa-Nqakula reverses a decision to build a further four privatised prisons, which G4S had also tendered for. She's concerned that the DCS has 'no control over what happens. At the end of the day, you have no idea what monster we are producing from the correctional facility,' she's quoted as saying.[220] Figures are also given for what Mangaung and Kutama cost the taxpayer per year in operational costs – R800 million a year.

Vincent Smith, chair of the Portfolio Committee on Correctional Services, repeats these figures in 2013, when there's about 14 years left on the 25-year contracts the DCS has with G4S and GEO Group. 'The annual costs of the two centres is R800-million a year,' Smith is quoted as saying. 'At the rate of R800-million for the next 14 years it will probably be in the tune of R12-billion that we are going to have to expend […] After 25 years, all we get is just two correctional centres, that's all we get […] R21-billion could have bought us 18 prisons if you take the rate we pay for Kimberley [prison].'[221]

The opposition to private prisons is sparked, in part, by one of the companies vying for a prison tender – a South African company known as Bosasa Operations. In 2003, Bosasa was accused of bribery and corruption to the value of R2 billion involving Correctional Services tenders,[222] as well as allegations of tender rigging. Bosasa tried to obstruct the investigation, and later, the public release of the investigative report, just like G4S several years later attempts to obstruct the release of the investigation report into allegations of abuse in Mangaung prison.

When former director of Bosasa, Angelo Agrizzi, blows up the toxic contract between the private prison company and the state by spilling ALL the beans on tender corruption and kickbacks before the Zondo Commission, Vincent Smith is caught with his metaphorical pants down.

Smith is known as a vocal opponent of prison privatisation, but Agrizzi alleges he accepted R45 000 and R100 000 every month from Bosasa in kickbacks.[223]

The private prison project in South Africa is not rooted in majority decisions or collectiveness and came about through improper tender processes.[224] Not surprisingly Mangaung has become a space where money is made while rights are trampled on.

G4S in war and conflict zones

After merging with the American company Armorgroup in 2008,[225] G4S moved into war and conflict zones. G4S is part of a lucrative global military industrial complex, where the company carries out tasks in 'complex environments'. It accepts jobs that national armies are not trained to do. G4S often provides security for critical supply chains and crucial national assets.

In Nigeria, for example, G4S provided security for Shell[226] and currently provides security for Chevron's oil operation in the Niger Delta,[227] siding with paramilitary forces who have for decades oppressed and fought against the local population.[228]

In South Sudan, G4S worked with the Sudan People's Liberation Army (SPLA),[229] which later became the South Sudanese army that has been accused of war crimes. G4S also holds contracts to provide security in Iraq and Afghanistan, at times siding with warlords who stand accused of war crimes.[230]

In November 2018 the Taliban bombed a G4S compound in Kabul.[231] Six people died and 19 were injured when the suicide bomb went off. The company's website mentioned that its 26 000 square feet Afghan headquarters is situated in a Kabul Business Park.[232] The BBC reported that the company employs about 1 200 members of staff in Afghanistan and have been in the country since 2003. The UK Ministry of Defence, however, has not qualified or quantified G4S's deployment of 1 200 workers to Afghanistan. Governments refer to national security and the company to corporate confidentiality when faced with requests for transparency.

The American Department of Defense estimated there were approximately 400 private contractors in Iraq in 2018 and more than 4 000 in Afghanistan.[233] What they are doing exactly and how much they are earning remains a mystery.

Not surprisingly, things can go wrong in this murky world, most infamously when American military contractor Blackwater shot dead 17 people in 2007 in Iraq.[234] Iraqi authorities claimed the guards had opened fire on the civilians without any provocation.

Maybe also not surprisingly, the UK is one of the biggest clients of *private military contractors. According to an article on the website Open Democracy, it spends approximately £50 million annually on the business of war.*[235] *South Africa, on the other hand, is a country that produces a lot of mercenaries for hire, often unemployed former apartheid (police and army) officers.*

The UN called for better regulation of private mercenaries in 2011. 'Iraq (is) a major theatre of operations by private military and security companies; South Africa a major source of people with extensive military skills and experience unwilling or unable to find jobs since the end of apartheid in 1994,'[236] *the UN report read. It was produced by a UN working group with very long name: Working Group on the use of mercenaries as a means of violating human rights and impeding the exercise of the right of peoples to self-determination.*

The chair of the working group flagged the lack of a legal framework regulating private security companies in war zones as the main problem: 'Mr. Gómez said there is a legal "gap" between recognized international conventions on the use of mercenaries, and the control of private security companies that are often used by governments and non-governmental organizations (NGOs).'[237]

13

The shareholders, the contract and the government

'The prison is present in our lives and at the same time, the prison is absent in our lives' – Angela Davis[238]

FOR YEARS, VERY FEW people know that the DCFM contract was not awarded to G4S alone. Dan, who started working in Mangaung in 2008, only ever negotiated with G4S. Up until his dismissal in 2013, he was unaware that the British multinational is actually one of five BCC shareholders including Old Mutual, and Fikile Mangaung, Ten Alliance Mangaung and Ikhwezi Community Trust, three empowerment companies. He's familiar with Old Mutual, one of the country's biggest and oldest insurance companies.

While G4S is one of the five shareholders, it is also subcontracted to manage the prison on a daily basis and is therefore the most visible of all of them.

The shareholders are a bit like the Bloemfontein illuminati. Inmates, G4S guards and DCS officials tell me they are corrupt and politically connected. But no one can provide evidence. And no one seems to know who is hiding behind previously disadvantaged enterprises Fikile Mangaung, Ten Alliance Mangaung and Ikhwezi Community Trust. The BCC board of directors is at first headed up by Lebogang Mokoena, and his brother Pappie takes over the position in 2014. The two are also directors of two other shareholder companies: Ten Alliance and Ikhwezi. In other words, the brothers' companies receive 40 per cent of the profits the contract generates. Because they are the public face of BCC, I try to speak to them, but they decline my calls. I ask everyone and anyone if they know anything. I speak to the local branches of the Economic Freedom Fighters and the Democratic Alliance, but they have not heard of the shareholder companies, but they do know the brothers. Otherwise, my sources come up with nothing.

Rumours keep swirling though, of prominent political figures who finance BCC. Famous and infamous politician's names are bandied about. But when I ask my sources for proof, they usually shrug.

Fikile, Ten Alliance and Ikhwezi all list the G4S South African headquarters as their address. They're originally registered a few days within each other – in July 1999, after BCC had won the tender and was busy negotiating the details of the contract with government. It's hard to believe the three companies were set up for any other purpose than the prison contract.

I start looking up as much as I can find on the obscure companies. Fikile seems to have a bona fide track record in the construction sector.

Ikhwezi is more obscure. When it signs the contract in 2000, BCC is known as Ikhwezi Bloemfontein Correctional Contracts. In isiXhosa, iKhwezi means morning star. The Ikhwezi Community Trust (ICT) as a corporate entity does not seem to have any business experience or presence or actually a track record in any field. A 2004 BCC submission to parliament[239] reveals that ICT 'was established as a vehicle for identifying needs in the local community and using the dividends generated by the company, to address those needs'. The submission also states that the trust, which is listed as a charity, received an R11 708 donation. It's unclear where that money originated from or what this donation was used for. The overview of ICT's plans to spend initial funds was then listed: 'education and training (R75 000 a year); home-based care services (R10 000 a year), feeding schemes (R20 000 a year); small, medium and micro-sized enterprises development (R50 000 a year); and lastly business growth and expansion.' BCC promises this money *would* be spent. No additional information is provided.

Eventually, I manage to get a response from Pappie Mokeona about Ikhwezi's charitable projects. 'ICT as a community development trust was granted a donation of R 150 000.00 by the sponsors of the project to assist with setup costs and as a contribution towards community projects that ICT intended to provide,' he writes in an email dated 15 February 2019. 'I am aware that ICT has over the years embarked on a number of successful community upliftment projects.'

I press him for details that I can verify and check. But he doesn't or can't provide any further information on the nature of these upliftment projects, despite repeated emails.

I check online and find that ICT is not registered as a charity with the Department of Social Development (DSD). Charitable organisations in South Africa have to be registered with the DSD.

I dig up more about Ten Alliance Holdings, the mother company of Ten Alliance Mangaung. It is set up in the early '90s as a vehicle for tenders and PPPs throughout the country. It had shareholders in every province. In 1998, Ten Alliance is part of a consortium vying to launch a new television network called Station for the Nation. It also buys shares in Zama Resources Company, which in 2002 is accused of funding the legal costs of an ANC chief whip, Tony Yengeni, who organised lucrative deals for the company while he was a shareholder.[240]

Then I find some more interesting information. The year is 2009. If the newspaper report is to be believed, two high-profile officials who had worked in Correctional Services and who were later elected as MPs to parliament, stood accused of not declaring their interests properly before joining Parliament. The two accused were Ten Alliance shareholders Xoliswa Sibeko, who was National Commissioner of Correctional Services from October 2008 to December 2009, and

Thabane Jali, a former judge who chaired the commission of inquiry into corruption, maladministration, violence and intimidation in the DCS in the early 2000s.[241]

'The database links National Commissioner of Correctional Services Xoliswa Sibeko and former judge turned businessman Thabani Jali to the company, which runs the privatised prison in Bloemfontein,' the article reads.

It is striking that two officials with such close ties to Correctional Services seemingly had shares in a for-profit prison.

BCC and Ten Alliance catch another bit of bad news, which was widely reported on in 2013, when it becomes apparent Hildagrade Ndude from the Congress of the People party (COPE) also held BCC shares. In 2013, the Asset Forfeiture Unit seized her assets, including her shares in BCC and Ten Alliance. She was accused of defrauding her party of R2 million, was later axed from COPE and sentenced to eight years in prison, of which five were suspended.[242]

The next person linked to BCC again doesn't enhance their public profile. Towards the end of 2013, during the widely covered trial against Czech fugitive and crime boss Radovan Krejčíř, a transaction of R12 million was flagged. MoneyPoint, a business connected to Krejcir, had allegedly received that amount from BCC. When I query the chairperson of BCC, Pappie Mokoena, he responds: 'BCC was the victim of a fraud by an ABSA employee whom it appears may have had some relationship to Radovan Krejcir. BCC has no "links" or other relationship to Radovan Krejcir whatsoever. BCC recovered the money (…). I understand that the criminal case is still ongoing.'[243]

Of all the people involved with BCC, Dan had only heard of the Mokoena brothers.

Pappie is the eldest and the more visible of the two. He was mayor of Bloemfontein from 2002 to 2005. On his Facebook page 'The Journey', @PapsMokoena[244] writes about growing up around

Bloemfontein, how his parents split when he was three and Lebogang only six months old. An ambitious adolescent, Pappie was head prefect in high school and led student protests that followed in the wake of the 1976 Soweto uprising. He matriculated with exemption and graduated as a pharmacist.

When he became mayor, he was working as a registered pharmacist at Pelonomi Hospital, and he also had two retail pharmacies in Bloemfontein. He took up his position as mayor with little to no experience in politics. He writes on 'The Journey' how some of his ANC comrades pulled him out of a meeting to tell him he'd been chosen as the mayor and that he was completely surprised. 'Thus began my rollercoaster in local government. An area that I had no aspirations for, neither any insight,' he writes.

He left the ANC after his tenure as Bloemfontein mayor ended and he founded his own party, the Afrikan Alliance of Social Democrats. On 'The Journey', he pulls no punches when it comes to the ruling party, revealing that within ANC ranks, there was talk of the 'mortgaging' of the organisation to business interests and that Bloemfontein was at the 'epicentre' of this corrupt constellation.

Interestingly, during the run-up to the last municipal elections, in March 2019, he spoke about human rights at a rally in Botshabelo, a small town close to Bloemfontein. 'The rights of citizens have been emasculated. The constitution says that there are certain fundamental human rights which are entrenched even in the Bill of Rights. More importantly, the government cannot do anything without participatory democracy and consultation.'[245]

I wonder if Pappie has ever considered the constitutionality of what transpired in the prison he chairs.

There is more human rights talk on 'The Journey'. Pappie hopes 'future generations will hold all of us just as guilty as the perpetrators of injustice, if, out of fear of material and financial deprivation, we condoned the subjugation of others and the undermining of our human rights-based constitutional democracy.'

Pappie's political career ends rather ignominiously in handcuffs. In 2005, Pappie and his wife, Granny, are arrested for corruption involving about 10 per cent of the R1.5 billion municipal budget for Bloemfontein. He is initially convicted but appeals and is acquitted in 2012.[246] Ten other co-accused lose their appeal.

If you ask around about Pappie's younger brother Lebogang, people will tell you they know him as a businessman. He holds positions in various investment, construction and trading companies, of which the most well-known is Bidvest, a rental, distribution and trading company. He's appointed non-executive director at Bidvest in 2003, serving alongside President Cyril Ramaphosa. He resigns in 2014. He's listed as holding directorships of PEO Projects, Sesiu Investment Holdings, Culca Investments and Dinatla Investment Holdings.

It is Lebogang who picks up the phone in 2013 when the majority of the guards strike and things go belly-up at the prison. BCC is suddenly faced with a crisis. Rumours are rife that the consortium is going to lose the contract. At first, the DCS insists that BCC should be held accountable and are bound to uphold the provisions of the contract.

Dan meets Lebogang and one of BCC's other directors, Doreen Medupe, in a municipal office in town in 2014. 'They told me they were not aware of any riots or stabbings, and that these issues had not been mentioned during the shareholders' quarterly meetings,' Dan says. When Dan shows them photos of injuries and damaged property, both seem shocked. Medupe was anxious, Dan remembers. 'She said to me: "This is too big for us."'

Sometime after this meeting, Dan receives a call from Lebogang, who tells him that the strikers should go back, so that, 'We can save the contract.' And when Dan tells Lebogang that he'd discuss the return with the POPCRU leadership, Lebogang apparently warns him that G4S will tap his communication. Dan tells me Lebogang says that G4S is a big company and 'They will destroy you.'

The shareholders crawled out of the woodwork when a termination of the contract, or, at the very least hefty fines, seemed an imminent possibility. Inmates, guards and DCS officials alike learned about the brothers Mokoena who had earned a living off the operation while managing to remain nearly invisible.

In the end, the shareholders were guaranteed profits, despite abuse and torture taking place in the correctional facility. The links to powerful businessmen and politicians remained rumours. The shareholders ensured that the leaked video footage and other evidence of forced injections and assaults did not affect the money flow negatively. And to achieve that, they didn't even need to bare their teeth. The lengthy, opaque contract, with its endless records of change, kept the government in a legal stranglehold. Had they wanted to terminate the contract based on non-compliance, the government couldn't even afford to do so.

The department found this out the hard way. It claimed BCC owed them roughly R110 million. DCS had delivered all the prison services during their take over from October 2013 to August 2014 and so, they figured, they were under no obligation to pay BCC the monthly fee for the period that DCS was in charge at the prison. Nearly all G4S staff had been fired and DCS officials were carrying out their work. BCC, however, felt it was under no obligation to repay DCS for their services. It kept paying G4S for the operation of the prison, while G4S was not operating the prison. The department dealt with this impasse by withholding monthly fee payments to BCC in 2017. Angered by this decision, BCC took DCS to court.

The judge ruled in favour of the shareholders.[247] It agreed with BCC that withholding R110 million from the shareholders would cause 'irreparable harm': 'The financial instability caused to the applicant (BCC) by the non-payment places the continued operation of the prison at risk. The prison is a maximum-security facility. Given the number and status of the persons incarcerated at the prison, the risks of loss of control and operation of the prison are too great to be born. If control of the prison is lost, there is a considerable risk of lives being lost, of injury to inmates and to staff, and of significant damage to property. The applicant states that this is not speculation because these things have happened in the past,' the judge reasoned.

That last sentence is interesting. BCC evidently had alerted the judge to the fact that it had previously lost complete control of the prison and that people had been hurt. BCC highlighted this with untouchable arrogance. Probably because it knew that it would not be held responsible for the serious transgressions that had taken place at the prison. Instead, BCC demanded that the Department of Correctional Services keep paying them a service fee while DCS was running the prison. And this is how the shareholders escaped any legal liability for the transgressions, while at the same time continuing to rake in money.

G4S: Too big to fail

Considering G4S's long litany of scandals, deaths, strikes and the extensive evidence of poor contract compliance, it should be classified as a failed company. But it is not. It continues to rake in lucrative contracts and governments keep paying the company for its services.

Journalist Simon Hattenstone argued in the Guardian[248] *that this is because G4S is 'too big to fail ... While the British government argued that banks had to be bailed out otherwise the economy would suffer, it appears to believe that G4S has to be bailed out of trouble otherwise the nation's security is at risk.'*

Lastly, as the Mangaung case clearly illustrated, outsourcing contracts are often drafted in such a way that escalating costs are embedded in the provisions and withdrawing from the contract is either financially crippling or impossible.[249]

This co-dependence between private companies and the government means a company like G4S can continue messing up their work and the government will continue awarding new work to the company. In 2019, for example, the Australian government extended an electronic monitoring contract to G4S,[250] *for the electronic monitoring of inmates in South Australia. In the UK, however, the serious fraud office investigated the company over the 3 000 'phantom' inmates G4S claimed it was monitoring.*[251]

Because G4S is such a behemoth of a company, more likely than not it will win tenders and bids from their competitors, because it can offer competitive pricing of services, due to its size. Clearly, size matters.

14

G4S in South Africa

'And so it goes on. Massive contracts, huge profits, humiliating exposés, big financial penalties, massive contracts, huge profits ...'[252]

'G4S has no idea of how things work in Africa.'

2016 WAS THE YEAR that 'state capture' became a catchall phrase to describe the rot in South African politics. On 2 November, Thuli Madonsela, the Public Protector (an office comparable to an ombudsman) released 'State of Capture', a 'Report on an investigation into alleged improper and unethical conduct by the President and other state functionaries relating to alleged improper relationships and involvement of the Gupta family in the removal and appointment of Ministers and Directors of State-Owned Enterprises resulting in improper and possibly corrupt award of state contracts and benefits to the Gupta family's businesses.'[253]

This report with the unbelievably long name details the deep ties that the Indian brothers Ajay, Atul and Rajesh Gupta established with the political and business elite in charge of South Africa. Zuma and the Guptas, comically known as the Zuptas, looted state energy supplier Eskom, South African Airways and various other state-owned enterprises.[254] The Indian brothers manoeuvred themselves into the heart of power, handpicking and firing ministers and other officials.

By 2016, an army of journalists, opposition politicians and independent oversight bodies such as the Public Protector were focused on the Zuptas. Whistleblowers released leaks and exposed corrupt money trails. Zuma's downfall seemed imminent.

Around the time the state capture report was published, Zuma's tentacles had also reached into my private life.

One Sunday morning in September 2016, I woke up to explosive news. I opened my eyes and saw the *Sunday Times* spread out across the bed. I rubbed sleep out of my eyes and took a closer look at the newspaper. A picture of my then husband's mother with a look of surprise on her face was plastered across the front page, with the words BUSTED above it. My mother-in-law, Hazel Ngubeni, had been appointed High Commissioner (ambassador) in Singapore in 2013.[255]

When the lease on our rental house lapsed, my then husband and I decided to rent the house Hazel had just bought in the Johannesburg suburb Northcliff.

That Sunday morning, as I woke up in her house, I learned that from 1999 to 2001 Ngubeni had spent time in a New York jail following an arrest for trafficking cocaine while she was working as an air stewardess for SAA, the article laid out. There was mention of a previous arrest in 1995 for trafficking heroine. That first case was dropped when a crucial witness refused to testify against her. The second time, however, she went to jail. She had lied to President Zuma and the Singaporean president about her two years behind bars. Now investigative journalist Mzilikazi wa Africa had busted her lies wide open. It was surreal. Spread out on the bed, her surprised face on the front page looked back at me.

Hazel was recalled and then fired. Zuma denied knowing her,[256] but a quick google search reveals this was a lie. In a 2008 *Mail & Guardian* article, he mentions his comrade and Hazel's father, Michael Ngubeni, who was incarcerated with him on Robben Island.[257]

How could a drug trafficking stewardess end up being appointed the South African ambassador in Singapore? The short answer is Zuma.

Around the same time that Zuma's influence reaches into my private life, I also find out that his friends and associates are all over G4S South Africa. Sandile Zungu is one of them; his company Zungu Investments has a 13 per cent stake in G4S South Africa. Zungu bankrolled Zuma's presidential campaign[258] and is a known business partner of the Gupta family as well as former president Zuma's son Duduzane Zuma.[259] Not surprisingly, G4S provided security for practically every Gupta enterprise, including three Gupta-owned mines: Optimum Coal in Mpumalanga, the Brakfontein Colliery and the Shiva uranium mine in Hartbeesfontein.[260] The company also provided private security at the Gupta residence in Johannesburg,[261] as well as for the family computer business, Sahara Computers,[262] ANN7 and their Oakbay office. Strangely, when I sent G4S South Africa a list of questions about the Gupta contracts at the mines in Brakfontein, G4S denies it had provided security for the Gupta mines: 'G4S has not provided security services to either of the mines detailed in the enquiry. G4S previously had a small number of contracts with the Gupta family to provide security officers at city locations totalling less than 40 officers. G4S no longer has any contracts with the Gupta family.' I have clear evidence though – contracts, invoices and emails – that prove G4S provided security for most of the important Gupta businesses and assets.

More than once, G4S has hired people working for 'the other side', mostly South African government officials. This practice is called a 'revolving door' and it refers to 'the movement of individuals back and forth between public office and private companies,' according to a 2010 Transparency International Report.[263]

G4S hired Frikkie Venter immediately after he, as a DCS official, had drafted a prison contract that has favoured the BCC shareholders. Xander Snijders, a DCS official who worked at the controller's office, was hired by G4S. The company also poached Thabang Molise, who used to work for the union and now works at G4S's HR department. Transparency International flags this practice as problematic because of: '(…) increased opportunities for corruption. A rise in conflicts of interest, and the creation of a "revolving door" in government, demonstrates the thinning of boundaries between the public and private spheres.'

I suspect the company nearly made me an offer.

During the strike, G4S Africa HR director Elanie Kruger contacts me. I'd seen the Afrikaans-speaking blonde in a video interview she gave when G4S achieved Top Employer status in 2012. She looks like she's in her late forties. Her hair is neatly trimmed, a fringe balances on her eyebrows, and her tone of voice is soft and friendly. She's the one person in the company the workers don't seem to hate with a vengeance. They demand she resolve the strike by firing G4S HR director Stephen Page. Kruger flies into Bloemfontein[264] and addresses the striking workers at the Koppie, but Page is not fired.

Shortly after the first big exposé is published in October 2013, she invites me for a coffee 'to discuss' things. I'm interested. We make arrangements to meet at a coffee shop in Sandton, but she cancels when I tell her my boss will be joining us. I have always wondered whether she was about to offer me a job.

At the executive level, I only ever interact with Baker and Kruger. The two prisoner directors: Frikkie Venter and Johan Theron never cross my path.

Venter is appointed director of the prison shortly after it opens its doors. He resigns – some say he's fired – early in 2011. Venter is an old-school correctional services official. He claims he served as a prison guard for Nelson Mandela and Walter Sisulu on Robben Island.[265] After apartheid he climbs the DCS career ladder. He eventually becomes national director within the DCS. His last assignment is to negotiate the contract between the state and BCC.

And before the ink has dried, G4S appoints Venter to run the prison.

'Everything we do at Mangaung is driven towards supporting the government's drive to rectify the imbalances of the past,' Venter states in G4S's 2008 annual report.[266] This was a mere three years after prison managers had allegedly made Isaac Nelani's murder appear like a suicide.

Frikkie Venter is loud and colourful. His Facebook profile is set to public, giving the viewer an in-depth view of his gallery of reasonable amateur photography. Venter also speaks to the press and presents in Parliament.

In a 2004 parliamentary submission,[267] Venter speaks about the prison in glowing terms, striking an upbeat and confident tone. 'We have invested heavily in the rehabilitation of offenders, to enhance the safety of the community,' Venter tells the gathered parliamentarians.

In 2004, however, unimaginable violence shook the prison. In October 2004, a 28-gang member murders a rival gang member in broad daylight. It is so horrific that eyewitnesses can barely speak about the disembowelment and murder. Shakes is called to the incident and finds the dying man on the floor, his internal organs exposed, his lungs heaving in his chest. Meanwhile, the gang general is parading around the cells with the rival's intestines draped around his neck.[268] Warders and inmates flee the scene screaming. Shakes collects the organs in evidence bags. An eyewitness writes in an affidavit that the deceased had asked to be transferred to another unit because he didn't feel safe, but the prison had ignored his request. This affidavit also claims prison officials were notified beforehand of the impending gang fight, but that they'd taken no action.

Johan Theron serves as Venter's deputy before succeeding him as prison director. Compared to Venter, Theron is faceless and invisible. He's practically non-existent online. He has no profile picture on LinkedIn and no photo gallery on his Facebook page. His Facebook profile picture shows Theron, his wife and his grandson sitting in the sun, with a sunflower placed in a heart-shaped vase on a table in front of them. All his LinkedIn page reveals is that he, like Venter, has worked for the DCS since 1979.

During the eight years I investigate the prison, I barely get to speak to any G4S representatives. So, when Bernard* contacts me, I'm surprised to say the least. Bernard used to work at G4S headquarters as a manager, alongside people like Baker and Kruger. He knows them well. Bernard had contacted me through LinkedIn. He meets with me on a sunny afternoon in 2018 in a coffee shop in Melville, my Joburg neighbourhood.

G4S employment contracts include stranglehold confidentiality clauses, with a promise to sue any employee who divulges any information about the company to third parties. Bernard is taking a risk speaking to me.

Every day, Bernard tells me, he would drive to Centurion and enter the heavily secured building of G4S South Africa. It is situated in an office park in Centurion, a small suburban town between Johannesburg and Pretoria. The building is divided into two parts, square and white, with a huge black and red G4S logo facing outward. I look at the building on Google Earth. Seen from above, the South African head office resembles two ships facing each other. They are like two giant puzzle pieces that slot into each other. The top half of the building is a white box-like structure, supported by pillars. Beneath the white top there are big tinted windows, behind which G4S's office space is situated. The building is fortified with fences, cameras and security lights.

While sipping impossibly green wheatgrass juice, Bernard tells me how in 2015 a 'town hall meeting' is called within the bowels of the G4S ship. Townhall meetings in company speak mean that there's an urgent message that the entire company workforce needs to hear. Every single employee has to drop what they're doing and head to the main atrium in the highly secured building.

When all employees are gathered, Mike Muller, a former army colonel who trained with the Israeli Defence Force[269] but who is then

---

*   Not his real name

the newly appointed director of G4S's Secure Solutions, addresses the crowd.

'We were told not to mention Ruth Hopkins or her work and to not engage with her,' Bernard says. 'If the media asks questions about her, refer them to the HR department. We were basically told to act as if Ruth Hopkins and her investigation didn't exist.'

My prison exposé had dominated headlines for a few days, maybe weeks, in 2013, but then it died down. The DCS started 'losing' evidence soon after a team was appointed to investigate allegations of mismanagement and violations of prisoners' rights in Mangaung prison. What looked and smelled like a cover-up started. In May 2015, The minister who had ordered the investigation was moved to a position abroad.[270] The video evidence of what basically boiled down to torture was dismissed and ignored. The union who had supported the strikes and had demanded G4S leave the country changed its tune and started to urge workers to return to work, eliciting a mass exodus of members from POPCRU. All of this took place in plain sight, and I sat and watched as everything was swept under the carpet.

Bernard says he decided to reach out to me because he felt uncomfortable with how the company treats its workers: 'There was no humanity in the company. G4S stood for everything that was wrong. The people working for the company never knew where they stood. They could be fired any day.'

Bernard understands the company, having been positioned in the management structures of the company for two years, he knows it's not just management who are being poorly treated. 'The guards are not treated well,' he confirms. 'They're exploited and tired, and that is something you can see from management level.'

The company's profit model, Bernard says, is based on a poorly paid and disposable workforce at the low end and very well paid – and therefore loyal – executives at the top. 'They make a lot of money because they don't care about humans.'

Bernard sends me a batch of his work files. In the thousands of excel sheets, emails and other documents that, among other things, prove that G4S had multiple contracts with the Gupta family – I find an interesting report. The organisation NOSA has compiled it, a South African company that provides safety and security audits for businesses. Interestingly, NOSA audited Mangaung prison in November 2013, just one month after chaos had descended and the department had to take control of the prison. It provides an interesting time stamp of what must have been a chaotic time.

The department dealt with the chaos that had erupted at the prison by locking everyone up for 23 hours a day, also known as Lockdown. This, so the report details: '(...) has seriously impacted on the effectiveness of maintaining parts of the prison as due to current lockdown conditions when prisoners are unavailable to perform maintenance and related duties.' The auditors scrutinised safety, health and environment (SHE) standards and they flagged a high number of injuries that had taken place at the facility in the previous 12-month period (2013/2014). This signified: 'an urgent need to be addressed in order to curb the current trend injuries occurring between inmates and G4S Wardens and prevent a further worsening that could potentially result in fatalities.'

The report goes on to assess policies in the field of restraint of medical patients in the prison. The guiding policy document, however, the authors of the report point out 'does not refer to the staff of G4S, DCS or any of the medical practitioners at the MCC medical centre.' The auditors complain medical records are not accessible. 'Records, especially emergency orders, in the back up control/command room used by top management were not dated, thereby creating uncertainty whether they were the latest updated versions of emergency orders.' And: 'Availability of records (documented procedures and work instructions) for verification purposes in the medical station was challenging at times.'

Despite the serious concerns, the prison is awarded NOSA certification.

Bernard's discomfort grows when G4S managers boast about another certification: its status as a 'Top Employer' through the Top Employers Institute in Amsterdam, the Netherlands.[271] G4S hold this status from 2012 to 2018, during and after my investigation is published and the information about a massive strike, the use of electroshocking and forced medication with antipsychotic drugs is in the public domain.

Bernard attends the 2014 'Top Employer' function, shortly after my investigation of the strike is published. Two-thirds of the workforce are dismissed following the industrial action in this year, yet G4S still retains its Top Employer status, for the third consecutive year.

'G4S won that award in a year when many people were being retrenched and when employees were very unhappy with G4S,' Bernard complains. 'I knew about the prison, but nothing was done about it, and no one was allowed to speak out about it. So how can you be a top employer under these circumstances?'

Bernard says the Top Employer status is a farce. The HR department of the company fills in the forms and employees are not consulted. Companies that pay a handsome sum to the Top Employers Institute, Bernard alleges, are guaranteed this status.

A phone call with David Plink, the Global CEO of the Top Employers Institute that is based in Amsterdam, the Netherlands reveals that companies have to pay 16 600 euros just to enter the certification process. 'We send them questions around various HR topics such as acquisition, compensation and benefits and performance management. The Institute then performs an audit of the company,' Plink says. The vetting procedure is a theoretical exercise that excludes the views of employees. 'The process focuses on an audit of the HR strategies and practices that are in place to develop employees. No consultation of employees takes place as this is conducted via the organisation's own employee engagement survey,' the Top Employers Institute's spokesperson Billy Elliot added in an email in July 2019.

G4S employees, meanwhile, are not satisfied with their 'top' employer. A sore point for many South African G4S workers is the Employee Share Ownership Plan (ESOP) that was established in 2005. G4S employees are supposed to own 13 per cent of shares of

G4S South Africa through this plan. In 2018, the opposition party, the Economic Freedom Fighters (EFF),[272] however claims that this is a fake deal because employees have told them they are yet to see a cent. The Broad-Based Black Economic Empowerment (B-BBEE) Commission is, at the time of writing, investigating G4S's BEE obligations, even though the minister had promised parliament that this investigation would be finished by May 2019.[273] G4S South Africa's main shareholder, Sandile Zungu, claims in a WhatsApp conversation with me that the company has not been profitable and that G4S can therefore not pay shareholders their dividends. Why a successful billionaire businessman like Zungu would continue to invest in a company that is not profitable is a question no one can or will answer.

Bernard's discomfort with the company's moral attitude, meanwhile, comes to a head one day. The glass panels at the entrance of the building bear stickers with the words 'Integrity, Loyalty, Trust'. These are supposed to reflect the company's values. 'But I never saw any of those values adhered to,' Bernard says.

Bernard's urge to speak up grew. 'I told my team that we needed to come into the office during the weekend with soap and a bucket to wash these words off the windows.' He felt that the company's track record did not reflect the words stuck onto the windows. 'Shortly after that, I left the company,' he says.

Bernard says the British influence in G4S was 'overbearing'. G4S's 'Africa president' has always been a Brit. 'All our accounts are pegged to the British pound. All they care about is profit. G4S has no idea of how things work in Africa.'

How they get away with it

Researcher Andrew Bowman writes in his book **What a Waste**[274] *about outsourcing in the UK:* 'Outsourcing contracts are typically announced in press releases making unsubstantiated claims about the millions that will be saved. But questions about what exactly is going on and what is finally delivered cannot be answered because contracts are usually withheld on the ground of commercial confidentiality.'

Outsourcing risk portfolios such as defence, national security and the incarceration system benefits governments. Possible filled pockets and greased palms aside, the outsourcing of these politically volatile dossiers offers opportunities for political blame shifting, further enabled by vague legal definitions and murky chains of responsibility in outsourcing contracts.

As a global company, G4S is informed by the priorities of the financial markets and G4S's wealthy private investors, more often than not global hedge fund managers. G4S's investors seek high rates of return and growth in their capital values for their investments. Low risk margins, profitable contracts and easy exit strategies usually produce profits. This profit-driven focus means the company does not necessarily have the expertise and skills to operate within a certain sector.

Because of their tenuous legal ties with nation states and domestic legal systems, G4S easily escapes legal responsibility. British lawyers with the law firm Leigh Day[275] tried to sue G4S for the abuse committed in Mangaung prison, before the London High Court, but the company challenged the jurisdiction of the court. They assured the judge that G4S was not trying to escape accountability, as it had no problem appearing before a South African judge. Not surprisingly maybe, in the year 2020 still no one has been held accountable and not a single inmate has received compensation for the harm caused.

15

Plus ça change…

'Do you pray with a candle?' Lufuno Nembambula asks me. A sharply dressed, lawyerly type, buttoned up and alert, Nembambula is a regional coordinator working for JICS, the semi-independent prison watchdog. It's the end of March 2017, and we're in a drab office in the centre of Bloemfontein, waiting for others to arrive for the monthly meeting of the Independent Correctional Centre Visitors (ICCVs), the men and women who, on behalf of JICS, go into prisons to record prisoner complaints. On the oblong table around which we're seated there are paper plates with crisps, nuts and raisins and two-litre bottles of cooldrinks. We're making small talk.

Nembambula's question poses a familiar dilemma. I could have told her 'no I don't' and left it at that. But then there will be a follow-up questions like 'well, do you pray in darkness?' or something. I could have told her: 'I don't pray because I don't subscribe to the idea of a God.' That answer satisfies me, because it is honest. But I also know that it will set me apart, draw attention, raise eyebrows and quite possibly put people off me. And I am there as a journalist. After years of trying and phoning the wrong people, I have been invited to an ICCV meeting and I need to make a good impression. Peter Choma, an ICCV at Mangaung prison, takes a seat next to me. Welcome, *pastor* Choma, someone says. 'I don't really pray anymore, but I was raised a Catholic and they love candles,' I finally reply.

I manage to avoid probing questions about my spirituality, or perceived lack thereof, and steer the conversation to the differences in worship between Lutherans and Catholics and fire hazards.

My attempt not to stand out or draw attention is futile. I'm the only white person in the room and moreover have written damning reports on Mangaung, which I imagine most attendees have read or heard about.

As more people trickle in, I try to read their expressions. A wry smile, a tired look. Pastor Choma glances at me with a half-smile and keeps looking at me from the corner of his eye. From the corner of my eye, I try to read the complaint forms in front of him.

I scavenge the meeting for information, hoping to capture names, positions, dates, case numbers in conversations and documents. The chairperson, Ms M. Vumazonke, formally opens the meeting. A tedious discussion of a long list of admin issues follows.

The minutes of the previous meeting reveal that in January 2017, there were five incidents involving 'unplanned uses of force' in Mangaung, as well as two suicide attempts. The minutes also mention a two-year backlog at the Bloemspruit police station. The officers at Bloemspruit are the ones investigating all cases – of assault, mostly, but also other offences – that take place at the prison.

A tired-looking warrant officer A.M. Mofokeng is seated at the head of the table, together with her colleague officer Constable R. Mokhojoa. Mofokeng has dark bags under her eyes, uncombed hair, and she explains that there were five cases reported in the previous month: minor transgressions such as theft and damage to property. 'But you need to explain why this backlog hasn't been dealt with,' chairperson Vumazonke says. In a continued exchange between the two women, it is revealed that Bloemspruit has a backlog of more than 100 cases, stretching back two years. Mokhojoa tells the group he's two days into his new job there and offers his deepest apologies for the backlog. He solemnly promises to personally do something about it, adding, 'The founding principle of the SAPS is: to "protect and serve", isn't it?'

When I start investigating Mangaung in 2012, Bloemspruit already has a two-year backlog of cases. I found out that for a period of two years there was no one at the station tasked with investigating cases at Mangaung prison. The two officers on the Mangaung beat, who had themselves been convicted for armed robbery, were never replaced, and they'd been gone two years.

In 2015, I visit Bloemspruit to look at dockets of prisoners who'd opened cases, the 'lucky few' who had been assigned case numbers. The cases are usually dropped because of 'lack of evidence"

Inmates' requests to see a police officer are filled out on prison complaints and requests forms. But these forms usually disappear, so prisoners tell me. The few that reach the police compost in the backlog pile. This means the prisoners also know they're fair game to a frustrated, underpaid and overstretched workforce at the prison. The only avenue available to air their discontent and frustration is the language they know well: violence.

'I stabbed the warder, because we have no other way of expressing our anger,' prisoner Neo* tells me the day after the ICCV meeting. His feet are shackled, as are his tattoo-covered hands. His gang affiliation, the number 28, is marked in between his thumb and index finger. His eyes and body are jerky; he seems irritated. I catch him as he's leaving the Bloemfontein Magistrate's Court, where he's standing trial for stabbing a warder two years earlier, in 2015. None of the prisoners' cases I heard of or have investigated have, to my knowledge, gone to court. But when a prisoner stabs a guard or damages prison property, there is justice. His sentence is increased – by months and even years.

After a minute or two, a G4S warder gives Neo a little push. With the chains attached to his ankles, Neo stumbles and lunges forward, his arms outstretched, but they are also chained. The warder grabs his shoulder and averts a fall. Together they walk back to the van waiting to transport him back to the prison.

---

*   Not his real name

The next day I meet with Zakhele Mahlangu at Pelonomi Hospital in Bloemfontein. I speak to him while he's waiting to see the doctor. Eighteen months earlier, in September 2015, the Ninjas assaulted him after he'd ended up in a gang fight. 'They took me to Broadway,' he says. 'There, they kicked me and electroshocked me. A white man, I can't remember his name, kicked me in the balls.' The next day, Zakhele had blood in his urine, and he went to see the prison doctor. The doctor documented injuries to his head, kidneys and private parts. Zakhele reported it to the police, but no one followed up.

He still needs medical treatment for the injuries to his kidneys. G4S, BCC and the DCS do not respond to Zakhele's injuries, when I send them a list of allegations.

After I break the Mangaung story, I'm ready to move on to something new. Shortly after Minister S'bu Ndebele launches an investigation that would leave 'no stone unturned',[276] in November 2013, lawyers with the London-based firm Leigh Day contact me. They're interested in representing the prisoners before the High Court of Justice in London in a damage claim vis-à-vis G4S. They visit 43 prisoners in South Africa, take statements and also speak to Dan and other sources. Accountability seems to be on the cards.

Not only does nothing ever come from the DCS investigation, G4S also challenges the jurisdiction of the case set for the London court, claiming they would rather face a judge in South Africa. When it becomes clear that UK courts lack sufficient jurisdiction, the case is referred to the local Legal Resources Centre (LRC), but they lack the funds to pursue it. Not one of the 43 prisoners has thus far received any form of compensation or acknowledgement of their pain and suffering.

I start to lose hope that the wrongdoing I'd exposed would ever lead to any form of justice. It feels like a wall of silence and indifference has been erected around the prison.

This also means, however, that I just can't let it go. Like a dog digging for a bone, I keep investigating the prison and the cover-up. Prisoners and warders keep sending me their complaints.

Guards and prisoners tell me about one particularly bloody fight that happens in August 2016, almost three years after I thought justice would be served.

Melvin Faas, John Marbi and a man known simply as Hartzenberg attempt to stab three EST members. The Ninjas retaliate, and the three prisoners are taken to Broadway. A guard writes to me, explaining that guards on duty cuffed them, kicked and shocked them in front of prison management. 'Marbi's ribs are broken and Faas has internal injuries and broken teeth. Hartzenburg has bleeding ears,' writes the guard. He further claims the prisoners do not get to see a doctor but are rather held in Broadway for a month.

Around the same time, a prisoner called Alfred Matlala tries to stab a DSO in the Altcourse unit, which triggers retaliation by seven DSOs. Matlala is admitted to an external hospital with severe head injuries. 'He nearly died,' the guard who transported him to the hospital tells me.

Prison management suspends the seven DSOs following the assault on Matlala yet claims the three EST members acted in self-defence against Faas, Marbi and Hartzenberg. This, so many prison guards claim, is because the EST members are with the union POPCRU, and the seven DSOs signed up with a rival union. Dan's skinny soldier is one of the seven men who are suspended. Not long after that, Shakes is dismissed. Is G4S slowly getting rid of its troublemakers?

It is not just the inmates who are ending up in hospital with broken limbs and internal injuries. When the guards returned to Mangaung prison after the strike, they were disconcerted to find out the toilet pots were still ceramic, which meant inmates could still fashion lethal weapons out of broken shards. While the company had not replaced the toilet pots, except for a number of cells in the Wolds unit, it has kitted out every guard with a helmet and a pepper spray. They have also installed cages around the guards' workstations in the prison units, so DSOs can safely retreat. No one understands why G4S spent money on these things and not on the toilet pots, an issue guards have for years raised with management, to no avail.

In March 2017, when a prisoner stabs a warder in the head and chest, prison management immediately retorts that he was not wearing his helmet. He ends up with serious head injuries in the prison hospital's intensive care unit. 'I nearly died,' he tells me some days after he's released. He's not offered any significant counselling.

I keep having regular meetings with the guards. Since Dan's departure from the prison, though, there is little action. The guards seem drained, resigned. Many of them are suspended or dismissed. Without a fearless rabble-rouser like Dan, they seem worse off than before.

Briefly, a big man called Big Show tries to fill Dan's shoes. True to his name, Big Show is a looming big hulk of a man, with a pitch-black beard and round eyes. We meet one night in 2017 after he'd knocked off from his job as a vocational trainer at Mangaung. Although Big Show's size makes him an excellent candidate for the EST, he chose to work on educational projects with the prisoners.

He's the first person who could substantiate what I'd heard before: that prisoners were still being injected.

Plus ça change…

Around the same time, Thabo Godfrey Botsane tells me the same thing on the phone from Grootvlei – that the injections are continuing at Mangaung. Prisoners coming in and out of Mangaung have to go through Grootvlei first, as it is a processing prison.

Following his release from Mangaung in 2013, Thabo is now back in prison – in Grootvlei this time – on trumped-up mugging charges and awaiting trial.

After his release, Thabo joins the National Unemployed Voters Organisation (NUVO), an activist organisation advocating for the poor and unemployed. The popularity of NUVO irritates the local ANC, so they frame Thabo for a mugging that had taken place at ANC stalwart Thabo Manyoni's lecture at the Free State University in Bloemfontein in May 2017.[277] Manyoni is vying for the position of ANC chair of the Free State, a hotly contested seat that the incumbent Free State ANC chair Ace Magashule wants to retain. When someone is mugged outside the lecture hall, the Magashule supporters claim it is Thabo who robbed that someone of his cell phone and beat him up. It takes Thabo nine months in Grootvlei prison and a lot of money he doesn't have to get back home to his family.

But while he is in Grootvlei, he's my 'man on the inside', and during the nine months he's held at Grootvlei, he interviews approximately ten incoming prisoners. Grootvlei is a processing prison, which means that everyone on their way to or from Mangaung prison goes through Grootvlei. Practically every one of the inmates tells him he had been assaulted, electroshocked or both. Thabo also speaks to men who claim they've been injected.

My sources at Mangaung tell me that following my exposés, the injections are no longer carried out within the facility. Prison management have decided to send prisoners requiring an injection to Pelonomi Hospital, about twenty minutes down the road from Mangaung.

Officers responsible for transporting prisoners tell me they had driven inmates Vuyo Ntshobololo and Anelize Gana to Pelonomi for their injections. They say both Ntshobololo and Gana want to speak with me. I ask Thabo to talk to Ntshobololo in Grootvlei and he confirms he wants to see me.

Early in 2018, I visit Ntshobololo in Grootvlei. It is a Sunday, and there are maybe five other people waiting. A woman arrives and provides a name and prisoner number to the warders. Suddenly, she falls to her knees and starts wailing, 'Run away! Run away!' She's tugging at her hair and face. An elderly man and a middle-aged woman rush towards her. They cradle her head in their hands and splash some water on her face. The warders behind the counter watch the unfolding drama with blank gazes. The woman has just found out her brother died in Grootvlei, a few hours before she arrived. The prison had not yet informed her, and she was expecting to see him that day. I want to say something to her, but I don't know what. She's sliding off her chair again and onto the floor, and the wailing continues. I offer her my bottled water.

When I'm called for my visit with Ntshobololo, my mind is still going over what I had just observed. The woman's raw, exposed grief was somehow heightened by the vacant looks of the warders, who sat perfectly still behind the glass, one of them chewing gum. Incarceration is not just a punishment for the individual offender – it affects entire families.

Ntshobololo is small and thin. I wonder if his family is worried about him. He's already seated on a bench in the visitors' room when I arrive. When he starts speaking, I realise that he is not well. He tells me he suffers from 'Amafufunyana', an affliction known among the Zulu and Xhosa people. People affected by it are considered to be possessed by demons or evil spirits. Traditional healers are typically consulted to exorcise the demons or spirits.

Ntshobololo tells me he's the son of God. When I look at him, puzzled, he tries to clarify: 'I am the News of God.'

'I want to know what happened to you in Mangaung prison,' I explain.

'They sent me to a psychiatrist,' he says. 'But I didn't want those injections. They make me feel dizzy and sleepy. Like I am not myself.'

Plus ça change...

Guards at the prison had told me about Ntshobololo. They mentioned he's 'crazy' and difficult to talk to.

It makes me wonder how Ntshobololo ended up in prison in the first place. Was he considered fit to stand trial? He was clearly delusional and, according to South African law, should not be in prison, but in a psychiatric institution.

Ntshobololo provides the first indication that the injections are continuing following my investigation.

I try tracing Anelize Gana, but the guards tell me he'd been transferred, and no one seems to know where.

More names start trickling in. Thabo tells me about another inmate, who was briefly in Grootvlei with him and he said he had been injected several times, against his will and that he is desperate to talk to me. I find out he's also been transferred and no one knows where to.

The Department of Correctional Services, meanwhile, is still sitting on the report that was supposed to detail evidence of the allegations. Under the Promotion of Access to Information Act (PAIA) Wits lawyers started a case against DCS to retrieve the DCS investigation report.[278]

Then G4S makes a bizarre move. At the eleventh hour, days before the deadline for DCS answering affidavits would have expired, G4S asks to be added to the case. Curiously, G4S responded differently to a previous PAIA request by the South African History Archives (SAHA) in 2016,[279] related to the Treasury guidelines that stipulated that feasibility and affordability studies had to be carried out before PPP projects were embarked on. Specifically, SAHA demanded G4S provide documents pertaining to feasibility and affordability of the prison contract that they would have had to produce, had Treasury Regulation 16 been in place when the contract for Mangaung prison was awarded. Regulation 16, however, was only adopted in 2003,[280] long after the prison had opened its doors. Heinrich Hoffman, regional legal manager, claimed G4S was not subject to PAIA. 'I can also confirm that G4S Secure Solutions (SA) (Pty) Ltd is not a public body', he wrote to SAHA. The South African freedom of information laws apply equally to public and private bodies (as long as the latter carries out public services).[281]

In 2018, however, G4S changes its mind. It actively asks a judge to be added as a defendant in a PAIA case.

The company's first motion is to apply for an 'in camera' hearing during which the underlying evidence of the investigation would be presented to the judge. In camera means the hearing will not be public, there will be no (publicly available) court records, basically no one will be able to find out what the evidence is. The company claims it does not want to violate the privacy of inmates.

The judge denies the in-camera hearing. Then, in his final ruling on 7 February 2020, Judge Pierre Rabie deems G4S's petition to only release a redacted report 'irrelevant and futile'. The court marks its disapproval of the manner in which G4S has conducted this case, by ordering G4S to pay all legal costs of the applicants.

Meanwhile, Minister of Justice and Correctional Services Ronald Lamola reacts to the case as if he has nothing to do with it, while he is the main respondent in this case. Astoundingly, he tells the *Citizen* newspaper: 'The minister is disturbed to hear of such allegations of torture, said to have taken place at the Mangaung Correctional Centre,' (…) 'Should these be proven to be true, this surely goes against the values and principles of what our first democratically elected president, Nelson Mandela, stood for.'[282]

When I meet a man, whom I will call Karel, I realise that DCS does not intend to release the report, ever.

I meet with Karel at the café of the Wits Art Museum, known as WAM café, which is a canteen-like restaurant that serves some of the best vegetarian food in Johannesburg. WAM café is on the ground floor of the building that houses the Wits Justice Project. The café caters to visitors of the museum, as well as academic staff of Wits departments – including mine – in the building.

It is an unforgivingly chilly place in winter. The cold air seems to gather and multiply. The second-floor balcony looks down onto the art café leaving an airy two-storey space open to the elements. Facing the balcony is an equally high glass façade overlooking Bertha Street, the extension of Jan Smuts Avenue, leading into Braamfontein.

Karel claims several senior DCS officials have asked him to 'help' with the Mangaung case. They sent him to meet with me. 'They want justice,' he says. I ask him about the DCS report. 'All the evidence has disappeared,' he says. 'A "bakkie" full of files has gone "missing" …'

In August 2018, we meet again in a big busy mall on the outskirts of Johannesburg.

Karel used to work with the DCS task force that carried out the investigation at Mangaung prison. He isn't the first source I have encountered on the task team, but he certainly is the first source who contacted me, instead of the other way around. He has taken this step because, so he says, it bothers him that the investigation was obstructed. Things are not right and they need to be exposed, he says.

When the DCS team arrived at the prison in early October 2013, G4S welcomed them with a charm offensive. 'We would be offered tickets to Loftus (rugby), tickets to soccer, wine and whiskey,' Karel relates. On Fridays there were company braais, where DCS and G4S managers could mingle. Karel says he never accepted a bribe or attended any of the braais.

In a WhatsApp exchange with me, Karel writes he is feeling 'hot under the collar'. When I ask him to explain, he writes: 'I am building up anger, because I have seen records and interviewed victims and it just disappeared into thin air. I am traumatized, emotionally drained, I still hear the last screaming of Nelani from the video.' Isaac Nelani's last minutes were apparently captured on CCTV footage. His death formed part of the DCS investigation.

Karel also reveals what happened to the report: '3 copies were made, colleagues drove the evidence and the reports to Leeuwkop

Prison in February 2015, from Bloemfontein. They met at Leeuwkop Golf Course [...] and Modise and Jolingana came to sign all three copies and each took theirs and Modise took an extra one to Britta Rotmann who had to forward to Mokoena of BCC ... and indeed it was delivered coz [sic] when they responded they demanded that we attach the source documents, which we did [...] and it was then swept under the carpet till today and G4S never reverted back.'

In May 2019, Mervin West, a prisoner held at Mangaung, sends me what feels like a never-ending list of incidents that he started recording in 2017:

- On 6 October 2017, inmate Randy Hoogdstaander stabs an official by the name of Thami in street 6 in Wolds.
- On 10 October 2017, at 10.15 am, Buckley Hall, a prisoner by the name of Vuyo, a 26 gangster, stabs an official.
- On 12 October 2017, Wolds Unit, prisoner CK, a 27 gangster, stabs an official called Thami. CK is cuffed, but somehow one of the prisoners uncuffs CK, and that is how he manages to stab an official 'very badly in the face'.
- On 19 December 2017, in Mount Gambier, prisoner Kleinpa Papier, a 28 gangster, is stabbed, strangled and killed by gang members with different affiliations.
- On 20 December 2017, in Mount Gambier, seven 28 gangsters stabbed five Airforce gangsters.
- On 21 December 2017, also in Mount Gambier, 26 and 28 gangsters stab four officials.
- On 24 December 2017, in Wolds, street 5, a prisoner who goes by the name of Tsegisho is stabbed by a 26 gangster.
- On 24 December 2017, a prisoner commits suicide by hanging himself. The unit supervisor gets fired.
- On 24 December 2017, an official by the name of Segwai is stabbed on the soccer grounds by a 26 gangster.

Plus ça change…

- On 12 October 2017, in Port Phillip, an inmate by the name of Brandon stabs an official.
- On 26 December 2017, in Rye Hill, 26 and 28 gangsters stab four officials.

Internal prison documents pertaining to Wolds reflect that employees are assaulted there:
- On 7, 9 and 21 May 2018 two employees are assaulted.
- Two officials are assaulted in two separate incidents on 4 June 2018.
- On 10 June 2018, another employee is assaulted.
- On 23 September 2018, an employee is assaulted again.
- On 28 September, 7 and 12 October, 18 November and 5 and 7 December 2018 employees are assaulted again.

But it's not only the staff being assaulted in Wolds, the documents reveal:
- On 10, 13 and 14 December 2018, prisoners assault other prisoners.
- On 14 December 2018, a second assault takes place.
- On 21 December 2018, three gang-related attacks on other prisoners take place.
- On 22 December 2018, two prisoners are assaulted in two separate incidents.
- On 23 December 2018, a prisoner and an official are assaulted in street 5.
- On 28 December, two inmates are assaulted.

And the list goes on in 2019 …
- Then on 3, 5 and 12 January 2019, prisoners assault prisoners.
- On 17 January 2019, there are five incidents where prisoners assault each other using ceramic shards of broken toilets.
- On 8 February 2019, another prisoner is assaulted.
- On 14 and 17 February 2019, prisoners are assaulted.
- Then, on 5 February 2019, three employees are assaulted.

West also sends me photos of internal records from the Wolds unit, where he is held. These records confirm the attacks against guards in Wolds.

I send the list of allegations to Pappie Mokoena, who is legally responsible as the chairperson of BCC. He gets back to me with a two-page letter. 'As we have advised you in the past, we would not condone nor tolerate abuse at the Mangaung Correctional Centre and would deal with any such conduct should we become aware of it. Based on our previous engagements with you we do not believe that you intend to give BCC a fair opportunity to respond or that you intend to report in a balanced manner on matters that relate to the Mangaung Correctional Centre,' he writes.

His next point is bizarre. 'It is a matter of great concern that although you are on record as having been aware of such allegations you have failed to provide any substantive information that can be used to ascertain the merits of the allegations, outside of vague statements and unreasonably short publication deadlines.' I had previously sent him names of victims and perpetrators, prison numbers, dates and places and information on the legal and medical steps the affected person had been able to take. I gave him verifiable information that he never verified.

Mokoena rounds off his belligerent statement with a threat of legal action. He does not respond to a single allegation of abuse that I had sent him.

The men of Mangaung keep contacting me. And I keep asking them to provide details of their claims, so I can follow up, knowing full well that the DCS and G4S will probably never respond to my queries and that the Bloemspruit SAPS has not followed up on a single prisoner's case that I came across in my eight years of research.

The one thing this uneven playing field has left me with after eight years are names. I write down names of prisoners who died. Then my sources send me five names of prisoners who they claim are still being injected. Neither BCC, nor the DCS nor G4S has ever responded to these allegations, other than to deny them. I can't access the inmates' medical files and I can also no longer visit them in prison.

Meanwhile, on the national stage, a deep rot and corruption within the Department of Correctional Services surfaces when Bosasa's former operations chief Angelo Agrizzi spills the beans before the Zondo Commission on his payments to DCS officials. The correctional services system has become deeply implicated in state capture in South Africa. Agrizzi reveals a web of patronage. At the heart of it are people with familiar names: former national commissioner Zach Modise, former acting national commissioner Nontsikelelo Jolingana, deputy regional commissioner for the Free State Grace Molatedi, former head of contracts at the department, Joseph Maako, CFO of the department, Patrick Gillingham. This network of DCS officials were also responsible in their supervisory roles for Mangaung prison. While it feels like the net around the company is drawing close, G4S's silent strategy also seems to pay off. The red flags are all there, but a G4S whistleblower has yet to stand up.

Instead of engaging with me, G4S, the BEE shareholders to the prison contract and the Department of Correctional Services have chosen to deny, threaten, delay and intimidate, hoping I will back off.

In this system that is rigged to protect vested interests while simultaneously suppressing evidence of malfeasance and abuse, the prisoners have lost before they can even begin. Bheki Dlamini, James Mothulwe, Boxer Maphikisa, Thabo Godfrey Botsane, Ishmael Mohlomi, Francis Makatsa, Captain Rampa, Tebogo Meje – some of the men I met and whose cases I investigated – they never stood a chance. Their pain is not recognised by the criminal justice system or before civil courts. All that remains of their humanity is their names, a reminder to the world that they are not just criminals, offenders, inmates, prisoners. They are humans.

G4S financial

In 2019, G4S presented its financial results for 2018.[283] Though G4S had produced £7,3 billion in revenue, the company had more than halved its pre-tax profits because it was ordered to pay millions of dollars in compensation to workers and detainees in the US, UK and Australia. In previous years, the company had seen growth and profits. The company's overall growth increased by 17 per cent from 2013 to 2017.[284] It derives most of its income in the UK and Northern America, yet employs the highest number of people in Africa. G4S is focused on 'emerging markets' and sees future growth in Africa, Asia and Latin America.[285,286]

The security behemoth has an incredibly complicated, expansive business structure. On international corporate database Orbis, there are more than a thousand holding companies registered, close to a hundred shareholders and approximately 1 200 subsidiaries.

Its main shareholders are major equity and investment companies. Invesco owns nearly 11 per cent of the company.[287] Invesco is domiciled in Bermuda, a known tax haven. It manages assets worth a staggering $888 billion. BlackRock is the next prominent shareholder, with a 5.5 per cent share. BlackRock is an American firm and was named the 'company that owns the world' by Investigate Europe,[288] a collective of investigative journalists who looked into the company that manages assets worth $6.3 trillion. It has shares and voting rights not just in G4S, but in a host of other European companies in the fields of energy, security and transport. It is not just an investment company, it also audits and advises, sometimes to the same companies it holds shares in. Harris Associates[289] is a Chicago-based investment company that manages assets worth $141 billion. Mondrian Investment Partners,[290] a UK investment company, has a 5 per cent share in G4S. G4S has other corporate shareholders with not the best reputations in terms of human rights: UK defence company BAE systems and Dutch oil multinational Shell for example both own shares.

The £860 billion Norwegian Government Pension Fund Global (GPFG), one of the company's major shareholders, with 2.33 per cent of shares, divested from G4S in 2019. It cited concerns 'that the company contributes to, or is responsible for serious or systematic human rights violations'.[291] *Norway's Council of Ethics monitors investments in the country and advised GPFG to divest because of G4S's treatment of migrant workers in the Gulf states, mainly Qatar and the United Arab Emirates, where the company employs 18 000 mostly migrant workers from India, Nepal, Pakistan and the Philippines. The Council on Ethics investigated the treatment of migrant workers in Gulf states employed by G4S. The workers related how they had to pay a recruitment fee in their home country to obtain work for G4S in Qatar,*[292] *that they were misled about wages and working conditions,*[293] *that their passports were confiscated, that they were not allowed to switch employers, that they were pressured to work when ill and that they were not given consent to travel. The Ethics Council noted that G4S has drafted a statement on human trafficking,*[294] *but that it has not adhered to its own standards. '[T]he Council attaches more weight to the fact that the company does not seem to have followed up its own risk assessments and guidelines to improve the workers' situation.'*[295] *It advised GPFG: 'that G4S PLC be excluded from investment by the Government Pension Fund Global (GPFG) due to an unacceptable risk that the company is contributing to systematic human rights violations.'*[296]

G4S has registered holding companies in tax havens. The Guardian *reported in 2013 that the company had 14 registered holding companies in the British Overseas Territories and crown dependencies, all known offshore tax havens.*[297] *It also has companies registered on the Cayman Islands and in Luxembourg. While this doesn't prove that G4S is evading tax, it is near impossible to find out which taxes it does pay, as these places are known as 'secrecy jurisdictions', which means they barely disclose any financial information. In 2013, however, the* Daily Telegraph *reported that G4S paid no tax in the UK in 2012.*[298]

G4S promises on its website that it adheres to tax regimes throughout the world: 'We have established and maintain appropriate policies and compliance processes to ensure the integrity of our tax returns, and timely and accurate tax payments in all countries in which we operate.'[299]

But that was not always the case. In Australia, for example, the company earns a substantial amount from government contracts which are funded by taxpayers' money: G4S runs two private prisons and a forensic hospital and it provides various criminal law and migration related services, such as electronic tagging and migrant transport. It received an Australian $2.2-million rebate in 2012, despite not having paid any tax that year. The Sydney Morning Herald claimed that in the same year, G4S also paid zero taxes in the UK. Greg Barton, a professor at Monash University, was quoted in the article: 'there are reasons to be critical of G4S and sceptical of the way it structures its businesses and the services they provide.'[300]

At the time, financial investigative journalist Michael West, dissected G4S's 'dodgy accounting' for the newspaper Business Day. His investigation revealed that G4S had handed in their financial reports to the tax authorities late in several consecutive years. In 2011, the company had revalued its 'goodwill assets upward from 15 million dollars to 51 million dollars. Goodwill assets are the costs to purchase a business minus the fair market value of intangible assets. In Australia, these assets are never valued upwards. The auditor of the company, KPMG, did not provide any comments to the allegations. It did not flag the irregular accounting in its audit report. Actually, KPMG's accounting was not even mentioned in G4S Australia's 2011 annual report, again an irregularity that falls below Australian accounting standards. But there was more. West went on to expose a tax avoidance agreement set up between the Australian subsidiary and the British mother company, involving an intra-company loan. 'The upshot was that G4S PLC had created an Australian company with payables in excess of Australian $40 million to the British mothership. And when the mothership is repaid from untaxed Australian cash earnings it may not attract any tax in Australia.'[301]

These constructions are by no means a uniquely G4S strategy, as the ICIJ's Panama and Paradise Papers exposed.[302] Business-friendly trade and investment policies in most countries have led to a global power constellation where multinationals by far outweigh nation states in terms of their revenue. States are actively complicit in all of this. The Tax Justice Network found that the UK 'has "single-handedly" done most to break down the global corporate tax system which loses an estimated £400 billion to avoidance'.[303]

In 2018, an analysis by Global Justice Now (GJN) revealed that 'the

Plus ça change…

world's most profitable companies are raking in revenue "far in excess of most governments." (…) 69 of the top 100 economic entities in the world are corporations.'[304] *Not surprisingly, multinationals pay less tax than they did a decade ago, while the taxation of consumers and workers has only gone up, the* Financial Times *reported in 2018.*[305]

This global business-friendly environment enables multinationals to make impressive profits off tax payers' monies, without much pay-back into tax systems and without ever breaking the law. In 2015, in Estonia, G4S again moved €86 million in profits to the UK and paid no taxes in Estonia and Latvia that year, despite employing hundreds of people in the two countries.[306] *Transfer pricing, as this is also known, is a very common and legal tax strategy adopted by most multinationals.*

16

Fight or flight?

JAMES IS MY BOXING coach. He is a muscled, compact man from Nigeria with an intensity in his eyes that I feel channels the Igbo God of Thunder, who is said to manifest the wrath of the Supreme Being. I doubt James would ever entertain that comparison, as he is a devout Christian, who has repeatedly tried and failed to convince me that 'Jesus will save me'. After six years of training with him, James and I have developed a synchronicity. We dance inside the ring, his pads inviting my punches. I know when one of his spirited and crazy moments is going to start. His eyes will go into a trance and the sounds coming from his throat will not always necessarily form words. As he dances around the ring – moving in, moving out, towards me, away from me – sometimes hitting my head with his pad, providing a rough reminder that a boxer in the ring would have slammed a hook on my temple. Blows come my way that I either need to avoid by ducking or respond to with an equally hard slam against his pink-coloured pad swishing through the air with the speed of light and thunder. James will at times yell at me in the midst of our frenetic performance, or produce a high-pitched laugh that he pushes out in bouts. At other times he will instruct me: 'Be yourself! Don't be afraid. Show yourself!!' as his pad lands with a loud thud on my swinging glove. Timed perfectly to coincide with the slam of glove against pad, James will stomp his foot on the boards under the padded surface of the ring.

His erratic movements across the ring, his swinging pads, moving to attack, responding to my counter attacks, attract crowds of spectators at the Bronx gym in Hillbrow. Muscled men cease pumping iron and from the balcony above the boxing ring, to observe how James yells, dances and reprimands, his eyes not missing a beat, a lowered guard or a lifted foot.

James taught me how to fight. It was a long held wish. Growing up as a kid, I had to ward off bullies. My immediate response was physical; I usually chose to fight back. So when my tenth birthday neared, I dragged my father to the local toyshop and asked him to buy me a kids' boxing bag and gloves. He refused, because, so he said, 'boxing is not for girls.'

James, the Nigerian with fire in his eyes, showed me boxing *is* for girls.

Whenever James yelled 'be yourself', I was usually in the trance-like state that is the mid-point of any good boxing training; when your body is sufficiently warmed up and you are nearing the point of resistance, that moment when the body says: no, wait, just give me a second. In that cloud-like point of exhilaration, rubbing up against physical pain, suffering and exhaustion, I feel like my true self, or more precisely my naked self emerges. I am but my body, my intellect shuts down and I'm naked, fighting, giving what I have, all I have, my breath pushing my body forward. My thought patterns slow down to a single pinhole view of the pads and my blows, my body responding to a primal urge: to fight back. I feel how my heel pivots my body as I turn in for the hook, I feel my knuckles absorbing blows, my breathing catches up after combination punches. It is a pure, undiluted, physical presence in the moment.

This total shutdown of cognitive capacities that a good boxing workout will cause was very restorative. The flat-lining of thoughts, combined with exhausting and aggressive body movements, was so much more healing than all the years of yoga I spent twisting my body and trying to 'smile from my heart'.

In the 1920s, physiologist Walter Bradford Cannon coined the term 'flight-or-fight response';[307] the two basic reflexes humans, and in fact most living creatures, have developed to life-threatening situations. Danger triggers a cocktail of hormones and neurotransmitters in the brain that will course through veins to incite the body to either run as fast as it can, away from the danger, or to respond in equal measure to the danger by fighting back.

Humans find out which category they fall into when danger presents itself. Growing up, my response fell clearly in the fight category. My peers nicknamed me the red hulk, because my rising anger would make my face go red as I was hitting and punching my way through the throngs of mean kids. My sister, on the other hand, had a flight response to the same bullying. She would escape and disconnect. I remember my mother frantically calling search parties of concerned neighbours to find her. Eventually someone would see her somewhere, sitting on a pavement, staring into space, inhabiting an imaginary world in her head, oblivious to the panic her disappearance had caused.

My fight or flight response was tested again decades later in an attempted smash and grab in Johannesburg. Two men appeared at the door of my old Merc. I was waiting for a traffic light to turn green and was backed up behind other cars so I basically couldn't move. I had ignored the safety rules of Johannesburg traffic that dictate one should drive with windows up, doors locked and all possessions stored away safely in the boot of the car. My window was rolled down and my cell phone in sight. What happened next seemed to take place in slow motion. One of the men had lowered his body into my car and he was reaching for the phone. The other man walked around to the locked passenger's door and was yanking at it. I started screaming and I tried to push back the man who was reaching for my phone. He started pulling on the window.

'Give me the phone,' he yelled.

'I have a gun,' he added.

I saw his hand reach into his jacket and I screamed louder. I was outwardly completely hysterical as this was going on, but simultaneously I made a rational assessment. I decided I would give up my phone once I saw the gun. Without a gun, I decided – in a split second – I would fight this guy. The man kept reaching into his jacket as if he was going to produce a firearm, but he never actually did. Then the light turned green and I sped off. My window was damaged, but I still had my phone. After I was done crying from the shock, I marvelled at the laser-sharp observations my brain had made while my life was in potential danger.

The fight response is effective when the opponent is in front of you. But when the threat of danger is like a shadow on the wall, the fight reflex becomes unfocused and ineffective. The rapid heartbeat, heightened hormonal levels and flushed cheeks do not service an imminent attack and thus can spiral into a panic attack.

That thin line between caution and neurosis was a familiar one. When I was in Albania around 2004 investigating trafficking of women for the sex trade, I met a rough-hewn guy from Macedonia who – so it slowly unfolded – turned out to be the pimp and trafficker of the young woman whose case I was looking into. I spent a few afternoons and evenings at his watering hole. There were some rooms at the back where the waitresses would take the men. As I was sipping my beer and observing the comings and goings, he started hitting on me. He compared me to Nicole Kidman and from then on would yell 'Nicole!!' whenever he saw me. A few days later he wanted to take me out for dinner. I declined. Then, one evening we bumped into him at a bar in Tirana. 'Nicole!!' he yelled as we approached. I could see from his eyes and movements that he was drunk. He insisted I sit down and drink with him. We are going out for dinner tonight, he asserted with bloodshot eyes. When I declined, he lost it. He started yelling at me as I walked away. Later he sent me threatening messages, telling me I was a whore like the other girls and he knew what to do with whores. In the following days, I left my apartment wearing a headscarf and large sunglasses. For days I was nervous he would track me down and harm me. The pimp probably woke up the next morning with a hangover and no recollection of what he had said to me.

So nothing happened, other than me walking the streets of Tirana incognito, experiencing a prolonged panic attack.[308]

In Albania, I knew the 'who' and 'where' of the danger. In

Bloemfontein, however, danger had no name, face or location. During the period the prison descended into lawlessness and chaos and the state stepped in to take over, I was followed around Bloemfontein whenever I visited anyone. At first I was unaware of the men – always men – lurking in plain sight, seated at a table next to me or watching me from the bar.

The first time I noticed something was off was in 2015, when I sat with Dan talking to British lawyers in a hotel lobby in Bloemfontein. The lawyers were preparing a civil lawsuit against G4S on behalf of the inmates. I had joined them on a road trip, visiting prisons throughout the country to interview the affected inmates. A man sat at the hotel bar, within hearing distance, looking at us. Mid-conversation, Dan stood up and walked to the corner of the room. The lawyers and I exchanged a glance. I still didn't quite grasp what was going on. I looked at the man again and only then noticed his studied, guileless demeanour. We all moved to Dan's corner. The man followed our movements. We stared back at him. He hastily settled his bill and walked off. The bar staff told me later that the man didn't have a room in the hotel, but claimed to be waiting for a friend. When we started staring at him, he informed the bar staff that the friend had cancelled.

Once the penny dropped, we all backtracked through our day and ran to our hotel rooms to retrieve laptops, phones and other valuables. An uneasy paranoia invaded my consciousness and I saw men following us almost everywhere we went.

Because of this surveillance Dan had different number plates on his car that he used to get in and out of Bloemfontein and, most importantly, to his home in the township.

I met up with Dan again some time later. Routinely, we turned both our phones off and I placed them in a little kitchenette next to my room. We had both become paranoid since the strike had blown up and the state had taken over the prison. Dan was convinced spooks were following his cell phone signal, because, so he claimed, they would turn up wherever his car was parked. The Hawks had told him G4S had bugged his phone, and those of the other POPCRU rebels. He also told me the intelligence unit of the Free State police was keeping tabs, as well as the National Intelligence Service, and even the British MI6. The world Dan described was murky and unpredictable.

He said he had once spoken to the Free State spooks. They wanted to know two things: had there been any murders committed at the prison and did the strike mean there was a second Marikana massacre about to happen? His claims were impossible to verify and follow up on, but they did fuel my fight response with no clear adversary.

Some days, I told myself Dan had watched too many spy films. Other days, I was terrified.

That day, Dan sank into the chair and I sat on the bed. He looked tired, and rubbed his chin, which was covered in a black beard intended as a cosmetic measure to shake off his followers.

I had rented a room in a bed and breakfast, which was housed in an old family home. Built around the swimming pool, adjacent to the old house, there was a courtyard with several rooms. I was the only guest in the courtyard.

About half an hour into our conversation I saw something move in the corner of my eye. My brain short-circuited as I tried to figure out who this guy was, standing in my doorway. The man was dressed in grey trousers, a grey polo shirt and he was carrying a laptop in a grey cover. '*Ek soek iemand*,' he said to me. I was too baffled and taken aback to say anything coherent, but Dan jumped up, more out of protection than interest. They conversed in Sesotho outside the room for half a minute and the man left.

'He said he was looking for someone who looks just like you, the same face, hair, clothes, everything,' Dan said as he came back into the room. I was still startled but when I finally got my wits about me, I bounded off the bed and went to look for the stranger. There was no sign of him. The main house was locked up, the guesthouse staff had gone home for the night.

'How did that guy even get in here?' I asked Dan when I got back to the room. You could only get into the secured property if you had a gate remote.

'It's them again, he said. 'Let them. Let them see us together,' Dan said wearily, rubbing his eyes. 'Don't be scared.'

But I was scared. Especially after Dan had left and the courtyard was enveloped in darkness and noises sounded suspect and I started checking behind doors and in the wardrobe in my room. My heart was pounding, my cheeks flushed. I was ready, but for what?

This shadowy presence, this 'opponent', for lack of a better word, was omnipresent, yet fluid and elusive. It changed form and identity depending on the context. I focused on the literal, factual parts of the puzzle, with questions like: What are the names of the guards who beat up inmate X so badly he ended up with head injuries in an external hospital? How can I access his medical files? What is the chain of command in the prison, who gives orders and who carries them out? How much does G4S's UK head office know? The answers to these questions presupposed a playing field with actors who had self-evident agendas: inmates who wanted access to justice, prison guards who meted out violence and who were exposed to unnecessary levels of violence, an indifferent prison management and correctional department.

But when these shadowy men appeared at my door the script was flipped and I started drawing other conclusions and parallels. It was as if the *mise en scene* was blown up and the actors and props scattered. When these shadowy creatures reared their heads, I started to feel like Truman Burbank, who finally found out that the horizon was not where he thought the sky and the ocean met, when his boat punctured the film set and he found an exit door. When men in grey appeared unannounced at my door the unease it generated in me was not caused by actual danger, it was triggered by everything I couldn't know and never would be able to know. My presuppositions melted away and revealed a new world that was unseen. Who was this person, who sent him, what was he instructed to find out? Why are they always so damn clumsy?

The men in grey hinted at a parallel universe operating alongside the one I knew. They opened up a horror world, where there was no accountability, no names, no verifiable facts, no paper trail. It turned the chessboard upside down and left me wondering how much they knew about me, my private life, my address.

I should never take the same route home, I thought as I tried to fall asleep that night.

G4S's political ties

In many countries, G4S enjoys warm relationships with the political elite.

In South Africa, for example, G4S has close ties to the political elite around former president Zuma, the man who introduced the phrase 'state capture'. Sandile Zungu, who financed Jacob Zuma's presidential campaign, is the main shareholder. G4S, moreover, did good business with the Guptas; it provided security for their mines, as well Sahara Computers, ANN7, their Oakbay office and their private residency.[309]

In Gambia, the leak that exposed President Jammeh's stolen billions[310] (an investigation by the OCCRP into the president's embezzlement of nearly $1 billion in public funds), a payment made by G4S directly to the personal bank account of the president showed up.

The company regularly employs former ministers and others who are part of the elite. In the UK, for example, G4S hired John Reid,[311] a former defence secretary of state; former Metropolitan Police Commissioner Lord Condon;[312] former prison governor Tom Wheatley; and former energy regulator Claire Spottiswoode.[313] In 2012, they hired UK's former ambassador to Libya during the Arab Spring, Richard Northern,[314] to advise the company on security issues in the region. In South Africa, they hired Frikkie Venter to run Mangaung prison.[315] He was a high-level correctional official at the Department of Correctional Services (DCS) and had been responsible for the contract negotiations between G4S and DCS.

G4S also contributes to political campaigns. In America, where corporate contributions to political campaigns are more common than in European countries, the company has, from 2004 to 2018, paid the Republicans close to $200 000 and the Democrats close to $100 000, according to transparency organisation Open Secrets.[316] Not surprisingly, G4S shares fared well when Trump was elected.

While political campaign contributions are subject to legal restrictions, political lobbying is a murkier field. In the US, G4S employed the services of lobbying firm Kelley, Drye & Warren, paying them $40 000 dollars to lobby the federal government,[317] according to the Senate Office of Public Records. At a state level, it is much more difficult to tally all the state-level lobbying expenditures, as there are different laws governing disclosure and lobbyists often meet behind closed doors. In some states, the lobbyists have been very successful. A 2011 report on the lobby for the private prison industry 'Gaming the System', by the Justice Policy Institute,[318] revealed that lobbyists working for private prison contractor GEO group managed to convince the Florida state legislature to adopt a bill that would require the privatisation of all prisons in South Florida.

Probably their most powerful tool to influence politics and policy is G4S's membership in a wide array of think tanks and policy institutes.

In America, one of the more important kind of think tank is The American Legislative Exchange Council (ALEC)[319] whose mission it is to advance conservative principles of free market, limited government and individual liberty. State legislators, private corporations and business professionals are ALEC members. Collectively, the business members have paid $6 million in terms of membership fees. This buys them a seat at the table with lawmakers. G4S's American subsidiary Wackenhut is a long-time ALEC member. ALEC drafts around 1 000 legislative proposals a year, most of them promoting a privatisation agenda, with a strong focus on public safety and the criminal justice system. Most infamously, ALEC drew up proposals for the 'three strikes' law, bills focusing on mandatory minimum sentencing and truth-in-sentencing laws (which enable sentences without a chance of parole): all major drivers of mass incarceration.[320] According to the report 'Gaming the System' approximately 20 per cent of those proposals are eventually adopted.

Another prominent police institute is the Atlantic Council (AC),[321] widely considered NATO's think tank. G4S is not only a member, it also financially supports the council and several G4S shareholders have been appointed to the Executive Committee of the Council.[322] Nineteen out of 35 executive committee members are specialised in the global private security issues. They sit cheek by jowl with former US politicians, CEOs of capital investment firms and major news outlets. The Atlantic Council was established in 1961 as a voluntary alliance of member states of NATO. Former political leaders such as Madeleine Albright, Condoleezza Rice and Colin Powell are members, as are directors and CEOs of capital investment, oil and private security companies and various other *multinationals as well as major corporate media such as Bloomberg, Reuters and NBC. The AC produces policy reports, books and papers. It has a hawkish agenda, evidenced by its 2016 report 'The Future of the Army'[323] which basically recommended an increase in American troops and more deployments overseas. Included in that report are recommendations to hire private military companies to carry out some of the proposed warfare. In another 2016 report, the AC sets out what NATO's policy in the Middle East should be. Instead of working towards a withdrawal of troops, the report recommends continued US-NATO presence in Syria, Iraq, Yemen and Israel/Palestine.*

Professor Peter Phillips paints a horror scenario of where this invisible concentration of power and wealth could lead us in his book Global Giants: The Global Power Elite. *'(…) continuing concentration of capital and massive poverty will lead to nation-states facing legitimization crises that would require them to employ a vast host of coercive control mechanisms, including mass incarceration, various levels of martial law, and an increasing separation of classes into restrictive geographical zones. (…) Capital would be free to travel instantly and internationally to anywhere profits are possible, while nation-states would become little more than population containment zones with increasingly repressive labor controls.' He is basically outlining a future where global security providers have become the private police force of transnational capital.*

17

Interconnectedness-towards-wholeness

INCARCERATION IS A LIFE-altering experience. Very few people would disagree with that statement. How exactly it alters a life is not so self-evident. While most expect incarcerated people to be rehabilitated in prison, the reality is often far removed from that ideal. The complete loss of control over one's safety and security is terrifying.

I have had two very minor brushes with the law that taught me more about the terror of incarceration than my six-year slog in law school ever did.

In 1996, I was a first-year law student at the University of Amsterdam. A 24-year-old with a lot of energy to burn, I had recently moved to the city, occupying a tiny room in a flat with some very untidy housemates. The rush of living in the big city was still novel. It was spring, the chill in the air was disappearing, I had gone out with my best friend and we were, well, a bit merry. My flat was in a quiet neighbourhood on the outskirts of Amsterdam, where young families raised their brood and where students lived because rent was cheap. My friend and I were returning home from a night on the town. We had hopped off a tram and were walking down a quiet street.

I felt we had to celebrate spring. So, I decided to pick a flower for my friend, and I walked over to a neatly kept garden and picked a purple flower. As I presented it to her, I noticed clumps of earth falling on my shoes. I had uprooted the entire plant. We started laughing when, seemingly out of nowhere, a police car pulled up.

Two male officers got out, one of them was fat and had a moustache and the other was younger and tall. The fat one approached me and I could see he was furious. He started yelling at me:

'What are you doing with that plant? This is vandalism, I'm going to arrest you.'

'Officer, Officer,' I started.

'You are as drunk as a monkey!' he shouted. I stepped away from him and placed the plant back in the garden.

'Look officer, I put the plant back,' I tried.

'Give me your name, your date of birth and your address,' the officer was fuming. He got out his notepad.

'Officer, I am not a drunk monkey, I simply wanted to pick a flower for my friend and accidentally uprooted the plant. Look, I have returned the plant to its rightful place.'

'You are drunk and you are coming with me,' the officer yelled.

'No officer, I live around the corner, I am going home to my bed,' I said and I started walking away from him. The officer ran after me and he launched his heavy body on top of me. I fell and felt the texture of the cold pavement on my cheek as I landed.

As I was lying there face down, with a fat cop on top of me, I suddenly remembered the lecture on criminal law I had attended the previous day.

I stood up and I started reciting the legal provisions in Dutch criminal law that govern the execution of an arrest, in a dream-like state. 'The provision instructs the police to "place a hand on a shoulder" when arresting suspects. What you just did is a violation of my physical integrity and it can lead to your dismissal.' I heard myself pronounce the sentences. It was as if a sober person was speaking through me.

My words were effective. The men disappeared like they had appeared: out of nowhere. In a split second, they had put away their note pads, ceased their harassment, got into their car and driven off.

I was left behind, flabbergasted. Then I wobbled back home with my friend.

My second run-in with the police didn't end as well.

In 2012, I experienced an attempted smash and grab, when two men tried to steal my phone, claiming they had a gun. The next day I still felt frazzled and I met with two friends who suggested we buy a joint off a car guard in my neighbourhood Melville. As we sat puffing in my friend's car that was parked on the main strip, I saw two men walk towards the car and I vaguely registered something was off. It was a busy Saturday night and looking back I am stupefied at my ignorance, smoking weed like it was legal. I had lived in Amsterdam before I moved to Johannesburg and that liberal city had blinded me to the simple fact that the South African police actually can and will arrest you for *one* joint.

At first, I thought a second smash and grab was about to happen, as I watched the two men walking determinedly towards us. But they ordered us out of the car and started flinging carpets onto the street, flashlights scoured every corner.

The officers took us to Brixton police station, where they proceeded to book us in. By this time, we were phoning around frantically for a lawyer. When an officer told us he would take our phones away, I told him I had not yet reached a lawyer and that I had a constitutional right to legal representation. He looked at me as if he was going to hit me, grabbed my phone and then he pushed me towards the cell. I didn't mention the constitution again.

Both (near) arrests taught me more about how the law works than all those years of law school ever did, because it provided me an invaluable glimpse of what the criminal justice system is like once you're in it. No one in law school tells you how petrifying it is.

While I was subjected to actual police violence in the Netherlands, in South Africa, the promise of violence scared me much more. I remember sitting on a filthy mattress with a fleece-ridden blanket and thinking that this was the moment where I get raped. My friend and I were dressed up for a night out, with heels, skirts and makeup. The women's communal cell was empty. The officer who took our fingerprints was drunk, I could tell from his smell, bloodshot eyes and clumsy body movements. No one would hear a thing. Thankfully nothing happened, we found a lawyer, paid bail, went home and took showers that lasted for hours. But I will never forget the panic and fear that the loss of control over my safety and security caused.

In jail, one is at the mercy of the guards and their mood swings, their views, their alcohol intake and their interpretation of the law. In jail, there are no eyewitnesses. People entering prison have the odds stacked up against them. A priori, they are viewed as criminals and low lives. The Brixton police told our friends and relatives who tried to bail us out that we were drug dealers who should be behind bars.

The men in Mangaung faced much harder odds than I ever did. I think of Francis Makatsa, who went into Mangaung prison for an armed robbery. He was a soccer-loving healthy young man with a slender athletic build. When he came out of prison, he walked unsteadily with crutches, following a brutal attack that had permanently damaged his spine. He was in constant pain and his speech was slurred, probably from the tuberculosis that had spread to his brain. During the interview, Francis cried several times, describing the utter despair and hopelessness he experienced in prison when the symptoms of his ailments worsened, when he ended up in the prison hospital in a wheelchair. He had TB, HIV, couldn't walk and was incontinent. No one seemed to care. Until one doctor did. He awarded Francis's medical parole as he thought the young man was dying.

Abuse was wired into Francis's DNA. His mother abandoned him at a young age, he became homeless and was taken in by a social worker who ran a home for orphaned and homeless kids. His sister told me he never really found his place in life and cycled in and out of prison. During the interview he sat on his bed, tears streaming down his cheeks, trying to wipe them away with the back of his sleeve, much like a little boy or girl would do. I imagine his tears stemmed from a deep place of pain, where the disappointments and isolation that ran through his life had pooled. That sunken place, to quote the film *Get Out* (2017),[324] where darkness and pain render a person immobile. Where silence is an insulating cloak around violence. Abuse and neglect were threaded into his life experiences and they had become his language. He changed from perpetrator to victim and back again so many times, it ceased to hold any value: receiving pain, then dishing it out.

Francis came out of prison a broken man, literally and figuratively. While he arrived back home in a wheelchair, his mobility has improved somewhat over time. He still walks with crutches and his speech is slurred, but he is living with family and volunteering at a community centre in a small Free State town. Francis is making the most of it, but he will never work a proper job or play soccer again.

Life after prison is harsh anywhere, especially in South Africa and even more so in Bloemfontein. NICRO, a national organisation that aims to help formerly incarcerated people settle back into life after prison, does not even have a budget to help released prisoners from Bloemfontein find a job, they tell me. Formerly incarcerated people are clearly expected to sink or swim.

A criminal record is a lifelong punishment. Finding and keeping work, travelling and many other mundane things in life become impossible or very complicated. Former Mangaung inmate Thabo Godfrey Botsane, whom I have come to know quite well over the years, has faced the full gamut of trials and tribulations of post-prison life.

In 2009, Thabo experienced the outbreak of the hostage taking and ensuing riots in the Broadway unit. He says he was beaten up, electroshocked and injected in the aftermath. He is built like a brick and that might be one of the reasons he survived several alleged attacks in prison. Thabo was released in 2013 after he served eight years in Mangaung prison.

Since he got out, Thabo has taken baby steps, often two forward and three back.

I remember one particularly hot summer's day in 2016. I am driving into Grassland, one of the townships hugging the city of

Bloemfontein, with three silent men on the backseat of my car. The doors in my car are locked from the inside, a quintessential paranoid South African measure to keep the criminals at bay. Three former Mangaung inmates are seated behind me and I realise that I am actually doing the reverse: locking – former – criminals into my car.

We pull up to a car wash that Thabo is in the process of building. Two rusted metal arches cross on a concrete elevated square. All he needs now, he says, is a roof or netting, a vacuum cleaner and a high-pressure hose.

Across from his skeleton car wash a gaggle of men sit around a table. '*Hey, ons soek werk,*' they yell when they see me. 'You think every white person is Afrikaans,' Thabo shouts back at them, laughing. 'They sit around all day, drinking and taking drugs,' he says as we drive off. The men on the back seat stare out of the window at the dusty township. Unemployment is high in the Free State, pegged at 36.6 per cent in 2018.[325] The morning gatherings of young men with blood red eyes, seated around a gambling table, quarters of beer balanced on their laps has become a common sight.

I interview the men on my back seat, who were recently released from Mangaung prison, about their experiences in prison. They share stories of electroshocking and assaults with me, confirming what I had heard several times before, that the violence continued unabated after the prison was handed back to G4S in August 2014.

When I've finished interviewing the men, Thabo shows me around his home. The last time we met, about six months earlier, he had built three walls. Then his money had run out. There used to be a roof on the walls, but a storm had blown it off. At the time he was fretting about getting through the rainy season. Thabo desperately wanted to get out of the tin shacks where he and his wife lived.

Six months later, I walk into his yard and see Thabo's two-room house. Not only does it have a fourth wall, it has windows, a front door. And a roof.

Every time I meet him, his potbelly has grown. He pats and rubs it like it is his pet. It seemingly expands with every incremental slice of happiness: after his release he finds a loving wife, they have a baby and now he has built himself a home. These are big steps for anyone, but they are huge achievements for a formerly incarcerated person. His happy equilibrium, though, is a fragile one. He is still grieving his recently deceased mother, whose funeral he could not attend because he was incarcerated in 2017 and 2018 for nine months on trumped-up charges laid by corrupt politicians. These local politicians used his vulnerability as a parolee, leveraging the odds stacked against him effectively in court. He ended up paying them large sums of money. However, while he was still in Grootvlei prison,[326] awaiting the outcome of this case, the Department of Correctional Services did not grant him permission to attend the funeral. Thabo, his wife and his two daughters now survive on piece jobs. He struggles to pay the school fees or buy his kids presents for their birthday and Christmas. There's palpable desperation in his voice every time we phone.

On another day, I drive all the way to the town of Botshabelo with Thabo to speak to another man. We drive for an hour in the blazing sun and Thabo opens up about his childhood and youth growing up. Halfway through his story, he starts talking about the crime that had landed him in prison. I had not asked him before. He tells me he was in his early twenties, when he started hanging out with the wrong crew who then decided to rob a store. Despite being a communist and ANC card-carrying activist at the time, Thabo held a gun to the head of a store owner as the others robbed him. The police caught the men red-handed and a shoot-out followed, one policeman ended up injured. They caught Thabo. Now approaching his forties, having survived his prison sentence, Thabo says he is done with the life of crime.

'I got carried away,' he says, resting his arms on his potbelly.

'I was young and stupid.'

Thabo might have left his gun-slinging days behind him, but his political fervour remains as strong as ever. And he is a grassroots man. He takes to the streets toyi-toyi-ing against inequality, unemployment and poverty, with his comrades of the National Unemployed Voters Organisation (NUVO). Post release, I watch him grow into an informal counsellor in his neighbourhood. Women confide in him about their abusive husbands, mothers ask him advice on what to do with their difficult children and the men who have come out of prison turn to him for help.

Thabo became somewhat of a neighbourhood hero in 2016, when he led an invasion of a few thousand homeless people and displaced shack dwellers. They built shacks on occupied land that they claimed should have been allocated to township residents and Bloemfontein citizens. The protesters stayed for a week, after which the police evicted them. Before the bulldozers were sent in, the shack dwellers named a square after him, crediting him for his leading role in the invasion.

One day Thabo invites me to a meeting he has called with several other men who had recently returned after stints in Mangaung prison and elsewhere. They are all from around Bloemfontein. The men recline in camping chairs in his yard and they smoke, chat about life, discuss their pains and ailments. The sun is setting, casting a warm glow on the gathering in the sandy back yard, where a fire crackles to life in an upturned oil drum. Thabo hands out cold beers and the men crack the bottles open and toast. Small smiles appear on their faces. Thabo wants to keep these men on the straight and narrow, he later tells me.

I caught a glimpse of what it feels like to be at the mercy of a guard following my brief run-ins with the police. The dozens of men I have interviewed have become accustomed to that heightened state of fear in their lives. And this applies not just to the incarcerated men, the unarmed guards in Mangaung were equally at the mercy of prison gangs who randomly ordered attacks.

How do we end violence? This prevailing question informs much of my work and life. Prisons in general, and Mangaung prison specifically, are places where violence is not random, it has become an organising principle.

Violence in South Africa is, of course, intimately intertwined with and fuelled by race. My own thinking around violence and race deepened when I started to question what it means to be white.

Not being able to blend in is written into my DNA. I was born in the UK, grew up in an English family and when I was very young, we moved to the Netherlands, where my family lived for two decades, first in a village in the north, then a small town in the west of the country. I spent a decade and a bit in Amsterdam, before my departure to Johannesburg.

In the village we were known as the 'Red Family' quite possibly because there are four red-haired women in my family. Our foreignness and flaming locks were not well received. My childhood memories are filled with street fights, name calling and sturdy farm kids ambushing me on my way to school, whereupon they would trash me and my schoolbooks. If my sisters, mother or I ventured out, inevitably someone would yell '*Rooie!*' or worse, from across the street or the train platform, in supermarkets, classrooms and public libraries. I couldn't hide. I remember a fight, a scuffle, an ambush and beat down for every street corner.

Gradually, over the years, the hostility changed into admiration. The hair on my head that I detested with a passion became an object of adoration. People would, uninvited, touch it and drool over its beauty. That still didn't mean I blended in. Over the years I embraced and settled into that position of outsider, using it to my advantage.

After I moved to South Africa, the appellation I loved to hate (rooie/ginger/carrot head, etc.) disappeared. I was now 'that white lady'. My old otherness had created a natural compassion for people who were excluded, not accepted, and bullied for no reason. But at the same time, it had blinded me to my own whiteness. I had never given my race much thought.

In South Africa, I was reclassified as another 'other': a white person, belonging to a minority with a whole new set of signifiers. South Africa made me confront my whiteness and made me think about what the meaning is of 'my people' – that group of people I had never felt a part of. I'm a British national, born in the UK to a British mother and a father with Irish heritage, and I grew up in the Netherlands. The countries of my nationality and residence were responsible for the design of apartheid rule. While I grew up in a left-wing, politically conscious family, with parents who dragged me to anti-apartheid protests, moving to this country really opened my eyes to the destructive inheritance of that system still felt by most black South Africans to this day.

The dominant political discourse in South Africa today is one of decolonisation and of land and wealth redistribution. That discourse, sharpened and amplified at the site of my employment, Wits University, has had a profound effect on me and educated me about race and in what means to be white and European. It made me reflect on the crimes of my ancestors.

In a country with such a vibrant, often volatile, debate around race and wealth, it was fascinating to see a powerful British security conglomerate earn a profit off incarcerating South Africa's poorest citizens. Unfolding alongside my own racial awakening, my investigation into the British security company running a South African prison baffled me. Why had South Africa, with its dark past of racial domination and incarceration practices, invited an aggressively expanding multinational into the country? In the past, the British had imprisoned and tortured South Africans in the name of their expanding empire, and now they were back in corporate disguise, doing the same thing.

A 2013 article in the *Financial Times*[327] compared the security behemoth to the East India Company: '[G4S is] an organization of a scale and scope rarely seen in the private sector since the 18th century, when the East India Company ran its own army, ruled large parts of the British empire, and implemented some of the most controversial government policies of the age ... Damaging scandals are raising questions on how the third-largest listed private sector employer runs its empire,' the introduction to the article read.

In fact, the entire concept of incarceration was relatively unknown on the African continent before European settlers arrived. Nowadays, many South Africans prefer a tough law-and-order approach to crime, evidenced in responses by internet trolls to articles I've written on prison torture, in Mangaung prison and elsewhere. These trolls often encourage the practice of torture and are proponents of the death penalty. But, what they probably don't realise is that mass incarceration and privatised prisons are both western imports.

Some of the men I interviewed during my research had committed the most vicious crimes. James Mothulwe was a serial rapist. I never looked up his criminal record. He confirmed he was convicted of rape in an affidavit I read. Sources at the prison – both within the prison population as well as the workforce – told me he had raped several women. I didn't really want to know, because that information sent a cold current down my spine.

I didn't know what to feel or think when I interviewed him in Mangaung prison. An injured, broken man stumbled towards me. His neck was in a permanent spasm, his hands jerked involuntarily; spit dripped from the corners of his mouth. He struggled to speak; he could barely steady his eyes. The prison hospital, so he claimed, had overdosed him. They started injecting him in 2004 and continued until 2007, when he started developing the symptoms that he still has to this day. The prison ignored his complaints about the permanent side effects, so he had fashioned himself a neck brace that looked like it was made from a ripped-up pillow. They never replaced the medication they had forcibly injected him with, further substantiating the claim that the prison was not administering the drugs for any medical reason, but rather for purposes of crowd control.

If there ever was a shadow of a man, it was Mothulwe. He will probably never speak fluently again. His helplessness in the face of an invisible leadership, that used violence instead of arguments and that espoused a hierarchical command structure based on secrecy, effectively a feeding ground for cruelty, was profound. For whatever reason, Mothulwe was singled out for three years of weekly injections with antipsychotic drugs.

I spoke to Mothulwe alone; it was just he and I in the spacious and mostly empty visiting hall of Mangaung prison. And as I sat opposite him, watching his hands twitch and his neck bob, I realised that it is impossible not to be affected by this level of suffering. It renders someone so defenseless that all what remains of his or her humanity is bare and vulnerable, like raw exposed flesh. My empathy does not mean I condone rape. I didn't look his victims in their eyes, I didn't observe and connect to their humanity. I was in a huge meeting hall with a cold wind breezing through the cracks. And I looked James Mothulwe in his eyes. If I had spoken to his victims, I would have written a different story.

The broken man in front of me deserved to be treated like a human and not like a lab rat/object/nobody. If we treat incarcerated people like animals, they will respond like an animal. That's how we humans work: we observe and copy behaviour from the moment we're born. If we treat criminals as people who still have potential, then a more likely outcome than growing recidivism rates might be that they rediscover what it means to be human.

From a public or political perspective, I care deeply about a carceral system that is rooted in democracy and upholds human rights. Prison provides the perfect setting for human cruelty to be carried out with impunity, because it can go unnoticed for so long. Inmates exist outside the democratic system of checks and balances; in many states incarcerated people are not allowed to vote or exercise other democratic rights. In most countries, prisons fall within an unattractive political portfolio, which means the electorate will most likely not protest abominable conditions and abuse that take place inside prison. In other words, there is little to no political pressure to change. What makes this obfuscation from public scrutiny even more deeply entrenched is that it is incredibly difficult for the media to access inmates who complain about prison conditions.

These men had killed, raped and generally caused harm. But as they sat opposite me, they were stripped down, their naked humanity was all they had; they were stripped of bravado, stripped of their individuality through their prison uniforms, often stripped of their mobility, because their hands were cuffed. I was there to talk to these men about what had happened to them. They had been assaulted, raped and harmed and no one cared. The perpetrator was now a victim and many people felt: serves them right. An eye for an eye.

I might have felt the same, had I been their victim. I know that I spend a lot of time fantasising about revenge in my private life.

Whenever I heard or read about Holocaust survivors forgiving the Nazis who had imprisoned them and exterminated their loved ones, I understood, admired and marvelled at their revelations from a rational point of view. But I could never 'get' or *feel* what they meant. Forgiving is setting yourself free, they say, it's letting go of the pain, without expecting anything from the other in return or expecting anything to change.

Whereas I was in no position to forgive the men I interviewed, because they had not harmed me, my approach was reconciliatory, focusing on their human dignity and humanity, which I felt was tied in with what I felt was everyone's dignity and humanity. Nelson Mandela's statement that a nation should not be judged by how it treats its highest citizens, but its lowest, resonated with me. And, that: 'No one truly knows a nation until one has been inside its jails.'

Forgiveness is central to restorative justice, which is in many ways an African concept. Various reconciliatory forms of justice can be found in indigenous laws throughout the continent. The Igbo in Nigeria and the Songhai Empire of West Africa, for example, were known to have 'indigenous social control and justice strategies that focus on forgiveness, communalism, healing and restitution instead of retribution'.[328]

Prisons barely existed in Africa before colonization.[329] The coloniser introduced Roman-Dutch law in South Africa and its neighbouring countries, which is retributive in its nature and focuses on fact and truth finding, whereas restorative justice is aimed at reconciliation and addresses the community at large. 'Restorative Justice can be defined as a process whereby all the parties with a stake in the particular offence come together to resolve collectively how to deal with the aftermath of the offence and its implications for the future.'[330]

Ubuntu, in my understanding, is a group-oriented, organic form of justice that focuses on the well-being and unity of the group, which in turn produces individual well-being. In South Africa, the principle of Ubuntu informs many restorative justice initiatives, the most famous one being the Truth and Reconciliation Commission (TRC). Journalist, poet and academic, Antije Krog, chronicled the TRC hearings as they were happening and she wrote a great deal about the process, including the principle of Ubuntu. In her philosophical essay '"*This thing called reconciliation ...*" forgiveness as part of an interconnectedness-towards-wholeness', Krog describes the term 'interconnectedness-towards-wholeness' as a principle that is founded on various African notions of communitarianism and justice, including Ubuntu. '(It is) not a passive state of nirvana, but a process of becoming in which everybody and everything is moving towards its fullest self, building itself; one can only reach that fullest self though, through and with others which include ancestors and the universe.'[331]

Krog continues to explain the concept of 'interconnectedness-towards-wholeness' by referencing Cynthia Ngewu, one of the seven 'Gugulethu mothers' – mothers of seven young men who were lured into a sting operation of the South African apartheid security police and killed. One of the black perpetrators of this killing had asked for a meeting with Ngewu, because he wanted to ask her for forgiveness for the murder he had committed.

Ngewu responded: 'This thing called reconciliation ... If I am understanding it correctly ... if it means this perpetrator, this man who has killed Christopher Piet [her son], if it means he becomes human again, this man, so that I, so that all of us, get our humanity back, then I agree, then I support it all.'[332]

In her understanding of the concept of 'interconnectedness-towards-wholeness' Ngewu recognised that the perpetrator's forgiveness opened up the possibility for her and him to become fully human again.

Another example of the principle of Ubuntu is the so-called Victim-Offender Dialogue (VOD) in the criminal justice system. A space of forgiveness is created for incarcerated people and the victims, the relatives of the victim and the community, a space where pain is spoken and apologies can be made and accepted. In person.

Victims and offenders sit opposite each other and can see into each other's eyes, observe body language and connect, on some level, as humans. The way James Mothulwe and I sat opposite each other in the empty visiting hall. No words could ever convey the experience of observing his suffering from across the table.

These beautifully delicate and nuanced set of justice principles, firmly rooted in African soil, are in many ways deeply antithetical to the mission of G4S and its counterparts: to earn profits off the incarceration of bodies.

In the endless cycle of poverty-crime-incarceration-recidivism there is very little Ubuntu left. In a financial model where salaries are kept at a bare minimum, where racism is prevalent and where unskilled labour is barely upskilled, it should come as no surprise that violence and abuse are so widespread.

And despite my investigation into the prison, international media coverage of that investigation, a governmental investigation and a minister who stated the privatisation of prisons in South Africa had failed, Mangaung prison is continuing to operate in an environment of violence, while deriving profit off the bodies it keeps behind bars.

It is my hope that South African society will start noticing and discussing this particular form of disaster capitalism.[333] In an ideal world, the indigenous restorative justice principles found on the African continent will chart a way forward to a criminal justice system firmly rooted in human rights, rule of law and a sense of 'interconnectedness-towards-wholeness'. Because our humanity is tied in with their humanity.

The future of G4S

2018 was a bad year for G4S. It more than halved its profits due to compensatory pay-outs. Early 2019, a relatively unknown Canadian security company, Gardaworld, made a surprise bid to buy all or parts of G4S.[334] While the announcement led to a 30 per cent jump in G4S shares, it never materialised. When Gardaworld announced it was no longer interested, G4S shares experienced the worst slump in six months.[335]

G4S wants to sell of its $1.5 billion cash transportation business, as there is a sharp decrease in the use of notes in the developed world and a lot of violence and armed attacks on cash-in-transit staff in the developing world. They hope to separate the cash business from the rest in the first half of 2020.[336] American security company Brinks is a potential buyer.[337]

G4S's role on the financial markets has historically been divorced from its presence on the ground. The profits derived off the incarceration of people, the detention of migrants, the care for mentally ill patients and military support in various war and conflict areas, are funnelled to global financial markets where there is just one reality: money. News articles either document their lengthy and terrible human rights track record, or financial brokers and market analysts write about the company's financial health, the ups and down of G4S shares and its market capitalisation.

Mangaung prison in Bloemfontein and Brook House removal centre in London both earned impressive profits for the company and the exposure of the abuse going on in these centres did not change that. G4S's political ties shield them from many consequences. In South Africa the government seemingly covered up for the company, by not releasing the investigation report into the alleged abuse. In the UK, the company seems to survive despite a string of scandals. The Home Office in the UK even extended the Brook House contract with two years, following the BBC exposé.

However, there are some cautious signs of change. The divestment of the Norwegian Sovereign Wealth Fund in 2019 came as a big shock to the company. Earlier that year, a High Court judge in London ordered, for the first time ever, a public inquiry into claims of systemic abuse at Brook House.[338] The judge, Mrs Justice May, commented that immigrants were a 'uniquely vulnerable group of people'. And 'the full extent of the *discreditable behaviour has not been exposed to public view'.*[339] *A public hearing, she added, would contribute to the public's confidence in the rule of law.*

The two worlds of G4S: their boots on the ground and their role in financial markets never clash because G4S has not really been held accountable as a company for its many transgressions. A public inquiry that would scrutinise the accountability of the multinational for its maltreatment of migrants in combination with a financial investigation into how the company managed to derive a 20 per cent profit off the same centre and a staggering 40 per cent profit margin on another UK immigration removal centre,[340] *should merge these two worlds. This would (partially) answer the question how it is possible that this multinational is earning substantial profits off human rights violations ...*

A word of thanks

WHEN I FIRST VISITED Mangaung Correctional Centre in 2012 I did not expect that prison to take over my life. One and a half years later, when the *Mail & Guardian* and the *Guardian* published my investigation into the allegations of abuse, I thought my work was done. But it was far from over. The investigation report promised by the minister never materialised. The national commissioner of correctional services started sending me personal text messages. Government officials visited my office to tell me to stop talking to sources.

This meant I could not let go. For the next six years I kept investigating this prison, the government officials involved in the cover-up and the British multinational company deriving a profit off the incarceration of South Africans.

Many people joined me on parts of this journey and I would like to thank them for their help, support and belief in this investigation. First and foremost, I want to thank the men incarcerated in Mangaung prison, for their candour and courage, for sharing their stories of pain and suffering with me. Incarcerated people in most societies find themselves at the bottom of the food chain. Very few people care about prisoners, because so they figure, they have committed harm, so it is acceptable to harm them. The Mangaung men attempted to break through this wall of indifference and impunity. Most of them spoke to me on condition of anonymity. Thabo Godfrey Botsane, Francis Makatsa, Tebogo Maje and Bheki Dlamini are some of the former inmates who allowed me to use their names. I am deeply grateful to them and to the many other anonymous inmates. A special thanks to the family Bereng, who lost their son and brother Tebogo Bereng and to the Nelani family whose son and brother Isaac Nelani died under suspicious circumstances. My gratefulness also extends to all the men who were injected with substances that made them walk, talk and feel like a zombie: Siphiwe Ambraal, Aubrey Buthelezi, James Mothulwe, David Kambule, Willem Boetie Vis, Joseph Maruping, Sello Mogale and many more.

I would also like to thank the guards working at the prison. They too were victims of violence, indifference and impunity, their complaints went unheard and their trauma untreated. Many thanks to the warders who spoke to me off the record: you know who you are. Dan Mbelwane and Shakes Audick Letsoara spoke to me on the record. Their courage and determination to expose the endless cycle of violence and corruption in Mangaung prison inspired and energised me. I could not have written this book without them. Former guards Pule Moholo and Dehlazwa Mdi also deserve my gratitude. Tatolo Setlai, who used to work as a DCS controller at the prison, also provided crucial evidence of corruption, abuse and irregularities. Many more DCS sources spoke to me off the record. I salute these whistle-blowers and their courageous mission to expose wrongdoing. I would also like to extend a word of thanks to the medical staff working at the prison hospital, who spoke to me off the record.

A thank you to the fixers and translators who accompanied me to Bloemfontein: Xoli Matomela and Fusi Mofokeng.

This book was conceived of and developed during my time at the Wits Justice Project, based at Wits University, where I worked from 2012 to end of 2018. My colleagues provided invaluable support and insight. Nooshin Erfani-Ghadimi, Carolyn – Fruity – Raphaely, Robyn Leslie, Simoniah Mashangoane, Paul Mc Nally, Anton Harber, Frantz Kruger and the many talented interns and volunteers at the Wits Justice Project: I thank you. A very special thanks to Deejay Manaleng, who viewed and transcribed all the leaked, and often quite graphic, footage shot in the prison.

Various lawyers have also helped me and influenced the course of this investigation. Human rights attorney Egon Oswald was there from the start, providing legal advice and support. Tessa Gregory and Sarah Clarke, lawyers with British law firm Leigh Day, were involved in the case for some time and though it sadly did not lead to a desirable outcome, it did elevate this investigation and they helped me corroborate many allegations. Lawyers with the Centre for Applied Legal Studies (CALS) at Wits University were instrumental in documenting prisoner complaints in Mangaung prison, Kokstad prison and other correctional facilities. They also pursued a freedom of information request pertaining to the DCS investigation report, through the courts for nearly six years. Thandeka Kathi, Gina Snyman, Palesa Madi, Sithuthukile Mkhize, Megan Niewoudt, Bonita Meyersfeld and all the other CALS lawyers: these fearless women never gave up. I salute you. The future is female.

I would like to thank the supervisors and my fellow students enrolled in the MA in creative writing at Wits University that I completed in 2019. I wrote this book during the MA and without the input from Robyn Aronstam, Wesley Thompson, Olivier February, Bronwyn Law-Viljoen, Phillippa Yaa de Villiers, Michelle Adler, Donato Somma and Ivan Vladislavich, this book would never have been born. A special thanks to my supervisor Elsie Cloete.

My friends; I am because of you. My 'lady writer group': Heather Mason, Eve Fairbanks, Ryan Brown, Greta Shuler and Caroline Wanjiku Kihato, thank you for reading my work and for always providing considerate feedback. Nkosikhona Kumalo: thank you for being you. Baz Dreisinger, thank you for your unending belief in a more humane world with fewer prisons. I am grateful to the 'Wildebeest' Femke and Ilse van Velzen for deciding to produce an amazing documentary film about this investigation (*Prison for Profit*) and for seeing it through to the end.

I would like to thank all the journalists that are part of the Private Security Network, a transnational network of investigative journalists that I set up with Femke and Ilse van Velzen. We are all looking into G4S's services in approximately 30 countries. This network has furthered the work I started in Bloemfontein and will shed light on how private security contractor G4S operates throughout the world. A special thanks to the Organized Crime and Reporting Project (OCCRP), for providing research support.

Lastly, I would like to thank my family for instilling a sense of justice and curiosity in me from a young age. My parents Brian and Janet Hopkins were, are and continue to be a great source of inspiration and love in my life. To my sisters Eve and Anna and their children Eva and Samuel: I am proud to call you my family.

I am blessed with many enduring deep friendships with people from all corners of the world. So, to everyone who I have not mentioned, but who has held my hand, heard me rant, missed my face at their events because I was holed up writing: I thank you.

Appendix

Statement regarding Bloemfontein Correctional Contracts and Mangaung Correctional Centre

G4S SOUTH AFRICA HAS been contacted regarding a forthcoming documentary programme relating to Mangaung Correctional Centre (MCC) in Bloemfontein and provides the following statement MCC provides for the safety and security of approximately 3,000 maximum security prisoners by providing safe custody, care and development through a number of programmes aimed at the rehabilitation of the people in its care.

In 1998, G4S South Africa became a minority shareholder in Bloemfontein Correctional Contracts (BCC) – the concessionaire company responsible for the management of MCC. It is anticipated that G4S South Africa's investment will end in 2026, when BCC's contract expires. In line with the G4S Group strategy, G4S South Africa has no plans to invest further in correctional services in South Africa.

BCC is committed to the respect and protection of the human rights of those in its care and has a zero tolerance policy towards the mistreatment of prisoners.

In 2013, G4S South Africa received reports of alleged mistreatment of prisoners at MCC and, in response, proposed that a retired judge carry out an independent investigation into the allegations. In the event, BCC reviewed the allegations and concluded that there was no evidence to support the allegations.

MCC is operated in accordance with the standards set out in the Correctional Services Act (CSA) and is subject to rigorous independent oversight including:

- An on-site Controller and support staff (appointed by the DCS) to monitor compliance with all contractual requirements and daily operations, including any use of force which are reported to the Controller for review – the Controller reports directly to the National Commissioner of DCS
- The office of the Inspecting Judge appoints a number of Independent Correctional Centre Visitors (ICCV) who are on-site at the centre and responsible for monitoring compliance with the contract and the standards set out in the CSA
- All reports of use of force and requests for segregation are within the scope of the on-site Controller who provides information to their regional office and the Inspecting Judge
- All prisoners have access to a 24/7 complaint and request system and can escalate a complaint or request, confidentially, directly to the Centre Director. Prisoners wishing to raise concerns to the attention of the Inspecting Judge, Public Protector or Commission for Human Rights are provided with support in doing so.

MCC is recognised as a well-managed correctional services centre. The Human Rights Commission "National Preventive Mechanism" committee, under the chairmanship of the Human Rights Commissioner Chris Nissen visited MCC on 7 September 2019. During the visit, the Commissioner took the opportunity to discuss the treatment of prisoners, medical services and the quality of the facilities directly with several inmates. Following the visit, the Commissioner recognised MCC as a centre of excellence in ensuring the human dignity of prisoners.

For as long as G4S South Africa remains a minority shareholder in BCC, it will continue to work with BCC to promote the best possible care for the people at MCC.[341]

Postscript

ON 28 FEBRUARY 2020, MERE hours before this book went to print, the lawyers at the Centre for Applied Legal Studies (CALS) sent me the contentious DCS investigation report into the allegations of torture, assault, forced medication with anti-psychotic drugs and lengthy isolation of inmates at Mangaung prison. CALS applied to access the report in 2014 and they pursued the case through the courts for five and a half years. The High Court in Pretoria ordered the release of an unredacted report on 7 February. I will make this report available on www.ruth-hopkins.com, after redacting for privacy sensitive information.

I have not been able to thoroughly analyse the report, because of time constraints, but a quick first read throws up some crucial questions.

The 2014 Bloemfontein Correctional Contract's (BCC) interim report that was leaked to me, and is referenced frequently in this book,[342] is included in the unredacted DCS investigation report. DCS's investigation forms the first part and BCC's responses to and explanations of the allegations follow in the second part. On 19 February, however, Singabakho Nxumalo, spokesperson for DCS stated: 'It is important to highlight that what is currently in our possession is a preliminary report, which was shared with the service provider, asking them to provide answers on the alleged transgressions levelled against them. As a matter of principle we could not release the report without their voice responding to it.'

The BCC interim report, which is identical to the second part of the unredacted DCS report, was leaked to me in 2014. So clearly the contractor's 'voice' had been added to the report six years ago. Why did the department sit on the report for all these years? Why did Nxumalo state this was a preliminary report? Nxumalo declined to answer my follow-up questions.

The report also contains incorrect information. It refers to a pathologist's report into the death of Isaac Nelani.[343] According to the report, the pathologist ruled that Nelani had a 'head wound' that might have been the cause of his death. However, in the inquest report that I have in my possession there is no mention of a head wound. The pathologist, Dr Book, mentions Nelani's 'bruising of the heart', which is uncommon in a hanging by the neck. The leaked BCC interim report also referenced this head wound. When I discussed this discrepancy with two sources who worked on the DCS investigation team, they said that the department had appointed a law firm to write up the report, but that the report they produced was 'hogwash'. According to these two sources, the department decided to appoint a DCS official to write a more accurate report. I met with this official and she showed me boxes of medical evidence stored in her car. So why has DCS included the report with incorrect information? Is this still the preliminary report? What happened to the second attempt to compile a report?

These questions remain unanswered.

The report lists many irregularities at the prison. Because I have no time to incorporate the details of the report in my book, I have summarised them here:

- Sello Mogale, whom I interviewed about the forced injections he underwent,[344] was assaulted on 13 November 2012 and admitted to hospital for injuries sustained during the assault. The report notes that there are no records of this use of force, the incident was not sanctioned by a senior official or reported to the controller or the Judicial Inspectorate of Correctional Services (JICS), as required by the Correctional Services Act as well as the prison contract.
- Aubrey Buthelezi and James Mothulwe,[345] whom I had also

interviewed about their forced medication, were assaulted by other inmates in 2010, 2011 and 2012. The report notes that no disciplinary procedures were started against the perpetrators, as is required by law.
- Gershwin Coutts,[346] also an inmate I had interviewed previously, was placed in an isolation cell, but the controller had not been notified.
- There are two taser guns at the hospital, but the report notes that Bennie van Aardt, the supervisor of the EST team, was issued a taser gun but he had not been trained in its use and there was no authorisation provided by the controller to use the weapons.
- The company is accused of having knowledge of a hostage taking of a guard in 2010, but not doing anything to stop it.
- The incident on 16 September where inmate Boxer Maphikisa lost sight in one eye and Captain Rampa was assaulted is also dealt with. The authors of the report point out that: the incident was never recorded nor reported to the controller; there was no authorisation for the use of force from senior members of staff or from the prison director; no evidence that the company disciplined the perpetrators; rubber bullets were fired in a building, which violates the law; and lastly, a firearm was discharged but there was no written report, as is required by law.
- Inmates Aubrey Buthelezi, Willem Boetie Vis and Bheki Dlamini[347] were forcibly injected with anti-psychotic drugs but there was no written application for this kind of treatment, which violates the Mental Health Care Act.
- One inmate was injected with expired Clopixol, a powerful anti-psychotic drug.
- Bheki Dlamini's forced injection was discussed. Apparently on 24 May 2013 a nurse obtained a telephonic prescription for Clopixol for Dlamini. According to the Medical and Related Substances Act, however, a verbal prescription needs to be followed by a written one, within seven days. Dlamini's prescription for the medication, normally indicated in cases of schizophrenia and psychoses, was never confirmed in writing.

- Willem Boetie Vis was also given Clopixol, but the DCS team found no records to confirm this medication was medically necessary.
- Several inmates were given overdoses of anti-psychotic medication, whereas others were not given enough medication.
- The DCS team also found evidence of falsification of medical records. In one instance, a nurse had documented in the medical records of an inmate that he had administered an injection, but employment records revealed the nurse was not on duty that day.
- Death investigation reports are not documented correctly; some reports are not available at all, others are not signed. The discrepancy – a head wound – in Isaac Nelani's death investigation is mentioned here as well.
- In the section titled Nutrition Investigations Findings, many irregularities are flagged. Inmates are only served one vegetable, instead of the legally required two; inmates are not receiving meat; fruit is only given 'once in a cycle'; inmates are not provided with suitable eating utensils.

Notes

1. The High Court in Pretoria, case no 37578/2015, in the matter between: Centre for Applied Legal Studies and the Acting National Commissioner of Correctional Services, the Minister of Justice and Correctional Services and G4S Correction Services Bloemfontein.
2. https://www.groundup.org.za/article/g4s-ordered-release-report-prison-torture-allegations/ (accessed on 8 February 2020)
3. See: https://www.rappler.com/news (accessed 10 February 2020)
4. https://gijn.org/2019/10/08/full-text-maria-ressas-keynote-speech-for-gijc19/ (accessed 31 December 2019)
5. https://www.g4s.com/en-za/what-we-do/services/care-and-justice (accessed 27 December 2019)
6. https://www.g4s.com/en-za/who-we-are/key-facts-and-figures (accessed 27 December 2019)
7. http://www.au.g4s.com/what-we-do/care-justice-services/justice/mount-gambier-prison/ (accessed 27 December 2019)
8. https://hmpaltcourse.co.uk/ (accessed 27 December 2019)
9. http://www.justice.gov.uk/contacts/prison-finder/buckley-hall (accessed 27 December 2019)
10. https://www.bbc.com/news/uk-20252359 (accessed 27 December 2019); https://www.telegraph.co.uk/finance/newsbysector/supportservices/9663733/G4S-loses-contract-to-run-Wolds-prison.html
    'An inspection of the prison earlier this year found that "performance accessed had deteriorated and we expressed concerns about a number of issues, including the availability of drugs, a lack of staff confidence in confronting poor behaviour, weaknesses in the promotion of diversity and limited work and training provision'. The report is online: https://webarchive.nationalarchives.gov.uk/20130207004734/; https://www.justice.gov.uk/downloads/publications/inspectorate-reports/hmipris/prison-and-yoi-inspections/wolds/wolds-2012.pdf (accessed 27 December 2019); https://www.mirror.co.uk/news/uk-news/g4s-loses-wolds-prison-contract-1426343 (accessed 27 December 2019); https://www.bbc.com/

news/uk-england-humber-19332782 (accessed 27 December 2019); https://pdfs.semanticscholar.org/8b0d/63e7003163f04795be9e984c204f2 34c2f7c.pdf (from p. 53) (accessed 27 December 2019)

11　Jonny Steinberg's book *The Number* (one man's search for identity in the Cape underworld and prison gangs) is a seminal book on the intricacies of South African prison gangs. Steinberg, J. (2004) *The Number*, Jonathan Ball Publishers, Johannesburg.

12　https://www.tandfonline.com/doi/abs/10.1080/03057070.2013. 765751?mobileUi=0&journalCode=cjss20 (accessed 27 December 2019)

13　https://www.g4s.com/en-za/who-we-are (accessed 27 December 2019)

14　Police and Prisons Civil Rights Union (2013) Petition: Immediate Upliftment of Suspension: Institutional Secretary: Dan Mbelwane and Four (4) Others, 9 September 2013. The list of complaints was part of this petition.

15　I wrote about their case in 2013: https://mg.co.za/article/2013-10-11-00-state-seizes-bedlam-riven-bloem-prison (accessed 28 December 2019)

16　https://www.g4s.com/who-we-are/our-people/our-employees (accessed 28 December 2019)

17　https://corporatewatch.org/g4s-company-profile-2018/ (accessed 28 December 2019)

18　https://www.youtube.com/watch?v=yWD6_PrMNA0 (accessed 28 December 2019)

19　https://city-press.news24.com/News/Who-owns-the-land-Ownership-by-numbers-20150503 (accessed 4 March 2019)

20　Malfunctioning of Private Prison: Mangaung Correctional Facility, 18/10/2010, att: Britta Rotmann, Department of Correctional Services, T. Setlai.

21　Fax sent by Mr Setlai to Mr Theron. Subject: Discrepancies by offiicals at Mangaung correctional center, 2009-05-08.

22　Interpretation of Policy or Act: Mangaung Correctional Center, 5 September 2009, att: Tertius de Toit, from: Controller MCC.

23　Sworn statement made by Mr Setlai at the DCS Regional Commissioner's office, 19 February 2010, Bleomfontein.

24　https://www.un.org/press/en/2011/gashc4014.doc.htm (accessed 28 December 2019)

25　http://www.bbc.com/future/story/20140514-how-extreme-isolation-warps-minds (accessed 20 November 2019)

26　Grassian, S. (2006) Psychiatric Effects of Solitary Confinement, *Washington University Journal of Law & Policy*, 22. See: https://openscholarship.wustl.edu/cgi/viewcontent.cgi?article=1362&context=law_journal_law_policy (accessed 27 December 2019); https://www.psychologytoday.com/intl/blog/almost-addicted/201801/solitary-confinement-torture-pure-and-simple (accessed 27 December 2019)

27　Email dated 8 May 2013. Subject: Concern: Judicial Inspectorate Inquiries: Mangaung Correctional Centre, Tertius du Toit.

Notes

28 Email dated 13 May 2013. Subject: Allegations of Unlawful Segregations of Inmates: Mangaung Correctional Centre, Judicial Inspectorate for Correctional Services, National Manager Legal Services, Umesh Raga.
29 https://www.theguardian.com/world/2013/may/28/g4s-south-african-prisoners-isolation (accessed 28 December 2019). The article is no longer available on the *City Press's* website, but you can still find it here: https://witsjusticeproject.wordpress.com/2013/05/27/prison-isolates-inmates/ (accessed 13 February 2020)
30 Ibid.
31 Email dated 7 June 2013, subject: High Care, sender: Tertius de Toit.
32 Statement: Update on Operations at Mangaung Correctional Centre, Kirsten van der Nest, 4 October 2013.
33 Solnit, R. (2014) *Men Explain Things to Me*, Haymarket Books, Chicago.
34 https://mg.co.za/article/2013-10-25-00-mangaung-prison-drugs-shock-and-torture-by-ninjas (accessed 28 December 2019)
35 https://web.archive.org/web/20170313195818/; http://www.dodig.mil/FOIA/ERR/09-INTEL-13_Redacted.pdf (accessed 28 December 2019, with the plug-in waybackmachine)
36 Also known as 'liquid cosh': https://www.esquire.com/uk/culture/news/a8144/strangeways-prison-riot-25-years-on/ (accessed 28 December 2019)
37 http://www.prisonreformtrust.org.uk/Portals/0/Documents/Woolf%20report.pdf (accessed 28 December 2019)
38 https://jjie.org/2012/03/16/behind-thorazine-shuffle-criminalization-of-mental-illness/ (accessed 28 December 2019)
39 https://caselaw.findlaw.com/us-supreme-court/494/210.html (accessed 28 December 2019)
40 https://www.cbc.ca/news/prisoners-given-powerful-drugs-off-label-allegedly-to-control-behaviour-1.2609940 (accessed 28 December 2019)
41 https://juris.ohchr.org/Search/Details/1596 (accessed 28 December 2019), Bradley McCallum vs South Africa, the UN Human Rights Committee, communication no 1818/2008, 25 October 2010.
42 Anton Piller was an English manufacturer who sold computer components to distributors and he had reason to believe that the distributing company was illegally selling trade secrets to competitors. The court granted Piller the right to enter the premises of the agent to secure evidence of this practice, without the consent of the agent. Crucially, for an Anton Piller order to succeed, there needs to be a real possibility that the material might be destroyed before any application can be brought.
43 *Willem Vis, Joseph Maruping, Sello Mogale and Dawid Khambule vs the Minister of Correctional Services, G4S and Faranani Health Care*, case no 1283/2013, High Court Bloemfontein.
44 https://mg.co.za/multimedia/2013-10-29-torture-and-drugging-in-mangaung-prison/ (accessed 28 December 2019)

45 https://www.theguardian.com/world/2013/oct/28/g4s-run-prison-south-africa-investigation (accessed 28 December 2019)
46 https://www.bbc.co.uk/news/world-africa-24699725 (accessed 28 December 2019)
47 https://www.pressreader.com/south-africa/cape-times/20131029/281496454030959 (accessed 28 December 2019), Carte Blanche has taken the footage off their website.
48 Bheki claims that a nurse was ordered to inject him and that she refused because there was no doctor's prescription. I have the transcripts of a video interview with him, as well as his affidavit before court. The affidavit clearly states that the G4S employees instructed the nurse to inject. The interview transcripts further claim that the nurse said there was no doctor's prescription. The video shows no doctor present, but does show Power Maluleke who says to camera that the injection has been approved. He only takes orders from prison management. Furthermore, when they pick up Bheki from his unit, they tell him he is going to another unit, not healthcare, where they end up taking him. If a doctor had ordered the injection, he would have been told he was going to healthcare.
49 https://pmg.org.za/committee-meeting/16724/ (accessed 28 December 2019)
50 *Bloemfontein Correctional Contracts* (PTY) LTE's response to the report dated 26 June 2014 Prepared by the Department of Correctional Services, Bloemfontein Correctional Contracts (not dated).
51 Strangely, on their website, they only mention the UK and Australia as countries where they run Care and Justice programmes: https://www.g4s.com/what-we-do/services/care-and-justice (accessed 28 December 2019)
52 http://pmg-assets.s3-website-eu-west-1.amazonaws.com/docs/2003/appendices/030318correctreport.htm (accessed 28 December 2019)
53 https://www.g4s.com/what-we-do/services/cash-solutions (accessed 28 December 2019)
54 https://uk.reuters.com/article/us-g4s-m-a-brinks/brinks-co-considering-1-23-billion-takeover-of-g4s-cash-business-sky-news-idUKKCN1VR1MT (accessed 28 December 2019)
55 https://www.g4s.com/what-we-do/services/security-services-and-systems (accessed 28 December 2019)
56 https://www.theguardian.com/commentisfree/2016/dec/23/g4s-prisons-contracts-hmp-birmingham (accessed 28 December 2019); https://www.theguardian.com/business/2014/mar/12/g4s-repay-overcharging-tagging-contracts (accessed 28 December 2019); https://www.cips.org/en/supply-management/news/2013/december/review-of-g4s-and-serco-contracts-reveals-deficiencies-in-key-controls/ (accessed 28 December 2019); https://www.ft.com/content/3eacae52-5628-11e9-a3db-1fe89bedc16e (accessed 28 December 2019); https://www.telegraph.co.uk/finance/newsbysector/supportservices/10070425/Timeline-how-G4Ss-bungled-Olympics-security-contract-unfolded.html (accessed 28 December 2019); https://www.theguardian.com/australia-news/2018/dec/27/australian-government-and-g4s-hit-with-

multiple-lawsuits-from-manus-island-staff (accessed 28 December 2019). G4S used to provide all immigration-related contracts in Australia and it ran juvenile detention centres in the US. It no longer runs these because of repeated scandals and mismanagement.

57 https://www.nationnews.com/nationnews/news/242184/g4s-strike-threat (accessed 28 December 2019); http://www.startribune.com/union-guards-at-xcel-s-monticello-nuclear-plant-locked-out-by-employer/559291062/ (accessed 28 December 2019); https://www.namibian.com.na/82608/read/G4S-employees-down-tools (accessed 28 December 2019); https://www.nation.co.ke/news/G4S-workers-threaten-to-strike-over-pay-/1056-1086850-byrryy/index.html (accessed 28 December 2019)

58 In 2013, G4S's own CEO blamed the aggressive acquisition strategy for the many scandals: https://www.ft.com/content/69f49998-45ea-11e3-9487-00144feabdc0 (accessed 28 December 2019). This overview of their history shows how they have always been obsessed with size: https://www.encyclopedia.com/books/politics-and-business-magazines/group-4-falck (accessed 28 December 2019)

59 See for example their sale of the Israeli businesses: https://www.independent.co.uk/news/business/news/g4s-sells-israeli-business-for-88m-after-pressure-from-campaigners-a7452836.html (accessed 31 December 2019); juvenile detention services in the US: https://www.theguardian.com/business/2016/feb/26/g4s-to-sell-controversial-youth-jail-contracts (accessed 31 December); and UK: https://www.ft.com/content/ae8fd378-dcac-11e5-827d-4dfbe0213e07 (accessed 31 December 2019); and their recent announcement they would cease their involvement in immigration-related contracts in the UK: https://www.theguardian.com/business/2019/sep/24/g4s-to-leave-immigration-sector-after-brook-house-scandal (accessed 28 December 2019)

60 Inquest, no 6/2010, Geregtelike Doodsondersoek, Magistrate's court Bloemfontein, magistrate R Botha, 7 April 2010.

61 Supra note 50.

62 Group 4 Correction Services SA (Pty) Ltd, Policy Document: Deaths in Custody.

63 https://www.theguardian.com/sport/2012/jul/12/london-2012-g4s-security-crisis (accessed 28 December 2019)

64 https://www.sfo.gov.uk/cases/g4s/ (accessed 28 December 2019)

65 https://www.bbc.co.uk/news/uk-26541375 (accessed 28 December 2019)

66 https://www.thelondoneconomic.com/news/g4s-offered-privatised-tagging-contract-despite-facing-multi-million-taxpayer-fraud-probe/11/07/ (accessed 28 December 2019)

67 http://www.au.g4s.com/media/1844/media-release-sa-em.pdf (accessed 28 December 2019)

68 https://www.independent.co.uk/news/business/news/nick-buckles-pockets-16m-as-he-finally-quits-g4s-8625716.html (accessed 28 December 2019)

69 https://www.telegraph.co.uk/finance/newsbysector/supportservices/8863291/G4Ss-deal-for-ISS-buckled-under-the-weight-of-shareholder-anger.html (accessed 28 December 2019)
70 https://www.bloomberg.com/profile/person/3647801 (accessed 28 December 2019)
71 https://www.youtube.com/watch?v=wbx3xQVgXLw (accessed 28 December 2019)
72 https://www.ft.com/content/cb14b056-e4da-11e4-bb4b-00144feab7de (accessed 28 December 2019)
73 https://corporatewatch.org/g4s-company-profile-2018/ (accessed 28 December 2019)
74 https://www.thetimes.co.uk/article/g4s-faces-shareholder-revolt-over-retirement-payment-to-chief-executive-ashley-almanza-8p08xtcgl (accessed 28 December 2019)
75 https://www.theguardian.com/business/nils-pratley-on-finance/2016/mar/09/g4s-long-way-from-home (accessed 28 December 2019)
76 Abridged death certificate for Teboho Daniel Bereng, date of issue: 04/04/2013, SAPS.
77 Department of Forensic Medicine, Dr. C. Liebenberg, Postmortem, BDR 288/2013.
78 https://www.securityfocusafrica.com/buyersguide/force-products/ (accessed 28 December 2019)
79 The website no longer contains this information, I have a screen shot of the old website.
80 https://www.dailymaverick.co.za/article/2014-05-30-the-measure-of-a-nation-st-albans-the-shame-of-south-africas-prisons/
81 Summary of evidence of Tiene Labuschagne in terms of Rule 36 (9) (b), in the matter between *Duru & Others vs the Minister of Correctional Services*, case no: 1421/2008
82 https://www.theguardian.com/world/2014/aug/19/manus-unrest-two-guards-charged-murder-reza-barati; https://www.theguardian.com/australia-news/2017/jun/14/government-to-pay-damages-to-manus-island-detainees-in-class-action; https://www.theguardian.com/australia-news/2017/jul/05/manus-island-detention-centre-closing-down-with-refugees-still-inside (accessed 28 December 2019)
83 https://www.bbc.co.uk/news/uk-scotland-glasgow-west-24727644 (accessed 28 December 2019)
84 https://www.opendemocracy.net/en/shine-a-light/g4s-guard-bludgeoned-woman-to-death/ (accessed 28 December 2019)
85 https://www.theguardian.com/uk/2010/oct/14/security-guards-accused-jimmy-mubenga-death
86 https://www.inquest.org.uk/jimmy-mubenga-jury-conclusions. (accessed 28 December 2019) The inquest: http://iapdeathsincustody.independent.gov.

uk/wp-content/uploads/2013/12/Rule-43-Report-Jimmy-Mubenga.pdf (accessed 28 December 2019)
87 https://www.theguardian.com/uk-news/2014/dec/17/jimmy-mubenga-racist-texts-not-heard-case. (accessed 28 December 2019)
88 https://www.opendemocracy.net/en/shine-a-light/g4s-guard-bludgeoned-woman-to-death/ (accessed 28 December 2019)
89 https://www.bbc.co.uk/news/uk-england-manchester-29481130 (accessed 28 December 2019)
90 https://www.bbc.co.uk/news/uk-scotland-19730387 (accessed 28 December 2019). The allegations were revealed in a BBC documentary about the case.
91 https://www.mirror.co.uk/news/uk-news/brit-paratrooper-jailed-iraq-killing-20938745 (accessed 28 December 2019)
92 Onderzoeksraad voor de Veiligheid, *Brand cellencomplex Schiphol-Oost*, Eindrapport van het onderzoek naar de brand in het detentie- en uitzetcentrum Schiphol-Oost in de nacht van 26 op 27 oktober 2005.
93 https://www.g4s.com/nl-nl (accessed 28 December 2019)
94 https://www.theguardian.com/commentisfree/2014/apr/19/gareth-myatt-died-prison-restraint-children-rainsbrook (accessed 28 December 2019)
95 https://www.inquest.org.uk/gareth-myatt-close (accessed 28 December 2019)
96 https://www.opendemocracy.net/en/shine-a-light/g4s-guard-fatally-restrains-15-year-old-gets-promoted/ (accessed 28 December 2019)
97 https://www.theguardian.com/commentisfree/2014/dec/22/g4s-convictions-deaths-employees-racial-overtones (accessed 28 December 2019)
98 hooks, b. (2001) *All About Love, New Visions*. First Harper Perennial: New York, p. 231.
99 High Court Bloemfontein, Appeal Number: A184/2014, 12 December 2014.
100 https://www.dailymaverick.co.za/article/2019-09-04-extent-of-overcrowding-at-sa-prisons-revealed/ (accessed 28 December 2019)
101 https://www.bbc.co.uk/news/uk-england-birmingham-45240742 (accessed 28 December 2019)
102 https://www.newsandstar.co.uk/news/16738590.prisons-minister-rory-stewart-speaks-of-his-visit-to-birmingham-jail-after-g4s-stripped-of-right-to-run-it/ (accessed 28 December 2019)
103 Ibid.
104 https://www.bbc.co.uk/news/uk-45214414 (accessed 28 December 2019)
105 https://www.bbc.co.uk/news/uk-england-kent-35260927 (accessed 28 December 2019)
106 https://www.bbc.co.uk/news/resources/idt-sh/g4s_brook_house_immigration_removal_centre_undercover (accessed 28 December 2019)
107 https://www.parliament.uk/business/committees/committees-a-z/commons-select/home-affairs-committee/news-parliament-2017/nao-report-published-17-19/ (accessed 28 December 2019)
108 https://www.parliament.uk/business/committees/committees-a-z/

commons-select/home-affairs-committee/news-parliament-2017/nao-report-published-17-19/ (accessed 28 December 2019)
109 https://www.bbc.co.uk/news/uk-england-sussex-50304234 (accessed 28 December 2019)
110 https://www.theguardian.com/uk-news/2019/jun/14/public-inquiry-into-abuse-claims-at-immigration-removal-centre-g4s-brook-house (accessed 28 December 2019)
111 https://electronicintifada.net/blogs/adri-nieuwhof/g4s-equips-apartheid-wall-israel-confirms (accessed 28 December 2019)
112 https://www.theguardian.com/world/2014/jun/04/g4s-complicity-israel-abuse-child-prisoners (accessed 28 December 2019)
113 https://www.jpost.com/Israel-News/Police-Academy-goes-to-Beit-Shemesh-388083 (accessed 28 December 2019)
114 https://rochdaleherald.co.uk/2018/08/20/g4s-win-contract-to-run-guantanamo-bay/ (accessed 28 December 2019)
115 https://reprieve.org.uk/press/police-asked-to-investigate-g4s-over-guantanamo-role/ (accessed 28 December 2019)
116 https://www.g4s.com/investors/news-and-presentations/regulatory-announcements/2019/03/12/2018-full-year-results (accessed 28 December 2019)
117 This is an unpublished essay
118 Jonny Steinberg wrote a book about this case: Steinberg, J. (2019) *One Day in Bethlehem*, Jonathan Ball Publishers, Johannesburg.
119 For an overview of the investigation into Zuma's Nkandla homestead, including the court ruling, see: https://africacheck.org/how-to-fact-check/factsheets-and-guides/a-compendium-of-nkandla-reports-court-papers/ (accessed on 28 January 2020)
120 Based on interviews with guards during the strike
121 Letter written by Dan Mbelwane, addressed to Johan Theron, Managing Director, subject: Grievance of entire shop stewards, 17 August 2013.
122 Letter written by Dan Mbelwane, addressed to Johan Theron, Managing Director, subject: Grievance of Rye Hill, 19 August 2013.
123 https://www.politicsweb.co.za/party/g4s-fires-300-popcru-members-for-staging-strike--c (accessed 28 December 2019)
124 Labour Court of South Africa, G4S Correction Services Bloemfontein (PTY) LTD vs Police and Prisons Civil Rights Union (POPCRU), those individuals listed in annexure "A", Dan Mbelwane, San Mahoko and Moses Mphephuka, case no. J 1864/13, 19 September 2013.
125 Labour Court of South Africa, case no J1864/13, 13 September 2013.
126 https://careers.g4s.com/2012/11/introducing-andy-baker-regional-president-africa-region/ (accessed 28 December 2019)
127 https://mg.co.za/article/2013-10-03-mangaung-prison-hostage-set-free-no-injuries-reported (accessed 28 December 2019)

128 According to medical files from Dr Loubser at Pelonomi Hospital contained in the police docket. CAS number: 215/10/2013. Loubser saw Boxer on 16 September 2013.
129 Medical files from Pelonomi Hospital contained in the police docket, CAS number: 226/10/2013.
130 Memorandum. Subject: Discrepancies by officials at Mangaung correctional centre, Investigation report: inmates Boxer Maphikisa and Captain Rampa, Monday 4 November 2013, Clement Motsapi
131 Email written by Ronnie Molelekoa, addressed to Wilson Gustav (DCS Regional Head: Corrections), subject: Investigation report: inmates Boxer Maphikisa and Captain Rampa, 4 November 2013.
132 Letter dated 26 September 2013, subject: suspension of G4S Care & Justice employees, from Kobus Fourie, managing director.
133 https://mg.co.za/article/2015-11-26-tortured-mangaung-prisoners-seek-justice (accessed 28 December 2019)
134 http://www.pressreader.com/south-africa/the-star-south-africa-early-edition/20150220/281706908123747 (accessed 28 December 2019)
135 Labour Court of South Africa, case no J1864/13, 19 September 2013.
136 https://www.bizcommunity.com/Article/196/369/101695.html (accessed 29 December 2019); https://www.youtube.com/watch?v=jEeFZZ0jnxw (accessed 29 December 2019)
137 https://www.iol.co.za/news/prison-handed-back-to-g4s-1729398 (accessed on 29 December 2019)
138 https://www.pressreader.com/south-africa/the-star-south-africa-early-edition/20130911/281797101674408 (accessed 29 December 2019)
139 In Namibia: https://www.namibian.com.na/82608/read/G4S-employees-down-tools (accessed 29 December 2019); in Kenya: https://www.standardmedia.co.ke/article/2001304987/g4s-guards-down-tools-over-pay (accessed 28 December 2019); in Nepal: https://www.scmp.com/article/667918/100-nepali-security-guards-sacked-amid-strike-wage-increase (accessed 28 December 2019); in India: http://www.policing-crowds.org/uploads/media/G4S-Security-The_inequality-beneath-Indias-Economic-Boom.pdf (accessed 28 December 2019); in Barbados: https://www.nationnews.com/nationnews/news/242184/g4s-strike-threat (accessed 28 December 2019)
140 https://www.thisismoney.co.uk/money/markets/article-6801029/G4S-forced-pay-100m-security-guards-got no-meal-rest-breaks.html (accessed 28 December 2019)
141 This section is based on two books that have been written about the global labour union campaign: McCallum, J. (2013) *Global Unions, Local Power: The New Spirit of Transnational Labor Organizing*, ILR Press, London; Brookes, M. (2019): *The New Politics of Transnational Labour: Why Some Alliances Succeed*, ILR Press, London.

142 https://mg.co.za/article/2006-03-23-security-strike-turns-violent-in-pretoria (accessed 28 December 2019)
143 https://www.gov.uk/government/publications/uk-ncp-initial-assessment-complaint-by-a-uk-ngo-against-a-company-in-the-security-sector (accessed 28 December 2019)
144 McCallum (2013) *Global Union, Local Power*, p. 90.
145 https://waronwant.org/sites/default/files/Who%20Protects%20the%20Guards.pdf (accessed 28 December 2019)
146 https://www.g4s.com/media-centre/news/2008/12/16/g4s-and-uni-sign-global-agreement (accessed 28 December 2019)
147 https://www.theguardian.com/australia-news/2017/sep/06/judge-approves-70m-compensation-for-manus-island-detainees (accessed 28 December 2019)
148 https://www.g4s.com/investors/news-and-presentations/regulatory-announcements/2019/01/22/g4s-secure-solutions-reaches-agreement-to-settle-california-employee-class-action (accessed 28 December 2019)
149 https://www.g4s.com/-/media/g4s/corporate/files/financial-presentations/2019/2018-full-year-results-announcement.ashx (accessed 28 December 2019)
150 https://www.thejournal.ie/hse-wrc-discrimination-case-3382945-May2017/ (accessed 28 December 2019)
151 https://www.theguardian.com/world/2013/oct/09/g4s-sacked-south-africa-prison-mangaung (accessed 28 December 2019)
152 https://mg.co.za/article/2013-10-25-00-mangaung-prison-drugs-shock-and-torture-by-ninjas (accessed 28 December 2019)
153 https://www.theguardian.com/world/2013/oct/28/g4s-run-prison-south-africa-investigation (accessed 28 December 2019)
154 https://www.bbc.co.uk/news/world-africa-24699725 (accessed 28 December 2019)
155 https://www.pressreader.com/south-africa/cape-times/20131029/281496454030959 (accessed 28 December 2019)
156 https://pmg.org.za/committee-meeting/16696/; https://mg.co.za/article/2013-11-05-parliament-concerned-about-r12bn-bill-for-private-prisons (accessed 29 December 2019)
157 https://pmg.org.za/committee-meeting/16696/ (accessed 29 December 2019)
158 https://www.dailymaverick.co.za/article/2015-05-05-mangaungs-hellish-prison-g4s-not-held-accountable-for-human-rights-violations/ (accessed 29 December 2019)
159 A consultant working at a sustainable investing company that advises potential investors on ethical and sustainable investments, leaked the presentation to me.
160 Email dated 23 June 2014, subject: MCC – DCS report, sender: Itumeleng Pappie Mokoena.
161 The High Court in Pretoria, case no 37578/2015, in the matter between: Centre for Applied Legal Studies and the acting National Commissioner of Correctional Services, the Minister of Justice and Correctional Services and

G4S Correction Services Bloemfontein.
162 Letter dated 25 May 2005, from J. Maako, contract management, subject: whither [sic.] breach of policies and procedures should lead to a breach of contract: (...) Mangaung correctional centre. Addressees: messrs. Venter and Korabie. Reference: 12/8/1 BLM.
163 Affidavit by Thembekile Shane Buso, prison number: 209069932/201400423, 10/07/2014.
164 Phalamende Mgungu Mujahid Madi and others, affidavit 30/10/2015.
165 Ebongweni Centre of Excellence Correctional Facility Consultation, 31 July 2014, Ms Megan Geldenhuys and Ms Wandisa Pharma, Centre for Applied Legal Studies (CALS), Wits University.
166 http://www.saflii.org/cgi-bin/disp.pl?file=za/cases/ZAFSHC/2014/98.html&query=%20MejeMeje and Another v S (A264/2013) [2014] ZAFSHC 98 (29 May 2014) (accessed 29 December 2019)
167 https://mg.co.za/article/2014-10-16-still-no-progress-on-mangaung-prison-abuse-claims (accessed 29 December 2019)
168 Idem.
169 https://www.g4s.com/en-gb/what-we-do/employment-services/screening-and-vetting-services (accessed 29 December 2019)
170 Evidence of this practice: https://www.glassdoor.com/Jobs/G4S-unarmed-security-officer-no-experience-necessary-Jobs-EI_IE35039.0,3_KO4,52.htm (accessed 20 November 2019); and: https://www.theguardian.com/uk/2012/aug/06/g4s-untrained-screen-olympic-visitors (accessed 20 November 2019)
In this article, Frikkie Venter, the then prison director at Mangaung prison, admits he specifically recruited 'inexperienced' staff to work in the prison: http://www.writerstudio.co.za/lana-jacobson-portfolio/corporate-social-investment/87-mangaung-maximum-security-private-prison.html (accessed 20 November 2019)
See also this recent investigation into G4S's lack of screening and vetting of their employees in the United States: https://www.jsonline.com/in-depth/news/2019/10/30/five-takeaways-from-investigation-into-g-4-s/4057981002/ (accessed 20 December 2019); and: https://www.jsonline.com/in-depth/news/2019/10/30/five-takeaways-from-investigation-into-g-4-s/4057981002/; https://www.usatoday.com/in-depth/news/investigations/2019/10/30/dangerous-guards-low-cost-security-g-4-s/3994676002/ (accessed 20 December 2019)
171 https://www.reuters.com/article/us-usa-florida-shooting/security-firm-that-employed-orlando-club-killer-fined-for-inaccurate-forms-idUSKCN11G0UJ (accessed on 29 December 2019)
172 https://www.usatoday.com/in-depth/news/investigations/2019/10/30/dangerous-guards-low-cost-security-g-4-s/3994676002/ (accessed 29 December 2019). It is not possible to view all *USA Today* content in Europe.
173 https://www.jsonline.com/in-depth/news/investigations/2019/12/15/private-security-guards-g-4-s-lost-and-sold-guns-criminals/4204016002/

(accessed 29 December 2019). It is not possible to view all *USA Today* content in Europe.
174 https://www.theguardian.com/world/live/2014/oct/16/oscar-pistorius-trial-prosecution-calls-witnesses-sentencing-hearing-live?page=with:block-543f7fd5e4b03829d13c20c6#block-543f7fd5e4b03829d13c20c6 (accessed 29 December 2019)
175 https://pmg.org.za/committee-meeting/17606/ (accessed 29 December 2019)
176 https://www.youtube.com/watch?v=9qMlRVyLKH4 (at 1:05) (accessed on 23 December 2019)
177 Modise's background is discussed during the sentencing hearing: https://www.youtube.com/watch?v=9qMlRVyLKH4 (from 10:50) (accessed on 29 December 2019)
178 Commission of inquiry into alleged incidents of corruption, maladministration, violence or intimidation into the department of correctional services appointed by order of the President of the Republic of South Africa in terms of Proclamation no. 135 of 2001, as amended, Mr. Justice T.S.B. Jali, December 2005, p. 75.
179 Idem, p. 749.
180 https://www.timeslive.co.za/news/south-africa/2014-03-31-graftbuster-punished/ (accessed 29 December 2019)
181 Letter written by DCS Deputy Regional Commissioner of the Free State and Northern Cape, Mr L.M. Ncongwane, subject: alleged incitement of the inmates at Mangaung private correctional centre to embark on a mass action by Mr Setlai, T.A., addressed to Mr T.A. Setlai, date: 19 May 2010
182 Email written by Zach Modise, addressed to Jennifer Schreiner (the then DCS National Commissioner), subject: urgent feedback and advice to commissioner: Grievance by Mr Z. Modise: RC FS/NC, 17 August 2009.
183 https://www.facebook.com/groups/473821679374431/ (accessed 29 December 2019)
184 Email dated 24 April 2015, subject: RESPONSE TO MEDIA INQUIRY: please confirm receipt, sender: Logan Maistry.
185 https://www.opendemocracy.net/en/shine-a-light/g4s-abuses-in-south-african-prison-still-ignored/ (accessed 29 December 2019); and https://www.dailymaverick.co.za/article/2015-05-05-mangaungs-hellish-prison-g4s-not-held-accountable-for-human-rights-violations/ (accessed 29 December 2019)
186 https://www.presscouncil.org.za/department_of_correctional_services_vs_mail_guardian_2849/ (accessed 29 December 2019)
187 https://www.telegraph.co.uk/news/worldnews/africaandindianocean/southafrica/11847153/G4S-accused-of-torturing-inmates-to-death-in-South-Africa.html (accessed 29 December 2019); and https://mg.co.za/article/2015-09-03-prison-inmate-tortured-to-death (accessed 29 December 2019)
188 SCOPA transcripts: https://pmg.org.za/committee-meeting/24627/ (accessed 29 December 2019)
189 https://www.news24.com/SouthAfrica/News/insider-claims-collusion-with-

r378m-prisons-tender-20170626 (accessed 29 December 2019)
190 https://www.news24.com/SouthAfrica/News/minister-announces-zach-modises-retirement-20170629 (accessed 29 December 2019)
191 https://www.dailymaverick.co.za/article/2019-01-22-bosasa-inc-more-songs-about-bribes-cooked-tenders-and-major-cover-ups/ (accessed 29 December 2019)
192 Commission of Inquiry into State Capture, 28 January 2019, day 41, p. 8 of the transcripts: https://www.sastatecapture.org.za/site/files/transcript/44/28_January_2019_Sessions.pdf (accessed 29 December 2019)
193 Commission of Inquiry into State Capture, 24 January 2019, day 40, p. 4 of the transcripts: https://www.sastatecapture.org.za/site/files/transcript/43/24_January_2019_Sessions.pdf (accessed 29 December 2019)
194 Commission of Inquiry into State Capture, 22 January 2019, day 38, p. 117 of the transcripts: https://www.sastatecapture.org.za/site/files/transcript/41/22_January_2019_Sessions.pdf
(accessed 29 December 2019)
195 Memorandum: stalling of corruption and maladministration case by the Hawks. Case no 85/05/2015, Bloemspruit Police Station Bloemfontein. Received by the National Prosecuting Authority on: 12/02/2019.
196 https://www.dailymail.co.uk/debate/article-4781880/KATIE-HOPKINS-sh-tshow-Athletics-Championships.html (accessed 29 December 2019)
197 Goyers, K.C. (2001) *Prison Privatisation in South Africa: Issues, Challenges and Opportunities*, Monograph, Institute for Security Studies (ISS), Pretoria.
198 https://africasacountry.com/2018/12/the-creation-of-black-criminality-in-south-africa (accessed 29 December 2019)
199 Greenberg, S. (2006) *The State, Privatisation and the Public Sector in South Africa*, Southern African Peoples' Solidarity Network (SAPSN), Harare.
200 https://www.gov.za/documents/growth-employment-and-redistribution-macroeconomic-strategy-south-africa-gear (accessed 29 December 2019)
201 In 1996, DCS announced that it would include the private sector in the financing, designing, construction and maintenance of prisons. The Treasury then presented a prison privatisation plan to Cabinet. It was not put to parliament. Nathan, S. (2007) A Snapshot of International Developments, Presentation at a colloquium on the implications for penal policy of the privatisation of prisons, Scottish Consortium on Crime and Criminal Justice Edinburgh, Scotland, 21 September 2007; Prussing, T. (2016) MAF 03: Public-Private Partnerships in South Africa: A Tale of Two Prisons, 2016 Southern African Accounting Association (SAAA) National Teaching and Learning and Regional Conference Proceedings; Massey, S. (2005) The Experience of Service Privatization in Developing Countries: The Case of South Africa's PPP Prisons, MA thesis in Development Studies, University of KwaZulu-Natal, December 2005; Open Society Foundation (2003) Seminar Report: Prison Privatisation, 26 August 2003, The Vineyard Hotel, Cape Town; Sloth-Nielsen, J. (2003) Policy and Practice in South African Prisons: An update, *Law, Democracy and Development*,

June 200; Goyer, K.C. (2001) *Prison Privatisation in South Africa*; Greenberg, S. (2006) *The State, Privatization and the Public Sector in South Africa*, Southern African Peoples' Solidarity Network (SAPSN) Harare, Zimbabwe, 2006; Coyle, A. (2008) Prison Privatisation African Context, *Review of African Political Economy*, Vol. 35, No. 118, *Public/Private, Global/Local: The Changing Contours of Africa's Security Governance* (Dec., 2008), pp. 660–665; Nikiwe Cenge, N. (2013) Enhancing Procurement of Security Services: A Comparative Case Study of Mangaung and Kimberly Correctional Centres, MA dissertation in Philosophy, Graduate School of Business, University of Cape Town, 2013; Ntsobi, M.P. (2005) Privatisation of Prisons and Prison Services in South Africa, Masters dissertation in Administration, University of the Western Cape, November 2005.
202 Sloth-Nielsen (2003) Policy and Practice in South African prisons, p.5: 'The Policy Review notes that the process of embarking on the privatisation route occurred extremely hastily, with the first tenders being awarded before enabling legislation was even tabled in Parliament.'
203 Specifically Treasury regulation 16, which provides for Public Private Partnerships: https://www.gov.za/sites/default/files/gcis_document/201409/257730.pdf (accessed 29 December 2019)
204 Prussing (2016) Public-Private Partnerships in South Africa.
205 Massey (2005) The Experience of Service Privatization in Developing Countries, p. 68.
206 https://mg.co.za/article/1996-03-01-priest-who-takes-no-prisoners (accessed 29 December 2019)
207 Ntsobi (2005) Privatisation of Prisons and Prison Services in South Africa, p. 74.
208 See for example: https://mg.co.za/article/1996-03-01-priest-who-takes-no-prisoners (accessed 29 December 2019); Peté, SA (2015) Penal Discourse and Imprisonment in South Africa: An Examination of the Evolving Discourse Surrounding Imprisonment in South Africa, from the Colonial Period to the Post-Apartheid Era, and its Effects on the Human Rights of Prisoners, PhD in Philosophy, University of Kwa Zulu Natal, November 2015, p. 393. Following a trip in 1997 to the US and UK, Mzimela observed: Wherever the private sector got involved, they have delivered a better service, and have done it at less cost to the taxpayer. – Referenced in Goyer (2001) *Prison Privatisation in South Africa*, p. 39. Munting, L. (2012) An Analytical Study of South African Prison Reform after 1994, PhD thesis, University of the Western Cape, January 2012, p. 125. That section also mentions there was very little debate around the privatisation of prisons when they were introduced.
209 Massey (2005) The Experience of Service Privatization in Developing Countries, p. 62.
210 Sloth-Nielsen, J. (2003). Policy and practice in South African prisons: an

update. *Law, Democracy & Development*, 9 (1): p. 6.
211 Conditions of Contract for the Design, Construction, Operation, Maintenance and Financing of a Prison in Bloemfontein, Government of the Republic of South Africa and Bloemfontein Correctional Contracts (Proprietary) Limited, 24 March 2000.
212 Prussing, T. (2015) Public-Private Financing in South Africa, Minor Dissertation, Masters in Commerce and Finance, University of Cape Town, May 2015, p. 52.
213 Nathan, S. (2003) Seminar Report: Prison Privatisation, Open Society Foundation for South Africa, p. 14.
214 Goyer (2001) *Prison Privatisation in South Africa*, p. 45.
215 This was the outcome of the 2003 Treasury investigation into the costs of private prisons. This was one of the conclusions. http://pmg-assets.s3-website-eu-west-1.amazonaws.com/docs/2003/appendices/030318correctreport.htm#_Toc24526583 (accessed 29 December 2019)
216 http://pmg-assets.s3-website-eu-west-1.amazonaws.com/docs/2003/appendices/030318correctreport.htm (accessed 29 December 2019)
217 Nathan (2003) Seminar Report: Prison Privatisation, p. 12.
218 https://pmg.org.za/committee-meeting/3180/ (accessed 29 December 2019) and https://pmg.org.za/committee-meeting/2009/ (accessed 29 December 2019)
219 Prussing (2015) Public-Private Financing in South Africa, p. 52.
220 https://www.dailymaverick.co.za/article/2011-10-28-government-surprises-by-scrapping-private-prisons/ (accessed 29 December 2019)
221 https://mg.co.za/article/2013-11-05-parliament-concerned-about-r12bn-bill-for-private-prisons (accessed 29 December 2019)
222 https://mg.co.za/article/2019-02-01-00-the-bosasa-tally-r12-billion (accessed 29 December 2019)
223 Commission of Inquiry into State Capture, 21 January 2019, day 37, p. 4 of the transcripts: https://www.sastatecapture.org.za/site/files/transcript/40/21_January_2018_Sessions.pdf
(accessed 29 December 2019), p. 87 and 94.
224 It was put to tender, but before the Treasury had adopted Regulation 16, which allows for tenders of this magnitude. Therefore, the tender was awarded before the enabling legislation had been tabled. This meant no feasibility studies were carried out, there was no costing or idea of affordability.
225 https://www.g4s.com/media-centre/news/2008/05/07/g4s-completes-acquisition-of-armorgroup-international-plc (accessed 29 December 2019)
226 https://platformlondon.org/wp-content/uploads/2012/08/Dirty-work-Shell%E2%80%99s-security-spending-in-Nigeria-and-beyond-Platform-August-2012.pdf (accessed 29 December 2019)
227 https://www.offshoreenergytoday.com/another-oil-and-gas-exec-heads-to-security-sector/ (accessed 29 December 2019)

228 Obi, C. (2009) *'Selling Security' or Engendering Conflict? Transnational Private Security Actors in Nigeria's Oil-rich Niger Delta*, Nordic Africa Institute, Uppsala.
229 https://www.vanityfair.com/news/business/2014/04/g4s-global-security-company (accessed 29 December 2019)
230 https://corporatewatch.org/g4s-company-profile-2018/ (accessed 29 December 2019)
231 https://www.bbc.com/news/world-asia-46377001 (accessed 29 December 2019)
232 https://www.g4scashreport.com/-/media/g4s/riskmanagement/files/about-us_services_glossies/afghan_glossy_16-07.ashx (accessed 29 December 2019)
233 For the fourth quarter of FY2018, DOD reported 4,172 private security contractors in Afghanistan, with 2,397 categorized as armed private security contractors (see Table 2). DOD reported 418 security contractor personnel in Iraq and Syria during the same period, none of whom were identified as armed private security: see: https://fas.org/sgp/crs/natsec/R44116.pdf (accessed 29 December 2019)
234 https://www.nytimes.com/2014/10/23/us/blackwater-verdict.html (accessed 29 December 2019)
235 https://www.opendemocracy.net/en/opendemocracyuk/britain-is-world-centre-for-private-military-contractors/ (accessed 29 December 2019)
236 https://news.un.org/en/story/2011/09/386572-outsourcing-private-security-contractors-threatens-rights-un-panel-warns (accessed 29 December 2019)
237 https://news.un.org/en/story/2011/07/381042-legally-binding-controls-needed-private-security-contractors-say-un-experts (accessed 29 December 2019)
238 Davis, A. (2011) *Are Prisons Obsolete?* Seven Stories Press, New York.
239 http://pmg-assets.s3-website-eu-west-1.amazonaws.com/docs/2004/appendices/040203bcc.pdf (accessed 29 December 2019)
240 http://www.armsdeal-vpo.co.za/articles01/yengeni_legal_fees.html (accessed 29 December 2019)
241 https://www.iol.co.za/news/south-africa/dodgy-database-links-two-to-state-contract-450292 (accessed 29 December 2019)
242 https://www.pressreader.com/south-africa/saturday-star-south-africa/20131221/281818576653885(accessed 29 December 2019)
243 https://mg.co.za/article/2013-11-19-krejcir-employees-fraud-case-postponed(accessed 29 December 2019)
244 https://www.facebook.com/PapsMokoena/ (accessed 29 December 2019)
245 https://www.bloemfonteincourant.co.za/pappie-wants-to-reconnect-community-with-constitution/ (accessed 29 December 2019)
246 https://www.iol.co.za/news/former-mayor-acquitted-of-fraud-1406164 (accessed 29 December 2019)
247 *Bloemfontein Correctional Contracts (Pty) Ltd vs the Minister for the department*

of correctional services, Group 4 correction services Bloemfontein (Pty) Ltd, the acting national commissioner: Department of correctional services, High Court Pretoria, case no: 54391/2017.

248 https://www.theguardian.com/commentisfree/2016/dec/23/g4s-prisons-contracts-hmp-birmingham (accessed on 29 December 2019)

249 Andrew Bowman et al describe this phenomenon in the UK in the book: Bowman, A. et al, (2015) *What a Waste! Outsourcing and How It Goes Wrong*, Manchester University Press, Manchester.

250 http://www.au.g4s.com/media/1844/media-release-sa-em.pdf (accessed 29 December 2019)

251 https://www.theguardian.com/law/2013/nov/04/serious-fraud-office-inquiry-g4s-serco-overcharging (accessed 29 December 2019)

252 https://www.theguardian.com/commentisfree/2016/dec/23/g4s-prisons-contracts-hmp-birmingham (accessed 29 December 2019)

253 http://www.saflii.org/images/329756472-State-of-Capture.pdf (accessed 29 December 2019)

254 https://www.economist.com/special-report/2019/04/25/a-decade-of-state-capture-has-damaged-south-africas-institutions (accessed 30 December 2019)

255 https://www.timeslive.co.za/sunday-times/news/2016-10-02-sa-high-commissioners-past-as-drug-smuggler-exposed/ (accessed 29 December 2019)

256 https://www.timeslive.co.za/sunday-times/news/2017-02-19-jailbird-ngubeni-fired-as-sas-high-commissioner-to-singapore-after-expos/ (accessed 30 December 2019)

257 https://mg.co.za/article/2008-05-25-mbeki-zuma-condemn-attacks (accessed 30 December 2019)

258 Zungu admits to bankrolling the presidential campaign in this interview: https://www.iol.co.za/business-report/economy/transcript-of-interview-with-sandile-zungu-807374 (accessed 30 December 2019)

It is also widely reported on in other media: https://www.timeslive.co.za/sunday-times/business/2010-08-15-zungu-denies-political-connections-in-arcelormittal-deal/ (accessed 30 December 2019); https://www.pressreader.com/south-africa/sunday-times-1107/20180819/282389810327172 (accessed 30 December 2019); https://www.pressreader.com/south-africa/sunday-times-1107/20141005/282329678173535(accessed 30 December 2019); https://www.bizcommunity.com/Article/196/524/76690.html (accessed 30 December 2019); https://www.businesslive.co.za/bt/business-and-economy/2018-08-18-this-is-the--bbc-adjusting-its-dial/ (accessed 30 December 2019); https://www.businesslive.co.za/bd/national/2019-02-27-black-business-council-helped-state-capture-says-sipho-pityana/ (accessed 30 December 2019)

259 https://mg.co.za/article/2010-08-13-zuma-jnr-heading-for-first-billion (accessed 30 December 2019)

260 This is evident from a batch of leaked documents from G4S South Africa, that

contain quotes, invoices and emails about G4S security contracts for these mines.

261 In addition to evidence in the leak of security contracts for the Guptas residences in Saxonwald, see also the state capture report under point 4.32. Thuli Madonsela suggests Mr Mjikijeli Kheswa, a G4S security guard at the Gupta family residence, should be subpoenaed, supra note 247.

262 There is evidence of these contracts in the leak, as well as in the Gupta email leak that aMabungane and Finance Uncovered received: https://www.gupta-leaks.com/ (accessed 30 December 2019)

263 http://www.cpahq.org/CPAHQ/CMDownload.aspx?ContentKey=42bb70f2-3ef7-4d3d-a76b-c482c0762f47&ContentItemKey=1212bdf6-f685-4a45-9a84-5b175cb56cbe (accessed 20 November 2019)

264 https://www.iol.co.za/news/bloemfontein-prison-warders-launch-strike-1576496 (accessed 30 December 2019)

265 http://www.writerstudio.co.za/lana-jacobson-portfolio/corporate-social-investment/87-mangaung-maximum-security-private-prison.html (accessed 30 December 2019)

266 https://www.g4s.com/-/media/g4s/global/files/annual-reports/ara_2008.ashx?la=en&hash=1B9EA171A012B6D9C8F74449A9EA1233, p. 13 (accessed 30 December 2019)

267 Supra note 233

268 Information derived from a sworn affidavit written by an inmate who witnessed the killing, dated: 24 October 2012.

269 https://www.pressreader.com/south-africa/the-star-early-edition/20150626/282673275971697

270 https://www.news24.com/SouthAfrica/News/ndebele-still-ambassador-to-australia-20160526 (accessed on 20 January 2020)

271 https://www.top-employers.com/en/ (accessed 29 December 2019)

272 https://pmg.org.za/committee-question/10050/ (accessed 29 December 2019)

273 https://pmg.org.za/committee-question/11096/ (accessed 29 December 2019)

274 Bowman et al (2015) *What a Waste! Outsourcing and How It Goes Wrong*.

275 https://www.leighday.co.uk/News/2015/February-2015/Legal-action-begins-against-G4S-after-claims-of-So (accessed 29 December 2019)

276 https://www.gov.za/no-stone-will-be-left-unturned-mangaung-investigation (accessed 30 December 2019)

277 https://mg.co.za/article/2018-04-13-00-free-state-anc-tramples-on-justice (accessed 30 December 2019)

278 *Center for Applied Legal Studies vs the Acting National Commissioner: in the Department of Correctional Services, the Minister of Justice and Correctional Services and G4S Correction Services (Bloemfontein) Pty Ltd*, Pretoria High Court, case no 37578/2015.

279 PAIA case number: SAH2016G4S0001, submitted 25 February 2016. SAHA did not follow up after G4S claimed the act was not applicable to it.
280 https://www.gov.za/sites/default/files/gcis_document/201409/257730.pdf (accessed 30 December 2019)
281 Part 3 of the Promotion of Access to Information Act deals with private bodies.
282 https://citizen.co.za/news/south-africa/government/2213238/private-prison-in-bloem-has-minister-concerned-after-allegations-of-torture/ (accessed 30 December 2019)
283 https://www.g4s.com/-/media/g4s/global/files/annual-reports/integrated-report-extracts-2018/g4s-full-integrated-report-2018.ashx (accessed 30 December 2019)
284 https://corporatewatch.org/g4s-company-profile-2018/ (accessed 30 December 2019)
285 See: https://www.financialsecrecyindex.com/en/faq/what-is-a-secrecy-jurisdiction (accessed 21 January 2020)
286 G4S Integrated Report and Accounts (2018) Integrated Solutions in a Connected World, London. https://www.g4s.com/-/media/g4s/global/files/annual-reports/integrated-report-extracts-2018/g4s-full-integrated-report-2018.ashx (accessed 13 February 2020)
287 Page 130 of the G4S 2018 annual report, supra note 273.
288 https://www.investigate-europe.eu/publications/blackrock-the-company-that-owns-the-world/ (accessed 30 December 2019)
289 https://www.harrisassoc.com/Harris.htm (accessed 30 December 2019)
290 https://www.mondrian.com/ (accessed 30 December 2019)
291 Recommendation to exclude G4S PLC from the Government Pension Fund Global (GPFG), 8 April 2019, p. 1. See: https://etikkradet.no/files/2019/11/G4S-tilr%C3%A5ding-engelsk.pdf (accessed 30 December 2019)
292 Idem, p. 7.
293 Idem, p. 8.
294 https://www.g4s.com/-/media/g4s/corporate/files/csr/slavery_and_human_trafficking_statement_2_pager_2017.ashx (accessed 30 December 2019)
295 GPFG report (2019), supra note 279, p. 14.
296 Idem, p. 16.
297 https://www.theguardian.com/news/datablog/2013/may/12/ftse-100-use-tax-havens-full-list (accessed 30 December 2019)
298 https://www.telegraph.co.uk/news/politics/10442231/Atos-G4S-paid-no-corporation-tax-last-year-despite-carrying-out-2billion-of-taxpayer-funded-work.html (accessed 30 December 2019)
299 https://www.g4s.com/social-responsibility/safeguarding-our-integrity/tax-strategy (accessed 30 December 2019)
300 https://www.smh.com.au/national/manus-operator-g4s-paid-no-2012-tax-but-got-a-refund-20140228-33rgs.html (accessed 30 December 2019)

301 https://www.smh.com.au/business/g4s-nabs-aussie-gold-with-questionable-tactics-20120731-23c2y.html (accessed 30 December 2019)
302 https://offshoreleaks.icij.org (accessed 30 December 2019)
303 https://www.independent.co.uk/news/business/news/uk-corporate-tax-avoidance-havens-justice-network-dodging-a8933661.html (accessed 30 December 2019)
304 https://www.globaljustice.org.uk/news/2018/oct/17/69-richest-100-entities-planet-are-corporations-not-governments-figures-show (accessed 30 December 2019)
305 https://www.ft.com/content/2b356956-17fc-11e8-9376-4a6390addb44 (accessed 30 December 2019)
306 https://www.aripaev.ee/uudised/2015/11/03/G4S-ekspordib-Eestis-teenitud-kasumit (accessed 30 December 2019)
307 https://home.cc.umanitoba.ca/~berczii/hans-selye/walter-cannon-fight-or-flight-response.html (accessed 30 December 2019)
308 I wrote about trafficking in Europe in the book: Hopkins, R. (2005) *Ik Laat je Nooit Meer Gaan* (*I Will Never Let You Go Again*), uitgeverij de Geus, Breda.
309 Evidence of G4S's alliance with Zungu and the Guptas can be found in the Guptaleaks as well as in the leak I received from a person who worked at the South African G4S headquarters.
310 https://www.occrp.org/en/greatgambiaheist/how-yahya-jammeh-stole-a-country (accessed 30 December 2019)
311 https://www.g4s.com/media-centre/news/2008/12/17/g4s-appoints-john-reid-as-group-consultant-united-kingdom (accessed 30 December 2019)
312 https://www.independent.co.uk/news/uk/crime/a-force-for-good-the-rise-of-private-police-7561646.html (accessed 30 December 2019)
313 http://www.g4s.com/en/media-centre/news/2010/05/28/appointment-of-new-director (accessed 30 December 2019)
314 https://euobserver.com/very-private/116407 (accessed 30 December 2019)
315 Gould, C. (2010) On the Record... Interview with Frikkie Venter, G4S Managing Director: Care and Justice Services, *SA Crime Quarterly*, no 33, September 2010.
316 https://www.opensecrets.org/orgs/summary.php?id=D000026342&cycle=2016 (accessed 30 December 2019)
317 https://www.sourcewatch.org/index.php/G4S#cite_note-10 (accessed 30 December 2019)
318 http://www.justicepolicy.org/uploads/justicepolicy/documents/gaming_the_system.pdf (accessed 30 December 2019)
319 https://www.alec.org/ (accessed 30 December 2019)
320 Cheung, A. (2007) Prison Privatization and the Use of Incarceration, the Sentencing Project. see: https://web.archive.org/web/20070714063407/http://www.sentencingproject.org/Admin/Documents/publications/inc_prisonprivatization.pdf (accessed 30 December 2019)

321 https://www.atlanticcouncil.org/ (accessed 30 December 2019)
322 Phillips, P. (2018) *Giants: The Global Power Elites*, Seven Stories Press, New York.
323 https://www.atlanticcouncil.org/in-depth-research-reports/report/the-future-of-the-army-2/ (accessed 20 January 2020)
324 https://www.imdb.com/title/tt5052448/ (accessed 30 December 2019)
325 https://www.bloemfonteincourant.co.za/fs-records-the-highest-unemployment-rate/ (accessed 30 December 2019)
326 https://mg.co.za/article/2018-04-13-00-free-state-anc-tramples-on-justice (accessed 30 December 2019)
327 https://www.ft.com/content/a6b46fc0-4cc0-11e3-958f-00144feabdc0 (accessed 3 March 2019)
328 Steyn, F. and Lombard, A. (2013) Victims' Experiences of Restorative Mediation: A Developmental Social Work Perspective, *Journal of Social Work*, 49(3), p. 333.
329 Ibid, p. 334; Wood, Steven (2006) Book Review: A History of Prison and Confinement in Africa. *International Criminal Justice Review*, 16(3), p. 209.
330 Venter, A (2005) Guidelines for Victim-Offender Mediation for Probation Offices in South Africa. MA dissertation, North-West University, p. 2.
331 Krog, A. (2008) '*This Thing Called Reconciliation...*' Forgiveness as Part of an Interconnectedness-Towards-Wholeness, *South African Journal of Philosophy*, 27(4), p. 355.
332 Ibid, p. 356.
333 Disaster capitalism is a phrase coined by the author Naomi Klein, in her 2007 book *The Shock Doctrine: The Rise of Disaster Capitalism* published by Penguin Books, London. It refers to private contractors, who often move into sectors following a disaster, to make profits off the chaos and disorder. Klein claims that this is not accidental, but rather integral to the operation of the free market and neo-liberalism. Journalist Anthony Loewenstein wrote a book about these phenomena: Loewenstein, A. (2015) *Disaster Capitalism*, Verso, London.
334 https://www.euronews.com/2019/04/11/g4s-soars-as-canadas-garda-world-security-considers-bid (accessed 30 December 2019)
335 https://www.bloomberg.com/news/articles/2019-05-07/g4s-falls-most-in-six-months-after-garda-world-scraps-offer (accessed 30 December 2019)
336 https://www.ft.com/content/a67e058e-ba6a-11e9-96bd-8e884d3ea203 (accessed 30 December 2019)
337 https://uk.reuters.com/article/us-g4s-m-a-brinks/brinks-co-considering-1-23-billion-takeover-of-g4s-cash-business-sky-news-idUKKCN1VR1MT (accessed 30 December 2019)
338 https://www.theguardian.com/uk-news/2019/jun/14/public-inquiry-into-abuse-claims-at-immigration-removal-centre-g4s-brook-house (accessed 30 December 2019)
339 https://www.theguardian.com/law/2019/aug/08/immigration-centre-abuse-

inquiry-must-be-held-in-public-court-says (accessed 30 December 2019)
340 https://www.theguardian.com/business/2017/sep/13/g4s-may-make-more-profit-than-allowed-from-removal-centres-figures-suggest (accessed 30 December 2019)
341 Available at: https://www.g4s.com/en-za/media-centre/mangaung-correctional-centre-statement (accessed 14 February 2020)
342 Bloemfontein Correctional Contracts (BCC) see pages ix–xi, 64–65, 66, 77, 79, 123, 131–132, 144, 162–165, 171–174, 176–178, 184, 196, 204, 206–207, 247–248
343 See chapter 6, page 67
344 Mogale, Sello see pages 51, 57, 244
345 Buthelezi, Aubrey see pages 47–48, 57, 65, 244; Mothulwe, James see pages 48–49, 53, 57, 207, 235-236, 239, 244
346 Coutts, Gershwin see page 113
347 Buthelezi, Aubrey see pages 47–48, 57, 65, 244; Vis, Willem Boetie see pages 57, 65, 244; Dlamini, Bheki see pages 54, 59–63, 71, 97, 130, 207

Index

11th Global Conference on Investigative Journalism xi–xii
26s 5–8, 13, 204–206
27s 6–7, 204–205
28s 6–7, 13, 185, 195, 204–205

A
ABSA 163–164, 174
Afghanistan 168
African National Congress (ANC) 7, 158–159, 173, 175, 199, 231
Afrikan Alliance of Social Democrats (AASD) 175
Agrizzi, Angelo 153, 155, 167, 207
Ahmedabad 128
Airforce 204
Albania 216
Albright, Madeleine 222
Allison, Eric 93
Almanza, Ashley 27, 80–81, 108
Altcourse 3, 59, 197
Ambraal, Simphiwe 45–48, 244
American Department of Defense 168
American Legislative Exchange Council (ALEC) 222
American Magnetics Corporation 42
Amnesty International 35
ANN7 183, 221
Anton Piller order 57–58
Argenbright 125–126
ArmorGroup 92, 168
Asset Forfeiture Unit 174
Atlantic Council 222

B
Baderoon, Gabeba 157
Baharti, Reza 91
Baker, Andy 63, 117–119, 122, 184, 186
Barton, Greg 210
BBC 62–63, 129, 186, 240
Beadnall, David 92
Bereng, Anna 83–86
Bereng, Bassie 83, 84
Bereng, Dikiledi 84
Bereng, Robert 84–86, 88
Bereng, Tebogo 84–94, 151, 244
Bermuda 208
Bernard 4–5, 186–187, 189–190
Bertha Street 203
Bethlehem 111
Big Show 198
Biko, Steve 26, 112
Bill of Rights 175
Birmingham Prison 107
Black Consciousness 116–117
Black Economic Empowerment (BEE) 159, 190, 207
Black Power 100
BlackRock 27, 80, 208
Blackwater 168
Blantyre 127
Bloem Plaza Mall 136
Bloemfontein Correctional Contracts (BCC) ix–xi, 64–65, 66, 77, 79, 123, 131–132, 144, 162–165, 171–174, 176–178, 184, 196, 204, 206–207, 247–248
Bloemfontein Magistrate's Court 96, 195

Bloemfontein Prison Trust 163–164
Bloomberg 223
Book, Robert Gene 70, 76–78
Bosasa Operations 153, 155, 166–167, 207
Boshof 146
Botha, Jan 51
Botha, Pappie 13
Botsane, Thabo Godfrey 44–45, 51, 198–199, 201, 207, 229–232
Botshabelo 175, 231
Bowman, Andrew 191
Braamfontein 203
Bradford Cannon, Walter 214
Brakfontein Colliery 183
Brandon 205
Brauteseth, Timothy 152
Brinks 66, 240
British Ministry of Justice 80
British Overseas Territories 209
British Serious Fraud Office (SFO) 80, 179
Brixton police station 227–228
Broad-Based Black Economic Empowerment (B-BBEE) Commission 190
Broadway 3, 13, 21–22, 32, 37–38, 45, 67–68, 71, 73, 74, 76, 135, 196, 197, 229
Brodsky, Joseph 54
Bronx gym 214
Brook House 108, 240
Buckles, Nick 80–81, 127
Buckley Hall 3, 21, 47, 119–120, 136, 204
Business Day 208
Buso, Thembekile Sane 133, 215
Buthelezi, Aubrey 47–48, 57, 65, 244

C
California 128
Care and Justice (division of G4S) 66
Carte Blanche 63, 129
Carter, Clive 91
Cayman Islands 209
Centre for Applied Legal Studies (CALS) 132, 135, 245
Centurion 186
Chicago 208

Choma, Peter 193–194
Christiansborg Castle 41
Citizen 202
City Press 41
Clomidep 45–46
Clopixol 52
CNN 63
Commission for Conciliation, Mediation and Arbitration (CCMA) 109–110
Commission of Inquiry into State Capture 152
Condon, Lord 221
Congress of the People (COPE) 174
Constitution of South Africa 34, 175
Copenhagen 41
Corporate Watch 27, 81
Correctional Services Act 34, 129, 131, 248
Correctional Services Amendment Act 102 of 1997 160
Council of Ethics 209
Coutts, Gershwin 113
Coutts, Sajeedah 113
Culca Investments 176

D
Daily Telegraph 151, 209
Danish Falck Group 41
Dastile, Sandile 119
David, Vuyo 71–72
Davis, Angela 171
Davis, Jon Christopher 27
De Beers Diamond Mining Company 157
De Klerk, Derrick 63, 109, 121, 123
Delport, Marius 51
Democratic Alliance (DA) 152, 172
Democratic Republic of the Congo (DRC) 125–127
Denmark 41, 125
Department of Correctional Services (DCS) ix–xi, 15, 22, 25, 30–31, 34–36, 39–40, 51, 52, 59, 63, 64–65, 70, 71, 72, 77–79, 88, 107, 118, 121, 123, 129–140, 143–155, 161, 163, 164–166, 171, 174, 176–178, 183–185, 187, 188, 196, 201, 202–203,

Index

206–207, 221, 244–245, 248
Department of Correctional Services Act 34, 40, 131, 248
Department of Finance & Tax, UCT 160
Department of Social Development (DSD) 173
Dewetsdorp Road 3
Dinatla Investment Holdings 176
Directorate for Priority Crime Investigations 154
Directorate of Special Operations 6
Dlamini, Bheki 54, 59–63, 71, 97, 130, 207
Du Toit, Tertius 35, 39–40, 63

E
East India Company 232
Economic Freedom Fighters (EFF) 190
Elliot, Billy 189
Emergency Security Team (EST) 23, 24, 45, 48, 51, 58, 59, 67, 73, 74–76, 78, 87, 96–97, 101–103, 109–110, 120, 133–134, 135–136, 139, 197, 198
Employee Share Ownership Plan (ESOP) 189
Erfani-Ghadimi, Nooshin 145, 244
Eskom 181
Estonia 211
Etomine 52, 53
European Union (EU) 66

F
Faas, Melvin 197
Falck, Sophus 41
Faranani Healthcare Solutions 47, 54, 57, 62, 63
Felepe, Mduduzi 135
Fence and Gates 152
Fikile Mangaung 162, 163, 171, 172
Financial Times 211, 234
First, Ruth 149
Fitzsimons, Danny 92
FMR 163
Force Products 89
Fourie, Kobus 121
Fraser, Arthur 165
Free State Agriculture 33

Freedom Charter 158
Freedom Square 98
FTSE 250 Index 27

G
G4S Cash Solutions 66
G4S ix–xii, 1–2, 15, 20–27, 31, 35–36, 38–40, 41–42, 44, 50, 62–65, 66, 67, 68, 70, 71, 72–73, 75–76, 77–779, 80–81, 84–86, 91–93, 97, 97, 101, 107–108, 109–124, 125–128, 129, 132–134, 136, 140, 141, 143–144, 148–149, 151, 162, 164, 166–167, 168–169, 171, 172, 176–178, 179, 181–190, 191, 195, 196, 197–198, 201–204, 206–207, 208–211, 217–218, 221–223, 230, 234, 239, 240–241, 247–248
Gana, Anelize 199–201
Gardaworld 240
Geneva 56
GEO Group 161, 166, 222
Ghana 125
Gillingham, Patrick 207
Global Framework Agreement (GFA) 125, 127
Global Giants: The Global Power Elite (Peter Phillips) 223
Global Justice Now (GJN) 210–211
Global Unions, Local Power (Jamie McCallum) 127
Goyer, KC 157
Grassland 164
Greenberg, Stephen 158–159
Grey 6, 8
Groenpunt prison 73
Grootvlei prison 31, 34, 72, 86, 134, 146–147, 153, 199–201, 231
Group 4 3, 42, 163
Group 4 Falck 42
Group 4 Securitas 42
Growth, Employment and Redistribution (GEAR) 159
Guantanamo Bay 35, 54, 108
Guardian 39, 62, 81, 93, 108, 129, 179, 209
Gupta, Ajay 15, 181, 183, 187, 221

Gupta, Atul 15, 181, 183, 187, 221
Gupta, Rajesh 15, 181, 183, 187, 221

H
Harding, Andrew 63
Harris Associates 208
Hartbeesfontein 183
Hartzenberg 197
Hattenstone, Simon 93, 179
Hawks 153–154, 218
Heathrow Airport 91
High Court of Justice 191, 196, 240
Hillbrow 214
Hoare, Darren 92
Hoffman, Heinrich ix, 201
Hogrefe, Marius 41
Home Affairs 78
Hoogdstaander, Randy 204
Hopkins, Katie 154
Hughes, Terrence 91

I
I Write What I Like (Steve Biko) 26
Ike, James 213–214
Ikhwezi Bloemfontein Correctional Contracts 172
Ikhwezi Community Trust 162, 171–172
Independent Correctional Centre Visitors (ICCVs) 193
India 125, 126, 128, 209
Indonesia 126
Inspectorate for Prisons 3
Institute for Security Studies (ISS) 81, 157
International Consortium of Investigative Journalists (ICIJ) 210
International Monetary Fund (IMF) 158
Invesco 27, 208
Investec 163–164
Investigate Europe 208
Iraq 92, 168–169, 223
Ireland 128
ISCOR 158
Israel 81, 108, 223
Israeli Defence Force 186

ISS 41

J
Jacobs, Elias 153–154
Jali, Thabane 146–147, 174
Jammeh, Yahya 221
Jan Smuts Avenue 203
Janse van Rensburg, Albert 51
Johannesburg 15, 32, 34, 56, 73, 74, 117, 182, 183, 202–203, 215, 227, 233
Jolingana, Nontsikelelo 121, 129–130, 132, 204, 207
JR 52, 54, 86–87, 123
Judicial Inspectorate for Correctional Services (JICS) 32, 38–39, 64
Justice Policy Institute 222

K
Kabul 168
Kabul Business Park 168
Kaler, Colin 191
Kambule, David 57–58, 244
Karel 202–203
Kelley, Drye & Warren 221
Kgopane 21
Khaphe, Tshepang 21
Kimberley 146, 166
King Moshoeshoe 32, 139
Kjøbenhavn Frederiksberg Nattevagt (the Copenhagen and Frederiksberg Night Watch) 41
Klerksdorp 146
Kokstad Ebongweni Centre of Excellence 31, 37, 73, 88, 135, 245
Korabie, Errol 133, 138
KPMG 210
Krejčíř, Radovan 174
Krog, Antjie 238
Kroonstad 34, 74, 99, 104
Kruger, Elanie 184, 186
Kutama Sinthumule Correctional Centre 161, 166

L
La Grange, Anneke 1–2, 121, 123
Laaken, Karel 13–14
Labour Court 113, 114, 117, 122

L

Labuschagne, Tienie 89
Lamola, Ronald 202
Langa, Malose 102
Largactil 55
Lash, John 55
Latvia 211
Legal Resources Centre (LRC) 196
Leigh Day 191, 196, 245
Leponex 45–46, 56
Leshabane, Papa 153
Leslie, Robyn 145, 244
Letsoara, Audick 'Bra Shakes' 97–98, 99–106, 109, 185, 197, 244
Letsoara, Kedibone 104–106
Liebenberg, Chantelle 88
Life Esidemeni 63
Loch Logan 53
Loftus 203
London 80, 196, 240
London Business School 80
London High Court 191
Louis Trichardt 161
Lund, Sue 165
Luxembourg 209
Lwazi 4–9, 11–14, 17, 19, 24–25, 30, 46, 56, 68, 71

M

Maako, Joseph 133, 207
Mabalane, Oupa 37–38, 73–74
Madondo 71–72, 75
Madonsela, Thuli 181
Magashule, Ace 199
Mahlangu, Zakhele 196
Mail & Guardian 26, 62, 78, 129, 145, 151, 182, 243
Maistry, Logan x, 80–81, 152–153
Makatsa, Francis 207, 228
Malawi 125–127
Maluleke, Power 60–61, 70, 74, 76
Mambazo, Paul 'Po' 7
Mandela, Nelson 7, 26, 100, 184, 202
Mangaung Correctional Centre (MCC) ix–xi, 2–9, 11–12, 15, 17–18, 22, 24, 30–40, 43–52, 54, 59, 64–65, 66, 67, 70, 72, 77, 79, 86, 96–97, 99, 101, 102, 104, 107, 111, 114, 116, 118, 121, 123, 129–140, 143, 144, 147, 148–155, 161–162, 165, 166–167, 171, 179, 185, 187–188, 191, 193–204, 206–207, 221, 228, 229–230, 232, 235–236, 239, 240, 247–248
Manus Island, Papua New Guinea 91, 128
Manyoni, Thabo 189
Mapetla 72
Maphikisa, Boxer 119–122, 207
Mapisa-Nqakula, Nosiwiwe 166
Marbi, John 197
Marikana 116, 218
Maruping, Joseph 57–58, 244
Maruping, Papi 73–76
Massey, Sarah 160, 162
Masutha, Michael 130, 132
Mateen, Omar 141
Mathee, Rudi 114
Matlala, Alfred 197
Matshaya, Ronnie 7
May, Juliet 240
Mbatyazwa, Hlello 88
Mbelwane, Dan 17–21, 23–26, 32, 40, 58, 68–71, 77, 97, 109–118, 122–123, 126, 132, 143, 145, 171, 174, 176, 196, 198, 217–219, 244
McCallum, Jamie 127
McGuigan, Paul 92
Mdi, Dehlazwa 21–23, 45, 244
Medupe, Doreen 176
Medway 108
Meje, Tebogo 135–137, 207
Melville 186, 227
Men Explain Things to Me (Rebecca Solnit) 41
Mental Healthcare Act 51
MI6 218
Mimosa Mall 20, 23, 30, 86
Mngomezulu, Hellen 49–50
Modecate 52
Modisane, Bloke 149
Modise, Moleka Zacharia Isaac (Zach) 36, 78, 123, 129–130, 131, 132, 143–155, 207
Modise, Tumi 143

Mofokeng, A.M. 194
Mofokeng, Fusi 110–111, 244
Mogale, Sello 51, 57, 244
Mohlomi, Ishmael 96, 207
Moholo, Pule 21–23, 45, 244
Mokhojoa, R. 194
Mokoena, Lebogang 172, 174–176
Mokoena, Pappie x, 131, 174–176, 206
Molatedi, Grace 207
Molise, Thabang 26, 116, 184
Monash University 210
Mondrian Investment Partners 208
MoneyPoint 174
Morocco 125
Morris, Gideon 160
Moshoeshoe, Masilo 139
Mothulwe, James 48–49, 53, 57, 207, 235–236, 239, 244
Motsapi, Clement 72, 121, 149
Motshelamadi, Tutu 21
Mount Gambier 3, 60–61, 204
Moyante, Joseph 63
Mozambique 125, 126, 127
Mpumalanga 183
Msinto, Lawrence 124
Mthethwa, Lucky 154
Mubenga, Jimmy 91–92
Mukahiwa, Emmanuel 50
Muller, Mike 186
Murray & Roberts Buildings 163
Myatt, Gareth 92
Mzimela, Sipo 161, 163

N
Nagel 115
Naidoo, Esandran 63
Nathan, Stephen 164
National Audit Office 108
National Broadcasting Company (NBC) 223
National District Hospital 50
National Empowerment Fund (NEF) 159
National Intelligence Services 218
National Treasury 66, 152, 160, 165, 201
National Unemployed Voters Organisation (NUVO) 199, 231
NATO 222–223

Nazareth Baptist Church 69
Ndaba, Mxolisi 73–74
Ndebele, S'bu 64, 130, 131–132, 196
Ndude, Hildagrade 174
Nel, Gerrie 144
Nelani, Isaac 12–13, 14, 19, 67–79, 91, 151, 185, 203, 244
Nembambula, Lufuno 193
Neo 195
Nepal 125, 126, 127, 209
Netherlands 92, 189, 227, 233–234
Newcastle 69
Ngewu, Christopher Piet 238
Ngewu, Cynthia 238
Ngubeni, Hazel 182
Ngubeni, Michael 182
NICRO 229
Niger Delta 168
Nigeria 168, 237
Ninjas *see* emergency security team (EST)
Nkandla 113, 130
Nongoloza 6
Northern, Richard 221
Norwegian Government Pension Fund Global (GPFG) 208–209
Norwegian Sovereign Wealth Fund 240
NOSA 188
Nthabi, Thabang 38
Ntshobololo, Vuyo 199–201
Nxumalo, Henry 149

O
Oakbay 183, 221
Old Mutual 162–163, 171
Open Democracy 169
Open Secrets 221
Open Society Foundation (OSF) 169
Operation Quiet Storm 147
Oppermann, Hendrik Beukes 163
Optimum Coal 183
OR Tambo International 117, 119
Orbis 208
Organisation for Economic Cooperation and Development (OECD) 127
Organised Crime and Corruption

Reporting Project (OCCRP) 221, 246
Oswald, Egon 56–58, 62, 122, 244

P
Page, Stephen 25–26, 112, 116, 123, 184
Pakistan 209
Palestine 108, 223
Pan African Congress (PAC) 39
Panama Papers 210
Papier, Kleinpa 204
Paradise Papers 210
Parliamentary Monitoring Group's Standing Committee on Public Accounts (SCOPA) 152
Parris, Helen 131
Parys 69
Pelonomi hospital 120, 175, 196, 199
PEO Projects 176
Philippines xi, 209
Philip-Sörensen, Erik 41
Philip-Sörensen, Jörgen 41
Phillips, Peter 223
Pistorius, Oscar 144–146
Plink, David 189
Poland 125, 126, 127
Police and Prisons Civil Rights Union (POPCRU) 19, 21, 26, 58, 109–110, 114, 116, 117, 123–124, 147, 176, 187, 197, 218
Port Elizabeth 56, 133
Port Phillip 3, 21, 86, 87, 113, 205
Port St Johns 7
Portfolio Committee on Correctional Services 166
Powell, Colin 222
Press Ombudsman 151–152
Prison Matters Facebook group 148
Promotion of Access to Information Act (PAIA) 132, 201–202
Protea Hotel 153
Prussing, Tim 160, 164
Public Protector 181–181, 248
Public Works Department 161
Pulse nightclub 141

Q
Qatar 209

R
Rabie, Pierre x, 132, 202
Rachel 8, 11
Raga, Umesh 39, 64
Rainsbrook Training Centre 92
Rakhetsi, Patrick 119
Ramaphosa, Cyril 176
Rampa, Captain 119–122, 207
Reid, John 221
Ressa, Maria xi
Reuters 63, 223
Rice, Condoleezza 222
Risperdal 52
Robben Island 39, 182, 184
Rocklands 116
Rotmann, Britta 148–149, 204
Roux, Barry 144–146
Rustenburg 116
Rye Hill 3, 114, 205

S
Sahara Computers 183, 221
Sambrook, Clare 91
Sampson 53–54, 59
Sandton 11, 47, 184
Sasolburg 69
SASSTEC 152
Satjawat, Khanokporn 91
Schiphol Airport 92
SCOPA *see* Parliamentary Monitoring Group's Standing Committee on Public Accounts
Scorpions 6
Securicor 42
Securitas 41
Security Solutions (division of G4S) 66
Segwai 204
Sehonka, Lawrence 87
Semenya, Caster 154
Senate Office of Public Records 221
Service Employees International Union (SEIU) 125–126
Sesiu Investment Holdings 176
Setlai, Tatolo 29–40, 147, 150, 153–154, 244
Shell 168, 208
Shembe *see* Nazareth Baptist Church

Shine a Light 91
Shiva Uranium Mine 183
Sibeko, Xoliswa 173–174
Singapore 182
Sisulu, Walter 184
Sizwe 52–53
Sloth-Nielsen, Julia 163
Smith, Vincent 166–167
Snijders, Xander 63, 72, 184
Sobukwe, Robert 41
Solnit, Rebecca 43
South African Airways (SAA) 181
South African Broadcasting Corporation (SABC) 31
South African Criminal Records Centre 78
South African History Archives (SAHA) 201–202
South African National Treasury 66, 165
South African Police Service (SAPS) 22, 70, 78, 194, 206
South Park Cemetery 83, 89, 90
South Sudan 168
Soviet Union 54, 158
Special Investigating Unit 31
Special Treatment Unit 42
Spottiswoode, Claire 221
St Albans prison 56, 89, 133, 134
Stalin, Joseph 54
State of Capture 181
State, Privatisation and the Public Sector in South Africa, The (Stephen Greenberg) 158
Steenkamp, Reeva 144
Stewart, Rory 107
Strangeways Prison 55
Strydom, Carol 155
Sudan People's Liberation Army (SPLA) 168
Sun City prison 73
Sunday Times 182
Sweden 41
Sydney Morning Herald 210
Syria 223

T
Taliban 168

Tax Justice Network 210
Team Mangaung: Keeping it Tight 138
Ten Alliance Holdings 173
Ten Alliance Mangaung 162, 171–172, 173, 174
Thami 204
Theron, Johan 34, 63, 121, 184–185
Thorazine 55
Tirana 216
Top Employers' Institute 184, 189
Transparency International 183–184
Tribelnig, Stuart 91
Truth and Reconciliation Commission (TRC) 238
Tsegisho 204

U
Uganda 125, 126, 127
UK Ministry of Defence 168
Umkhonto we Sizwe (MK) 7
UN Human Rights Committee 56
UN Special Rapporteur on Torture 37
Union Network International (UNI) 125
United Arab Emirates 209
United Kingdom (UK) 81
United Nations (UN) 56
United States of America (USA) 81, 161
Universitas 83
University of Amsterdam 225
University of Cape Town (UCT) 160
University of Natal 80
University of South Africa 135
University of the Free State 83
University of the Witwatersrand (Wits) 51, 56, 102, 132, 149–151, 201, 202–203, 234, 245
Urban Hotel 17, 18
US State Department 54
US Supreme Court of Appeal 55
USA Today 141

V
Van Aardt, Bennie 103, 120–121, 123
Van der Merwe, André 59–61
Van der Nest, Kirsten 117
Van Staden, Gerard 71, 74–75
Veloen, Heinrich 139

Index

Venter, Frikkie 183–185, 221
Victim-Offender Dialogue (VOD) 238
Vis, Willem Boetie 57, 65, 244
Vumazonke, M 194
Vuyo 204

W
Wa Afrika, Mzilikazi 182
Wackenhut 126, 222
Washington vs Harper 55
Wepener prison 139
West, Mervin 204, 206
West, Michael 210
What a Waste (Andrew Bowman) 191
Wheatley, Tom 221
Who Protects the Guards? 127
Wits Art Museum (WAM) 202
Wits Justice Project (WJP) 2, 4, 5, 44, 59, 72, 85, 87, 120, 135, 144–145, 150, 203, 244
Wolds 3, 35, 87, 113, 115, 198, 204, 205, 206
Wolela, Manelisi 137
Woolf Report 55
Woolf, Lord Harry 55
World Bank 158

Y
Yemen 223
Young Investigators 67

Z
Zali, Zoli 13
Zama Resources Company 173
Zastron Street 30
Zimbabwe 125, 126
Zondo Commission 153, 155, 167, 207
Zulus *see* emergency security team (EST)
Zuma, Duduzane 183
Zuma, Jacob 113, 130, 181–182, 183, 221
Zungu Investments 183
Zungu, Sandile 183, 190, 221
Zuptas 181–182